D1035877

# American Psychosis

# American Psychosis

*How the Federal Government Destroyed*

*the Mental Illness Treatment System*

E. Fuller Torrey, MD

OXFORD

UNIVERSITY PRESS

# OXFORD

UNIVERSITY PRESS

Oxford University Press is a department of the University of Oxford.
It furthers the University's objective of excellence in research, scholarship,
and education by publishing worldwide.

Oxford   New York
Auckland   Cape Town   Dar es Salaam   Hong Kong   Karachi
Kuala Lumpur   Madrid   Melbourne   Mexico City   Nairobi
New Delhi   Shanghai   Taipei   Toronto

With offices in
Argentina   Austria   Brazil   Chile   Czech Republic   France   Greece
Guatemala   Hungary   Italy   Japan   Poland   Portugal   Singapore
South Korea   Switzerland   Thailand   Turkey   Ukraine   Vietnam

Oxford is a registered trademark of Oxford University Press
in the UK and certain other countries.

Published in the United States of America by
Oxford University Press
198 Madison Avenue, New York, NY 10016

Library of Congress Cataloging-in-Publication Data

Torrey, E. Fuller (Edwin Fuller), 1937-
American psychosis : how the federal government destroyed the mental illness treatment system /
E. Fuller Torrey, MD.
pages cm
Includes bibliographical references and index.
ISBN 978-0-19-998871-6
1. Mentally ill—Care—United States—History.   2. Mentally ill—Services for—United
States.   3. Mental health policy—United States.   4. Mental health services—United
States—Evaluation.   I. Title.
RC443.T66 2014
362.1968900973—dc23
2013017565

For the ineffable women of my life
—Barbara, Martha, Torrey, and Olivia

All royalties have been assigned to the Treatment Advocacy Center in Arlington, Virginia.

# CONTENTS

# PREFACE

I don't know why other people write books, but for me, it is a selfish enterprise. I write to answer questions that are bothering me. For many years I have been appalled to watch the unfolding disaster of services for people with serious mental illnesses. The fact that my sister suffered from severe schizophrenia has certainly accounted for part of my interest. Year after year, I observed the consequences as public mental hospitals were being emptied. It was like watching the effects of a tsunami or a Category 5 hurricane in slow motion; although I knew what would happen next, I have re-run the tape in my mind, again and again.

I worked at the National Institute of Mental Health (NIMH) from 1970 to 1976, in the midst of the events described herein. Bertram Brown, then NIMH director, was my supervisor. Although I had no formal responsibilities for the federal community mental health centers program, I interested myself in it and visited some centers. Thus, I personally was acquainted with many of the players who were responsible for the program. With few exceptions, these people were intelligent, public-spirited, well-meaning, and dedicated individuals. That fact elicited the question that bothered me: How could so many well-meaning professionals have been so wrong and been complicit in creating such a disaster? This book attempts to answer that question.

I do not pretend to be a dispassionate observer. During my years of working in a public psychiatric hospital, I observed with increasing anger the effects on my patients of inadequate community services. I continue to become choleric when I read accounts like that of Charles Furry, diagnosed with schizophrenia and Lou Gehrig's disease, living by himself in suburban Virginia and dependent on Medicaid-funded home health aides:

> When we removed his socks maggots fell out. Hundreds fell out initially. There were some between his toes and under his skin. Furry's legs were swollen and his shirt was drenched in drool.[1]

This is not what President Kennedy had in mind 50 years ago when he promised that for people like Mr. Furry "reliance on the cold mercy of custodial isolation will be supplanted by the open warmth of community concern and capability."[2] The home health aides responsible for Mr. Furry's care were employed by Sierra Health Services, Inc., a highly profitable private company. We should not allow human beings to be treated in this manner if we claim to be truly civilized.

Having lived in the nation's capital for most of my adult life, I have also been intrigued by the federal angle to this story. Here is a case study of a federal policy that went astray. In most such cases, there is a course correction. Yet in this case, there has been none, even now, a half-century later. Why is that? Each day after work, thousands of government workers gather over drinks to discuss their Grand Idea for solving one national problem or another. Like Robert Felix, the first director of the NIMH, they wait for the stars to align and the approval of their supervisors to implement their Grand Idea. This is thus also a cautionary tale.

If we are to correct our errors, then it is necessary to understand how we got where we are. We have made many mistakes in how we care for the most vulnerable among us and, alarmingly, other countries such as Canada and Britain are following us down this path. What can we learn from the past?

# ACKNOWLEDGMENTS

This book would not have been possible without the generous donation of many people's time. Special thanks go to Bertram S. Brown, who unhesitatingly shared his ideas and memories for a book that he knew would not be flattering, and to Henry Foley, who retrieved his valuable 1972 interview tapes from his garage shelf and generously shared them. Others who kindly responded to my inquiries include Robert Atwell, Jerry Dincin, Matthew Dumont, Sister Ann Dyer, Rashi Fein, Mary Herbert, Robert Keisling, Anthony Lehman, Bentson McFarland, Frank Ochberg, Lucy Ozarin, Anthony Panzetta, Roger Peele, Steven Sharfstein, Alan Stone, John Talbott, and Claudwell Thomas. Archivists and librarians are a writer's best friends and I am specifically indebted to Tracy Holt at NIMH; Doug Atkins at the National Library of Medicine; Gary McMillan at the American Psychiatric Association; Amy Lutzke at the Fort Atkinson Public Library; and Eric Robinson at the New York Historical Society.

Faith Dickerson, Doris Fuller, Jeffrey Geller, Stephen Hersh, D. J. Jaffe, and Robert Taylor read portions of the text and contributed valuable comments. My best reader, as always, was Barbara Torrey, who contributed not only suggestions but everything else that makes writing a book possible. Sarah Harrington and Andrea Zekus at Oxford University Press made the revisions and publication of this book hassle-free, and it has been a great pleasure to work with them. Melissa Bolla is an excellent research assistant, and Judy Miller provided invaluable editorial and administrative assistance once again.

In addition to the above, I gratefully acknowledge the following:

- Chloe Raub, Special Collections Research Center, George Washington University, for permission to use the picture of Dr. Walter Freeman
- Michael Gorman, for permission to use the picture of his father
- Keith Ablow, MD, for permission to quote him from Fox News
- The *San Francisco Chronicle*, for permission to quote from "Homeless by the Bay"
- The American Psychiatric Association, for permission to quote from the *American Journal of Psychiatry* and *Hospital and Community Psychiatry*
- Mental Health America, for permission to quote from *Mental Hygiene*

# American Psychosis

# 1

## JOE KENNEDY: A MAN WITH PROBLEMS

September 1, 1939: Ambassador Joseph P. Kennedy was preoccupied with two deeply distressing problems. The first had become apparent at dawn that day, when German tanks rolled into Poland. This was a clear invitation for Britain to declare war, as Britain had publicly guaranteed Poland's independence. Two days later Parliament obliged, and Kennedy immediately telephoned the president. According to Michael Beschloss's history *Kennedy and Roosevelt*, "Roosevelt could barely recognize the choked voice from across the Atlantic.... [He] tried to comfort his old ally, but the voice was inconsolable. Over and over Kennedy cried, 'It's the end of the world...the end of everything...'"[1]

Joe Kennedy knew that "everything" included his own aspirations to run for president in 1940. Anticipating that Roosevelt would not run for a third term, Kennedy had spent the previous 2 years carefully positioning himself. A recent poll had ranked Kennedy fifth among possible Democratic nominees, and some pundits claimed that Roosevelt had appointed him as ambassador to Britain to remove him from the American scene. In London, Kennedy had joined Prime Minister Neville Chamberlain as a major voice for the appeasement of Hitler, even as the Nazis were sweeping over Austria and Czechoslovakia. According to Beschloss, "both Kennedy and Chamberlain interpreted Hitler's eastward expansionism as a bid mainly for resources and markets." Indeed, just 1 week prior to the German invasion of Poland, Kennedy had assured Roosevelt that Hitler had limited ambitions and that once these had been achieved Hitler would "go back to peaceful pursuits and become an artist, which is what he wanted to be." As Kennedy was painfully aware, Hitler's signing of a nonaggression pact with the Soviet Union and his invasion of Poland were not the acts of an artist.[2]

* * *

On that September morning, as his own political ambitions were being crushed beneath the treads of Hitler's tanks, Kennedy was also preoccupied with another problem, one that was profoundly personal. The problem was his eldest daughter, Rosemary, who would turn 21 years old in 2 weeks. Recently, he had received disturbing reports that something was wrong with her, something more than the mild mental retardation she had experienced since birth. The retardation had been a source of great distress for the

1

family, especially for Joe, who expected his children to be strong and accomplished, like himself. Few people knew of Rosemary's mild retardation, because superficially she looked normal and the family fiercely protected her. As Rosemary grew older, they placed her in convents, where, thanks to Joe Kennedy's bounteous bestowments on the church's hierarchy, they could be assured that she would be kept safe and out of view.

At the time, Rosemary was living in a convent in Hertfordshire, northwest of London. The convent trained Montessori primary school teachers, and Rosemary read to the children each afternoon. It was a highly structured environment, in addition to which Rosemary had a full-time female companion, hired by the Kennedys, to watch over her. In recent weeks, however, Rosemary had been exhibiting increasingly severe mood swings and had to be admonished to not be "fierce" with the children. Her recent letters had included "eerie ellipses," suggestive of an emerging thought disorder. Disturbed by the reports he was receiving from the convent, Joe consulted privately with London's leading child development specialists. He was perplexed and infuriated by what he was being told; mental retardation had been a family disgrace, but mental illness would be a debacle. Such things could not be allowed in the Kennedy family.[3]

With war now a certainty, Joe Kennedy would remain in London as ambassador, but it was necessary to send his wife, Rose, and the children—Jack, Kathleen, Eunice, Pat, Bobby, Jean, and Teddy—back to the States. Joe Jr. was already there, at Harvard Law School. That left only Rosemary, and it was decided to leave her at the convent in Hertfordshire; she was happy there, and it was far from the eyes of the American press. Two months later, reporters from the *Boston Globe* realized that Rosemary had been the only Kennedy child left behind in England and wrote to her, asking for an interview. Joe Kennedy's aide penned a reply for Rosemary, which she dutifully copied. She said that she "thought it [her] duty to remain behind with my Father." Further, Rosemary implied that she had responsibilities that necessitated her staying in England. "For some time past, I have been studying the well known psychological method of Dr. Maria Montessori and I got my degree in teaching last year. Although it has been very hard work, I have enjoyed it immensely and I have made many good friends." The reporters were apparently satisfied and did not pursue the matter further.[4]

## ROSEMARY'S BIRTH AND DEVELOPMENT

Rosemary had been born on September 13, 1918, at the Kennedy home in Boston. Jack had been born 15 months earlier; Rosemary and Jack were thus closer in age than any other Kennedy children. Joe Jr., the first of the nine Kennedy children, had been born 3 years earlier. As the eldest Kennedy daughter, Rosemary was christened Rose Marie after her mother; the family called her Rosie, but the rest of the world would know her as Rosemary (Figure 1.1).

FIG 1.1 Joseph Jr. (left), Rosemary (center), and Jack (left) as young children. Rosemary was born less than 16 months after Jack and the two were closer in age than any other of the Kennedy children. Jack and Joe Jr. were very protective of their younger sister. (AP Photo)

It was an inauspicious time to be born in Boston. Two weeks earlier, cases of influenza had been diagnosed among military personnel awaiting transportation to Europe. The disease spread quickly across Boston, and by September 11 there had already been 35 deaths. The epidemic was unusual in its predilection for young adults, its lethality, and its propensity to cause severe psychiatric symptoms as it spread to the victim's brain. At the Boston Psychopathic Hospital, Karl Menninger, who had just graduated from Harvard Medical School, was making notes on 80 patients who had been admitted between September 15 and December 15 with influenza and symptoms of psychosis. Menninger would subsequently publish five professional papers on these cases, thereby launching his psychiatric career.[5]

Probably of greater consequence for Rosemary was the fact that a milder wave of influenza had passed through Boston the previous spring. According to Alfred Crosby's history of the epidemic, "flu had been nearly omnipresent in March and April." This was when Rose Kennedy was in the third and fourth months of her pregnancy. Although it was not known at the time, a later study reported that "maternal exposure to influenza at approximately the third to fourth month of gestation may be a risk factor for developing mental handicap." Another study showed that the intelligence scores of individuals who had been in their first trimester of development *in utero* during an influenza epidemic were lower than the scores of individuals born at other times. Even more alarming was a study showing that individuals who had been *in utero* in mid-pregnancy during an influenza epidemic had an increased chance of being later diagnosed with schizophrenia. This specter would later haunt the Kennedy family. [6]

Rosemary was said to have been "a very pretty baby" but "cried less" than her brothers had and did "not seem to have the vitality and energy" her brothers had shown. She was not as well coordinated, was unable to manage her baby spoon, and later could not steer a sled down the hill in winter or handle the oars of a rowboat in summer. She tried to join in the games of her siblings and their friends, but "there were many games and activities in which she didn't participate" and often was remembered as being just "part of the background."[7]

By the end of kindergarten, it was clear that something was seriously wrong with Rosemary when she was not passed to the first grade. Rose Kennedy consulted the head of the psychology department at Harvard, the first of many such consultations. The experts were unanimous in their opinion: Rosemary was mildly retarded. Terms used for such people in the 1920s included "feebleminded" and "moron." The early 1920s was the peak of the eugenics craze; male morons were said to have a high proclivity toward criminality, and female morons, toward prostitution.[8]

Joe and Rose Kennedy determined to prove the experts wrong. From primary school onward, Rosemary was sent to convent schools and provided with special tutors. For example, at the Sacred Heart Convent in Providence, Rosemary was taught in a classroom by herself, "set down before two nuns and another special teacher, Miss Newton, who worked with her all day long." The Kennedys also "hired a special governess or nurse with whom Rosemary lived part of the time." When Rosemary was at home, Rose Kennedy spent hours with her on the tennis court, "methodically hitting the ball back and forth to her" and helping her "to write better, to spell, and to count." The intense work helped Rosemary eventually achieve a fourth grade level in math and a fifth grade level in English, but she could go no farther. To those outside the family, the Kennedys pretended that Rosemary was normal. In *The Kennedy Women*, Laurence Leamer claimed that "even cousins and other relatives beyond the immediate family did not know about Rosemary's condition."[9]

Among the Kennedy siblings, Eunice, almost 3 years younger, took a special interest in her older sister. Eunice was the most religious of the five Kennedy girls, and "many thought that Eunice would one day become a nun." She "made a special point of spending time with Rosemary...integrating her into their lives." According to one family friend, "Eunice seemed to develop very early on a sense of special responsibility for Rosemary as if Rosemary were her child instead of her sister." Ted Kennedy later recalled, "Eunice reached out to make sure that Rosemary was included in all activities—whether it was Dodge Ball or Duck Duck Goose....Eunice was the one who ensured that Rosemary would have her fair share of successes." As teenagers the two sisters became close, traveling in Europe together in the summer of 1935. As Eunice later recalled: "We went on boat trips in Holland, climbed mountains in Switzerland, went rowing on Lake Lucerne....Rose[mary] could do all those things—rowing, climbing—as well or better than I. She could walk faster and longer distances than I could. And she was fun to be with." Like her mother, Eunice was determined to make Rosemary seem as normal as possible.[10]

Responsibility for protecting Rosemary also fell to her older brothers, Joe Jr. and Jack, who was closest to her in age. This was especially true as she matured. She was described as "an immensely pretty woman," according to some observers the most attractive of all the Kennedy sisters, and amply endowed. This, combined with her sweet demeanor and natural reticence, attracted young men, and it fell to Joe Jr. and Jack to warn them off. In summers they would escort her to dances at the Hyannis Yacht Club. As described in *The Kennedy Women*, "Jack put his name at the top of his sister's dance card and went around the room, getting his friends to help fill out the rest of the card." When writing to her from college, Jack's letters were described as "sensitive and warm," and a biographer described him as being "as generous toward his sister as any of the children." Rosemary's problems were thus indelibly etched upon Jack Kennedy's conscience, as would later become clear when he assumed the presidency.[11]

During their first year in London, the Kennedys had continued to include Rosemary in all family social activities. On May 11, 1938, Kathleen, age 18 years, and Rosemary, age 19 years, were presented to King George and Queen Elizabeth in a formal ceremony at Buckingham Palace. A few weeks later, Rose held a coming-out party for Kathleen and Rosemary, complete with 300 guests and an embassy official as Rosemary's escort. In September, Rosemary joined Eunice, Pat, Bobby, and their governess for a 2-week tour of Scotland and Ireland. Then, in December, Rosemary joined the family for a ski holiday at St. Moritz. According to *The Kennedy Women*, "Rose's main concern at St. Moritz was her eldest daughter...a picturesque young woman, a snow princess with flushed cheeks...[who] was attracting the attention of young men who took her cryptic silences and deliberate speech as feminine demureness." In March 1939, Rosemary joined her family to attend the investiture of Pope Pius XII in Rome, and on May 4, Rosemary was in attendance at the dinner given by the Kennedys for the King and Queen prior to the royal visit to the United States. Thus, until mid-1939, when she was almost 21 years old, Rosemary was very much part of the Kennedy family, protected by them and apparently functioning at a socially appropriate level (Figures 1.2 and 1.3).[12]

FIG 1.2 Rosemary (right), with sister Kathleen and their mother Rose, arriving at Buckingham Palace to be presented to the Queen in June, 1938. Rosemary was mildly retarded but 1 year later she developed the initial symptoms of what became a severe mental illness. (Copyright Bettmann/Corbis/ AP Images)

## A KENNEDY PROBLEM

Rosemary's status within the family changed during the summer of 1939, as the earliest symptoms of her mental illness became manifest. She remained in England when all of her family, except her father, returned to the United States in September. And when

FIG 1.3 Rosemary and her father in London in 1938. (Copyright Bettmann/Corbis/AP Images)

Joe Kennedy traveled to the States on November 29 to join his family for Christmas, Rosemary remained at the Hertfordshire convent. The people who were increasingly in charge of Rosemary's life were Edward M. Moore and his wife, Mary. Moore had begun working for Joe Kennedy in 1915. He was not only Kennedy's most trusted assistant but also Rosemary's godfather and the namesake of the youngest of the Kennedy children, Edward (Ted) Moore Kennedy. During the 3 months when Joe Kennedy was absent from England, from December 1939 through February 1940, the Moores remained there and looked after Rosemary's needs. The distance between Rosemary and her family at that point can be measured by the fact that she only learned of her father's return to England when she read about it in the newspaper.[13]

Throughout the spring of 1940, the Nazis marched inexorably across Europe. Norway and Denmark fell, then Belgium and the Netherlands. It seemed just a matter of time before German bombs would fall on England, and Joe Kennedy predicted that the country would fall by July. Having the Nazis overrun England and capture Rosemary was not a welcome idea, so finally, in May of 1940, the Moores escorted Rosemary back to the States by way of Lisbon. Reporters were told that she had remained in England "to continue her art studies" (Figure 1.4).[14]

FIG 1.4 Rosemary, Jack, and younger sister Jean in 1940, shortly after Rosemary had returned from England. At that time, she had begun showing symptoms of mental illness, in addition to her mild mental retardation. (AP Photo)

Joe Kennedy remained in London for five additional months, returning on October 22, just prior to the election. Wendell Wilkie, the Republican nominee, was proving to be a tougher foe than Roosevelt had anticipated. Kennedy represented a significant block of American voters who wanted American to stay out of Europe's war, so Roosevelt strongly urged him to publicly endorse his reelection. Although Kennedy suspected that Roosevelt would bring America into the war if given the chance, he endorsed him. When later asked why he had done so, Kennedy replied: "I simply made a deal with Roosevelt. We agreed that if I endorsed him for President in 1940, then he would support my son Joe for governor of Massachusetts in 1942." Although he had not yet finished law school, Joe Jr. was regarded as the most promising of the Kennedy children and "had made no secret of his ultimate intention to become president of the United States." Because Joe Sr.'s own political career was by then "in ruins," he was ready to pass his mantle of aspiration to his oldest son. As historian Alonzo Hamby noted, "he expected his children to achieve his frustrated ambitions for social acceptance and political recognition and deliberately guided them along that path."[15]

What limited information is available suggests that things did not go well for Rosemary after she returned from England. According to Peter Collier and David Horowitz's *The Kennedys*, "the basic skills she had labored so hard to master in her special schools were deteriorating." She lived with the Moores, at a convent in Boston, at a "special camp" in Massachusetts, and with her family for various periods. One Kennedy guest recalled that "it was embarrassing to be around Rosemary....She would behave in strange ways at the table....She would appear there standing in her nightgown when everyone else was moving ahead so rapidly." For one dinner party, Rose "didn't feel comfortable having Rosemary around" and asked her governess to take her to her home for the weekend.[16]

By the summer of 1941, Rosemary's behavior had become increasingly alarming. According to Doris Kearns Goodwin's *The Fitzgeralds and the Kennedys*, Rosemary's "customary good nature had given way to tantrums, rages and violent behavior. Pacing up and down the halls of her home, she was like a wild animal, given to screaming, cursing, and thrashing out at anyone who tried to thwart her will." For no apparent reason, "she would erupt in an inexplicable fury, the rage pouring out of her like a tempest from a cloudless sky." One significant episode that summer involved her 78-year-old grandfather, John F. Fitzgerald. "Rosemary, who was sitting on the porch at Hyannis, suddenly attacked Honey Fitz, hitting and kicking her tiny, white-haired grandfather until she was pulled away." Fitzgerald had been a three-term member of Congress and three-term mayor of Boston and was still regarded as one of the most powerful men in the city.[17]

Shortly after the attack on her grandfather, Rosemary was sent to live at St. Gertrude's School for Arts and Crafts, one of the first schools in the United States offering academic training for retarded children. It was part of a Benedictine convent in northeast Washington, D.C., located on Sargent Road, adjacent to the campus of Catholic University. Rosemary's sister Kathleen had already moved to Washington in August to take a job with the *Washington Times-Herald*. In October, Jack also moved to Washington to work at the Office of Naval Intelligence and lived at Dorchester House, on 16th Street. Kathleen and Jack could both, therefore, keep an eye on their increasingly unpredictable sibling.

What had become painfully clear was that something had to be done. Joe and Rose were afraid that their daughter would become pregnant, a potentially disgraceful situation for a Catholic family with political ambitions in an era when abortions were not a realistic option. Their fears only increased when Rosemary figured out how to escape from the convent and wander the streets of northeast Washington at night. In Goodwin's *The Fitzgeralds and the Kennedys*, Ann Gargan, Rosemary's cousin on her mother's side, recalled the Kennedy dilemma:

> She was the most beautiful of all the Kennedys. . . . She had the body of a twenty-one-year-old yearning for fulfillment with the mentality of a four-year-old. She was in a convent in Washington at the time, and many nights the school would call to say she was missing, only to find her out walking the streets at 2 a.m. Can you imagine what it must have been like to know your daughter was walking the streets in the darkness of the night, the perfect prey for an unsuspecting male?

In *The Kennedy Women*, Laurence Leamer added that "the nuns would find her wandering in the streets, her story disconnected and vague, and they would bring her back to the convent, ask her to bathe, and warn her never again to walk into those nighttime streets. Soon she would be off again. . . . The family worried there were men who wanted her and men she may have wanted. . . . The family feared that Rosemary had lost all control. . . . They feared that she was going out into the streets to do what Kathleen called 'the thing the priest says not to do.'" Edward Shorter, who had access to the Kennedy archives for his book on them, claims that "apparently in the course of these wanderings [Rosemary] was having sexual contact with men."[18]

It is not possible to give a definitive diagnosis of Rosemary's illness without access to her files. The Kennedy Foundation has kept them closed and rejected applications to view them, including my own request in October 2010, despite the fact that all the principals had died. According to FBI files, Joseph Kennedy's attorney confirmed that Rosemary had suffered from a "mental illness" for "many years." In her autobiography, Rose Kennedy herself acknowledged that "there were other factors at work besides retardation" and added: "A neurological disturbance or disease of some sort seemingly had overtaken her, and it was becoming progressively worse." Dr. Bertram S. Brown, former director of the National Institute of Mental Health, indicated in a 1968 interview that Rosemary "may well have had a schizophrenic illness," based on his discussion with psychiatrists who had been involved with the Kennedy family. What can be said with reasonable certainty is that Rosemary had developed a severe psychiatric disorder with psychotic features that fit somewhere in the clinical spectrum of schizophrenia, schizoaffective disorder, and bipolar disorder with psychotic features. This development should not have been completely unexpected; several studies have reported that between 4% and 8% of children who have mild mental retardation subsequently develop schizophrenia or other psychosis when they reach maturity. And, as noted previously, individuals exposed to the influenza virus prior to birth have an increased chance of later developing schizophrenia. [19]

## THE LOBOTOMY

One of Joe Kennedy's goals in life was to achieve respectability for himself and his family. As an Irish American in Boston, he had grown up in an era when "Paddy" and "Mick" occupied the lowest rungs on the social ladder. At college, according to Beschloss, "Kennedy seemed to seek out wellborn Harvard men, one of whom told him that he was being watched for signs of the behavior commonly thought of as Irish. Perhaps to escape the Irish stereotype, Kennedy neither smoked, drank or gambled." In 1922, when Kennedy applied for membership in the Cohasset Country Club, his wife "was snubbed by the Cohasset matrons and Joe was blackballed." Years later, he remembered it clearly: "Those narrow-minded bigoted sons of bitches barred me because I was an Irish Catholic and son of a barkeep." On another occasion, after having been referred to in the newspaper as an "Irishman," Kennedy exploded: "Goddam it! I was born in this country! My children were born in this country! What the hell does someone have to do to become an American?"[20]

Joe Kennedy's Irish roots and Catholic faith were thus significant impediments to respectability. Rosemary's mental retardation was yet another barrier, given beliefs about the genetic origins of mental retardation that were prevalent early in the twentieth century. But to have a daughter who was seriously mentally ill and in danger of becoming pregnant out of wedlock was perhaps the greatest impediment of all. In 1941 Freudian theories regarding the cause of mental illness were prominent, and standard textbooks of psychiatry, such as Aaron J. Rosanoff's *Manual of Psychiatry and Mental Hygiene*, claimed that schizophrenia and related diseases were caused by "chaotic sexuality" resulting from "inborn psychosexual ill-balance...mainly between the factors within the individual which makes for maleness and those which make for femaleness." Joe and Rose Kennedy had grown up in an era when the epithet "crazy Irish" was commonly directed at families like their own. As early as 1854, a Massachusetts

Commission on Lunacy had reported that Irish immigrants were disproportionately represented in the state's asylums. In the Boston Lunatic Hospital, for example, 80% of the inmates were Irish, compared with 31% of Boston's population. For a socially and politically ambitious Irish family like the Kennedys, having an insane family member was the definitive disgrace.[21]

The decision of Joe Kennedy to seek a lobotomy for Rosemary should be viewed in this historical light. The operation, which involves surgically severing the connections between the frontal lobe and the rest of the brain, had been pioneered by Dr. Edgar Moniz in Portugal in 1935. It had subsequently been introduced in the United States in 1936 by Drs. Walter J. Freeman, a neurologist, and James W. Watts, a neurosurgeon, in Washington. By 1941 Freeman and Watts had done lobotomies on almost 100 mentally ill patients and were claiming good results for many of them, especially those with symptoms of agitated depression and obsessive-compulsive symptoms. As Freeman later described it: "Disturbed patients often become friendly, quiet and cooperative.... The results are usually quite good, especially from an administrative point of view." However, "patients...with schizophrenia fared poorly by comparison," according to Freeman's biographer, who examined his records.[22]

Joe Kennedy's decision to have Rosemary lobotomized was made after careful consideration. According to one account, "when he was in England he had talked with doctors about a pioneering operation called a prefrontal lobotomy," suggesting that he was exploring this option in 1940, even before leaving England. The first lobotomy in England would not be done until the following year. Kennedy probably also got information from his daughter Kathleen. In 1941 she had gone to work for the *Washington Times-Herald* and had befriended John White, who was writing a series on mental illness for the paper. According to White, Kathleen quizzed him "rigorously" about it. She would "draw me out on the details—not just draw me out but absolutely drain me." Later she told him "it was because of Rosemary. She spoke slowly and sadly about it, as though she was confessing something quite embarrassing, almost shameful."[23]

For Joe Kennedy a lobotomy offered a definitive solution to the one problem that had defied him. Rosemary's retardation had been a source of great frustration to him, for money alone would not fix it. For example, when Rosemary was 10 years old, actress Gloria Swanson, Joe's mistress at the time, recalled his becoming enraged when he offered to donate money to a hospital "if they would guarantee that it could cure Rosemary," which, of course, they could not. Joe Kennedy's frustration in the face of his daughter's severe mental illness must have been several times greater than that engendered by her mild mental retardation.[24]

Thus, in the fall of 1941, Joe Kennedy went to Dr. Walter Freeman to arrange for a lobotomy for Rosemary. Freeman's office was in the LaSalle Building at Connecticut Avenue and L Street NW and was described as "a palatial penthouse in which patients waited in a 50-foot-long living room." Freeman, 45 years old at the time, had graduated from Yale University and the University of Pennsylvania Medical School and had trained in neurology in Europe. He had been raised as an Episcopalian with a Catholic mother and had visited Germany just prior to the outbreak of war. Like Kennedy, Freeman had publicly said many favorable things about Germany, so much so that the Federal Bureau of Investigation in 1942 investigated Freeman's "patriotism and political beliefs."[25]

For Walter Freeman, Kennedy offered a rare opportunity to do a lobotomy on the daughter of one of the nation's most powerful and influential men. According to Freeman's biographer, "he yearned to make an indelible mark on the treatment of the mentally ill." At the time Kennedy approached him, Freeman was making the final corrections to his book, *Psychosurgery: Intelligence, Emotion and Social Behavior following Prefrontal Lobotomy for Mental Disorders*, which would be published in 1942. Freeman regarded his book as "absolutely necessary to the popularization of psychosurgery." Freeman was an aggressive self-promoter in trying to get lobotomies established as a standard psychiatric treatment, despite intense criticism from many of his medical colleagues. He even hoped to win a Nobel Prize in Medicine for his work; the award instead went to Moniz in 1949.[26]

Thus, in mid-November 1941, Rosemary Kennedy was operated on at George Washington University Hospital by Dr. Watts, with Dr. Freeman supervising. Because Freeman was a neurologist and not trained to do neurosurgery, Watts did all the actual procedures until 1945, when the two men parted company. Watts was interviewed in 1994, shortly before his death. As described in Ronald Kessler's *The Sins of the Father*, Watts confirmed that Rosemary did indeed have a severe mental illness. After mildly sedating Rosemary and drilling two small holes in the top of her skull, Watts inserted a knife and "swung it up and down to cut brain tissue.... As Dr. Watts cut, Dr. Freeman asked Rosemary questions. For example, he asked her to recite the Lord's Prayer or sing 'God Bless America' or count backward.... 'We made an estimate on how far to cut based on how she responded,' Dr. Watts said. When she began to become incoherent, they stopped." Given Joe Kennedy's desperation for a definitive solution and his propensity for offering large sums of money to those who might help him solve his problems, it seems reasonable to assume that Drs. Freeman and Watts would have erred on the side of cutting too much rather than too little.[27]

And err they did—the lobotomy was an unmitigated disaster. As one family member described it in later years, the operation "made her go from mildly retarded to very retarded." According to Ronald Kessler, Rosemary could no longer wash or dress herself and was "like a baby." She had also lost most of her ability to speak: "She is like someone with a stroke who knows what you are saying and would like to let you know that she knows but she can't." This was in stark contrast to the usual descriptions of her as "just chattering all the time" prior to the surgery. In *The Kennedy Women*, Laurence Leamer described the lobotomized Rosemary as "like a painting that had been brutally slashed so it was scarcely recognizable. She had regressed into an infantlike state, mumbling a few words, sitting for hours staring at the walls, only traces left of the young woman she had been" (Figure 1.5).[28]

The effect of Rosemary's lobotomy on her family was understandably profound. Rose, who had spent so many hours trying to help her daughter, was devastated. Years later, after Jack and Bobby Kennedy had been assassinated, Rose said that she was "deeply hurt by what happened to my boys, but I feel more heartbroken about what happened to Rosemary....The assassinations hurt, but it was a different kind of hurt." Eunice, who loved and cared for Rosemary perhaps more than anyone in the family, was probably the most profoundly affected. A student at Manhattanville College in Purchase, New York, at the time, she "began to act strangely...and distanced herself even more from life and study at the college. She missed so many classes that one of her schoolmates...tutored her in chemistry." After Christmas recess Eunice abruptly left Manhattanville and transferred to Stanford University. There she was joined by her mother, according to one Kennedy biographer, suggesting that the family was concerned about her. At Stanford, Eunice was remembered as "a silent, sullen presence leaving almost no deep mark on the lives of women with whom she had lived for three years," suggesting an ongoing depression.[29]

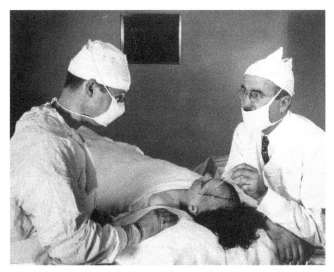

FIG 1.5  Neurosurgeon James Watts (left) and neurologist Walter Freeman (right), doing a lobotomy in 1942, a few months after having operated on Rosemary Kennedy. (Harris and Ewing Studio, courtesy of Special Collections Research Center, The George Washington University).

The effect of the lobotomy on Joe Kennedy is difficult to assess because most of his letters have not been made available. According to Amanda Smith, who had access to the Kennedy family files, "almost no mention of Rosemary survives among her father's papers after the end of 1940....Her correspondence ends, and she seldom appears except obliquely in the surviving family letters and papers." One letter, however, provides a clue. Written in 1958 to Sister Anastasia at St. Coletta's school and convent in Wisconsin, where Rosemary had been living for 15 years, the letter said: "I am still very grateful for your help....after all, the solution of Rosemary's problem has been a major factor in the ability of all the Kennedys to go about their life's work and to try to do it as well as they can."[30]

\* \* \*

Following her lobotomy, Rosemary was hospitalized for 7 years in Craig House, a private psychiatric hospital in Beacon, New York, best known for having had Zelda Fitzgerald as a patient. Because the hospital was only about 40 miles from Manhattanville College, that may be why Eunice abruptly transferred to Stanford 1 month after the lobotomy, to escape the painful reality of her sister's condition. In 1948 the Kennedys sought a permanent home for Rosemary and placed her in St. Coletta's School for Exceptional Children, a convent run by Franciscan nuns, in Jefferson, Wisconsin. Originally, the plan had been to place Rosemary in an institution in Massachusetts, close to her family, but the family was persuaded not to do so because of possible publicity. St. Coletta's, by contrast, was a thousand miles away in rural Wisconsin. There, on the grounds, the Kennedys built a private house and set up a trust fund to provide for four full-time staff to care for her. She also had a dog and a car in which she could be taken out for rides. In 1983 the Kennedys donated a million dollars to St. Coletta's, and Rosemary remained there until her death in 2005 at the age of 86.[31]

For the rest of their lives, the tragedy of Rosemary would hang over the Kennedy family, like Edgar Allan Poe's raven:

> And the raven, never flitting, still is sitting, still is sitting
> On the pallid bust of Pallas just above my chamber door;
> And his eyes have all the seeming of a demon's that is dreaming.

Rosemary essentially disappeared. According to Janet Des Rosiers, Joe Kennedy's secretary and mistress, "Rosemary's name was never mentioned in the house. I knew she existed because I saw the family photographs in the attic. But the name was never mentioned." According to Kennedy biographers who had access to the family's correspondence, there was "almost no mention" of Rosemary in Joe Kennedy's correspondence after the lobotomy, as noted above, and Rose Kennedy did "not mention her again in a letter for the next twenty years." In addition, according to David Nasaw's biography of Joe Kennedy, "there is no evidence that anyone in the family either visited or was in contact with Rosemary or the nuns for the first ten or so years" she was at St. Coletta's. In later years, Rose and other family members did visit, but Joe never did. Evidence of the lobotomy itself also disappeared. According to Walter Freeman's biographer, "Freeman's correspondence and private writings are silent on the question of her surgery and its outcome." It would be 20 years before the family would even publicly acknowledge that Rosemary had been mildly mentally retarded, and no family member has ever publicly acknowledged her mental illness.[32]

According to Laurence Leamer's *The Kennedy Men*, "the lobotomy is the emotional divide in the history of the Kennedy family, an event of transcendent psychological importance." Plane crashes took the lives of Joe Jr. in 1944 and Kathleen in 1948, and assassinations killed Jack in 1963 and Bobby in 1968, but none of these deaths had as profound an effect on the Kennedy family as Rosemary's lobotomy had. Plane crashes and assassinations can be viewed as acts of God, but the lobotomy was an act of a Kennedy. Rosemary's tragedy was a family sin that demanded expiation. That opportunity would present itself in 1960, when John F. Kennedy was elected president.[33]

# 2

## ROBERT FELIX: A MAN WITH PLANS

In the fall of 1941, at the same time that Rosemary Kennedy was undergoing a lobotomy in Washington, Dr. Robert H. Felix was writing his master's degree thesis at Johns Hopkins University School of Public Health in Baltimore, 40 miles away. Bob Felix's thesis consisted of a plan to fix the nation's mental illness treatment system by replacing overcrowded state mental hospitals with "properly staffed out-patient clinics" that would "eventually be available throughout the length and breadth of the land." As a member of the U.S. Public Health Service, Felix believed that such programs should be initiated at the federal level and not merely left up to the states. Twenty years later, the consequences of Rosemary Kennedy's lobotomy would intersect with Bob Felix's plan, leading to profound changes in America's mental illness treatment system (Figure 2.1).[1]

Felix, 37 years old at the time, had grown up in Downs, Kansas, which had a population of 1,427. His father and grandfather had both been country doctors, so it surprised no one when Felix continued his education at the University of Colorado School of Medicine. Graduating with honors, he then took psychiatric training under Dr. Franklin Ebaugh at the Colorado Psychopathic Hospital, one of a handful of special research psychiatric hospitals in the United States. Ebaugh was an outspoken opponent of traditional

FIG 2.1 Robert H. Felix, M.D.., the architect of the federal mental health program and first director of the National Institute of Mental Health (NIMH) from 1946 to 1962. In 1984, he acknowledged that the program's "result is not what we intended." Photo courtesy of the National Library of Medicine.

state hospitals and a proponent of mental hygiene and community treatment. Felix recalled his training as "one of the most important experiences in my professional career....We were steeped in community psychiatry and a philosophy of public service."[2]

Following his training, Felix entered the United States Public Health Service and worked in the federal prison in Springfield, Missouri; the federal narcotics treatment center in Lexington, Kentucky; and the Coast Guard Academy in New London, Connecticut. He became known for his expertise in treating alcoholism and drug addiction but apparently had little experience with other psychiatric disorders or state mental hospitals. In 1944 he became chief of the Mental Hygiene Division of the Public Health Service. At the time, the Mental Hygiene Division reflected the very limited involvement of the federal government in mental illness issues. The government screened immigrants for mental illness, provided services to federal prisons, ran two narcotics treatment hospitals, and ran St. Elizabeths Hospital, which provided psychiatric services for residents of the District of Columbia, merchant seamen, and Native Americans. Other than these, all other psychiatric services were provided by state and county governments.

In 1945, following congressional testimony on the disabling effects of mental illness on America's fighting forces, the Surgeon General "asked Felix to design a national mental health program." Felix merely had to take his master's degree thesis off the shelf. He was ideally suited to lead such an effort; medical historian Gerald Grob described him as "a gregarious, humorous, and charismatic personality...one of the shrewdest and most effective federal bureaucrats of his generation." Psychiatrist Alan Miller, who worked under Felix, remembered him as "one of the most engaging, persuasive, energetic, wide-visioned rascals I have ever met. A man of virtue, but nevertheless a rascal. He had strong principles, and when necessary he could rise above them." Bertram S. Brown, who also worked under Felix, likened his interpersonal skills to those of former president Bill Clinton and called Felix "an enormous human rolodex." Felix understood, Brown added, "that members of Congress and their families get sick too, and if you help them, then they will help you." Felix was an expert at cultivating key members of Congress, and when he went to Congress to get his programs passed, it was often a mutual admiration society. The following, for example, is an exchange between Senator Lister Hill and Felix, after Felix had become the Director of the National Institute of Mental Health:

Senator Hill: "I will give him [Felix] another quotation, if I may. 'An institution is but the length and shadow of an individual.' Here is the head of the National Institute of Mental Health and what you have just commented on shows this wonderful leadership there."

Dr. Felix: "Sir, shadows are cast by light and were it not for the glowing light that comes from this house [the Senate] and the House of Representatives, I would have no shadow at all."[3]

## A RADICAL DEPARTURE

The plan outlined by Robert Felix in 1941 and then formally proposed in 1945 was "to employ the prestige and resources of the national government to redirect mental health priorities." It is difficult today to comprehend just how radical such a plan was at that time. Since 1766, when the governor of Virginia asked the House of Burgesses for funds to open the first public psychiatric hospital in the United States, the care of mentally ill individuals had been the exclusive responsibility of state and local governments. This was in accord with the tenth amendment to the Constitution, which explicitly stated that "powers not delegated to the United States by the Constitution...[are] reserved to the States respectively, or to the people."[4]

The first half of the nineteenth century saw an ongoing debate among states, cities, and counties regarding their respective fiscal responsibilities for mentally ill individuals. Worcester State Hospital, opened in Massachusetts in 1833, was the first state hospital supported exclusively with state funds. Largely because of the advocacy of Dorothea Dix, 28 of the existing 33 states subsequently built one or more state psychiatric hospitals by 1860. Fiscal responsibility varied from state to state; Wisconsin, for example, built "a system of county asylums for persistently mentally ill patients and provided a [state] subsidy to cover part of the costs that were involved." Over time the states assumed increasing fiscal responsibility from the counties and cities, and in 1890 New York State passed legislation providing "for removal of all the insane from local poorhouses and jails to state hospitals, where they were to be supported and treated at state expense." Many states followed suit, so that "after 1900 state care of the mentally ill, with a few notable exceptions, became the general rule."[5]

Prior to 1945 there had been only one attempt to transfer state responsibility for mentally ill individuals to the federal government. In the first half of the nineteenth century, the federal government sometimes raised funds by selling federal lands. Beginning in 1847, Dorothea Dix and her supporters lobbied the federal government to use the proceeds of 12,225,000 acres of federal land to build state psychiatric hospitals. A bill was introduced and passed by Congress in 1854. However, it was immediately vetoed by President Franklin Pierce, who viewed it as contrary to the Constitution and a foot in the federal door for states to transfer their responsibility for mentally ill and other needy individuals. In his veto message, Pierce noted:

> If Congress have power to make provision for the indigent insane...the whole field of public beneficence is thrown open to the care and culture of the Federal Government....I readily...acknowledge the duty incumbent on us all...to provide for those who, in the mysterious order of Providence, are subject to want and to disease of body or mind, but I cannot find any authority in the

Constitution that makes the Federal Government the great almoner of public charity throughout the United States. To do so would, in my judgment, be contrary to the letter and spirit of the Constitution... [and] be prejudicial rather than beneficial to the noble offices of charity.

If the proposed legislation were enacted, Pierce predicted:

...the fountains of charity will be dried up at home, and the several States, instead of bestowing their own means on the social wants of their own people, may themselves, through the strong temptation, which appeals to States as to individuals, become humble suppliants for the bounty of the Federal Government, reversing their true relation to this Union.[6]

Pierce's veto ended discussion of this idea for almost 100 years. As a consolation prize for Dix, in 1855 Congress established the Government Hospital for the Insane, which became known as St. Elizabeths Hospital, for residents of the District of Columbia and other federal dependents, such as merchant seamen and Native Americans.

## THE NATIONAL PLAN

The 1945 plan of Robert Felix to involve the federal government in a wide range of mental illness-related activities was virtually without precedent. In 1906 Congress had passed the Pure Food and Drug Act, and in the 1930s it had set up the National Institute of Health and National Cancer Institute. Felix's plan proposed that the federal government create a mental illness research center to be called the National Neuropsychiatric Institute, that it use federal funds to train more mental health workers, and that it use federal funds for the early detection, treatment, and ultimately prevention of mental illness.

The detection, treatment, and prevention of mental illness was to be accomplished by two related programs—community mental health clinics and the modification of the environment to prevent future cases of mental illness. In a 1945 paper, Felix said the proposed clinics would treat "the non-psychotic and pre-psychotic patients with personality problems of varying severity, and the convalescent psychotic patients who need guidance and help in making successful adjustment to home, occupation, and community environment." To accomplish early detection and treatment, Felix added, "we must go out and find the people who need help," focusing especially on "the schools, the courts, [and] the welfare department." He likened his program for early detection and treatment to "the campaigns against venereal disease and tuberculosis" that were prominent at that time and widely regarded as having been successful. In

1947 Felix further quantified his plan, recommending "one out-patient mental health clinic for each 100,000 of the population" to provide "psychiatric treatment or psychological counseling for patients not in need of hospitalization and, most significant, for patients in the early stage of illness, when the prospect of cure is greatest."[7]

The idea of early detection and treatment of psychiatric disorders was seductive in 1945, as it still is today. It assumes, however, that early cases can be identified. In 1945 Felix and many other American psychiatrists were enamored with the ideas of Sigmund Freud and the mental hygiene movement, and from 1951 to 1955, Felix undertook formal psychoanalytic training. Freud and mental hygiene advocates believed that small problems in childhood, if untreated, led directly to big problems in adulthood, including schizophrenia, bipolar disorder, and major depression. As Felix later wrote, "As a tree is bent so it grows. And we like to do what we can while the youth is, figuratively speaking, a sapling." Thus, Felix supported and praised early experiments, such as one in the St. Louis public schools, "where the teachers are given mental health orientation so that they can help in case finding, and group therapy sessions are set up to work with and through the parents rather than the children." Such early treatments, Felix assumed, would prevent major problems from developing later.[8]

The second part of Felix's national mental health plan involved modifications of the social and cultural environment, which he believed would prevent the emergence of future psychiatric problems. As he wrote in a 1948 paper, "the content and the orientation of personality are powerfully influenced by the social setting." Thus, serious mental illnesses were caused by social factors, such as "areas of high mobility and disorganized community life." Felix believed that serious mental illnesses were also caused by cultural factors, and he cited the research of Margaret Mead, whom he was using as a consultant at the time. For example, the paranoid South Pacific culture described by Mead's second husband, Reo Fortune, in *The Sorcerers of Dobu* was cited by Felix as an example of a mentally unhealthy culture. Mead's claims were widely accepted in the United States at that time; it would not be until later that her cultural research would be shown to be fatally flawed and Reo Fortune's cultural observations in Dobu shown to be a product of his own paranoid personality.[9]

Because he believed mental illness could be caused by social and cultural factors, Felix deemed it to be the legitimate task of mental health clinics to correct such factors. Thus, he wrote:

> It should be made clear that mental hygiene must be concerned with more than the psychoses and with more than hospitalized mental illness....Our research attention should be directed not only to the psychotherapeutic sessions between doctor and patient, but also to the social world out of which the patient came, in which he is now living, and to which he will return. This focus

on the "individual in environment" means that psychotherapy should be supplemented in at least some of our experiments by what might be called "sociotherapy," observation and treatment of the patient's relevant social setting, both during his treatment and post-treatment periods.

As examples of such legitimate mental hygiene activities, Felix listed "parent education, the promotion of special classes for exceptional children, marriage counseling, therapeutic recreational activities, and cooperative projects with courts and other agencies." Indeed, there was no problem too big for psychiatrists who wished to promote mental hygiene. Felix cited approvingly the claims of C. Brock Chisholm of the World Health Organization:

> We have never had a really peaceful society in the world.... Can the world learn to live at peace?... With the other human sciences, psychiatry must now decide what is to be the immediate future of the human race. No one else can. And this is the prime responsibility of psychiatry.[10]

## THE NATIONAL NEUROPSYCHIATRIC INSTITUTE

In ordinary times, Felix's radical mental health plan would have quietly circulated in Washington among a few interested people, then died a natural death. But the postwar years were not ordinary times. The end of World War II confronted the nation with two disturbing facts: serious mental illnesses were much more prevalent than people had previously believed, and conditions in state mental hospitals were appalling. The first became clear from congressional testimony regarding the military draft. Among all men rejected for induction during the war, 18% had been rejected because of "mental illness," 14% more because of mental retardation, and 5% because of neurological diseases. Once in uniform, among all men discharged for disability, 38% "were due to mental disease." General Lewis B. Hershey, director of the Selective Service System, testified that "mental illness was the greatest cause of noneffectiveness or loss of manpower that we met."[11]

Conditions in state mental hospitals became public when more than 3,000 conscientious objectors—mostly Mennonites and Quakers—were assigned to alternative duty during the war in one-third of the nation's state mental hospitals. These idealistic young men were appalled by what they found and in 1943 began publishing their findings. The reports of the conscientious objectors included scenes such as the following:

> He opened the door to another room. I stood frozen at what I saw. Here were two hundred and fifty men—all of them completely naked—standing about the walls of the most dismal room I have ever seen. There was no furniture of

any kind. Patients squatted on the damp floor or perched on the window seats. Some of them huddled together in corners like wild animals. Others wandered about the room picking up bits of filth and playing with it.

Such conditions should not have been surprising, as the hospitals were grossly over-crowded and understaffed. The population of state mental hospitals had increased dramatically, from 150,151 in 1903 to 423,445 in 1940. In addition, up to half of the hospitals' professional staff members had been drafted for the war effort.[12]

Investigating commissions followed the published reports, and in 1945 a Grand Jury indicted the State of Ohio for "the uncivilized social system which enabled such an intolerable and barbaric practice to fasten itself upon the people." *Life* magazine picked up the story, and on May 6, 1946, published a sensational exposé, "Bedlam 1946: Most U.S. Mental Hospitals Are a Shame and a Disgrace." Included were Bosch-like photographs of naked patients. The story etched the problem of mental illness into the consciousness and conscience of the nation as nothing had previously done.

The prevalence of mental illnesses and conditions in state mental hospitals stirred Congress to action, and on September 18, 1945, just one month after the sur-render of the Japanese, congressional hearings opened on the proposed National Neuropsychiatric Institute Act and national mental health plan. Its purpose, as stated in the legislation, was "to provide for, foster, and aid in coordinating research relating to neuropsychiatric disorders; to provide for more effective methods of prevention, diagnosis, and treatment of such disorders; to establish the National Neuropsychiatric Institute; and for other purposes." A national institute to support research on neuro-psychiatric diseases had originally been proposed in 1939, shortly after the National Cancer Institute had been set up by Congress; its mission was to carry out "laboratory and clinical investigations of mental and nervous diseases." In congressional hearings on the newly proposed institute in 1945 and 1946, frequent references were made to the Manhattan Project, which had resulted in the making of the atomic bomb. Because research had made the bomb, surely a similar research effort could discover the causes of and treatments for mental illnesses.[13]

The proposed National Neuropsychiatric Institute, however, was intended to do much more than just research. That was assured by Felix, who with his colleagues had largely written the bill and then persuaded Representative Percy Priest, chairman of the Labor and Public Welfare Committee, to introduce it. In addition to research on neuropsychiatric disorders, the legislation said that the proposed institute would "pro-vide for more effective methods of prevention, diagnosis, and treatment of such disor-ders" and be used "for other purposes." Such vague language was intentional; as Felix later recalled in an interview, "I wanted [the bill] written in broad language…and the Act is broad. There is literally nothing I can't do." Insofar as it had a non-research as well as a research mission, the National Neuropsychiatric Institute would be different from the National Cancer Institute and other research institutes to be later created under the National Institute of Health.[14]

Felix knew precisely what his non-research agenda was going to be under a National Neuropsychiatric Institute. In congressional testimony, he proposed using "grants-in-aid to States…for the establishment of psychiatric out-patient clinical facilities, for demonstrations of approved community mental health programs." Such clinics would be used "to treat individuals before they reach the point where they must avail themselves of such asylum as is provided. If it would assist to stimulate the states to provide these outpatient facilities, I think it is proper for the federal government to contribute a certain amount of money." Thus, for the first time, the federal government would be taking on a fiscal role in the clinical care of individuals with mental illness, other than the federal narcotics hospitals and St. Elizabeths Hospital. It was a federal foot in the states' door, and it would never be closed again.[15]

Once passage of the National Neuropsychiatric Institute Act was assured, Felix and his psychiatric colleagues suggested changing the name of the new institute to more clearly reflect its intended mission. "Neuropsychiatric," they concluded, was too medical and too narrow. According to Gerald Grob, "the psychiatric establishment, because of its prevalent psychoanalytic emphasis, leaned toward mental health rather than neurology." Among alternative names considered were the National Mental Hygiene Institute and the National Institute of Mental Health (NIMH). The latter won out, and within NIMH mental *health* would thereafter take precedence over mental *illness*. This shift in priorities would prove to be crucial. On July 3, 1946, President Harry Truman signed the bill, and the federal government had officially gone into the business of mental health.[16]

Given the magnitude of the proposed departure from almost 200 years of the existing federal–state allocation of fiscal responsibilities, it is surprising that more questions were not raised during the 1945–1946 congressional hearings. The main voices of dissent were those of Senator Robert A. Taft and Representative Clarence J. Brown, both Republicans from Ohio. Brown, who had been the Ohio state statistician, secretary of state, and lieutenant governor, strongly agreed with the need for a national research institute but was highly suspicious of federal money being used to support psychiatric services:

I agree with everything that has been said as to the necessity for research and study of this problem, but it seems to me that we must always draw the line somewhere, or build a fence to define the field of activity in which the federal government can participate and the field in which the responsibility rests with the local and state governments and with the individual citizens themselves.

I believe the federal government should lead the way in research, in furnishing information and advice to the people of the states and their local subdivisions, but I don't think the federal government should take the responsibility of administering aid to the individual all the way through.

Representative Brown also observed that local and state governments would be quick to seize upon federal funds as a means of saving their own funds:

That is ... because a lot of our citizens are very short-sighted and don't seem to realize that when the federal government spends the money it costs them just as much, if not a little more, as when the local government spends the money, and they have to pay for it in the end anyhow.

Brown appeared to have been the only member of Congress who correctly understood Felix's true intentions and where his national plan was heading:

Men get strange ideas; they get hobbies and they decide the only way in the world they are going to solve all the problems of mankind is to do a certain thing and that their field is the most important.[17]

## THE MENTAL HEALTH LOBBY

Robert Felix's "hobby," the federalization of mental health services, was underway. By 1948 he was using his broad new authority to award $2.1 million ($19.0 million in 2010 dollars) to 45 states "for assistance in the development or expansion of community mental health services." The federally funded activities included, according to Felix, "the establishment and maintenance of out-patient community mental health clinics"; paying "mental health personnel who can serve ... in a consultant, supervisory, or service capacity to State and community health and welfare agencies, as well as to schools, courts, well-baby clinics, prenatal clinics etc."; setting up "short courses ... to demonstrate techniques of disseminating the latest psychiatric information to the practicing physician," especially "the newest accepted concepts of the role the emotions play in illness"; and finally, "education and preventive activity ... in schools, colleges and community groups such as the P.T.A. ... [in] cooperation with State and local mental hygiene societies." Based on Freudian and mental hygiene theories, the federal program was intended to carry the concepts of mental health to every corner of American society; this idea would dominate the psychiatric landscape for the next half-century. As Felix phrased it in 1957: "From the simple gesture of a helping hand we have gone on to create a network of community mental health services which has been woven into the structure of our society."[18]

It should be noted that the new federal mental health program did nothing to improve state mental hospitals. That was because Congress, fearful that NIMH would try to completely usurp the authority of the states, specifically stated that "federal funds could *not* be used to train personnel or obtain equipment for state hospitals." This exclusion was agreeable to Felix, and he may have even suggested it. As one historian noted, Felix was "from his early days as a resident... committed to abolishing the state mental hospital in favor of some form of community care." He would later predict that "public mental hospitals as we know them today can disappear in 25 years... [because] all the various types of emotionally disturbed patients can be handled in the community."[19]

By the late 1940s, Felix had developed a coterie of like-minded colleagues who shared his vision of a mentally healthy America. This group would become a powerful lobby and would be largely responsible for the unprecedented increase in federal mental health allocations over the next two decades. It consisted of three psychiatrists who had helped Felix write the original plan to create the National Institute of Mental Health—Jack Ewalt, William Menninger, and Francis Braceland—and a crusading journalist, Mike Gorman. They all shared a belief that psychiatric illnesses could be treated in the community and that state mental hospitals were no longer necessary. They also shared a belief that mental illness could be prevented using the principles of mental hygiene. Felix, Ewalt, Menninger, and Braceland had all been, or would be, trained in psychoanalysis, and all would become presidents of the American Psychiatric Association and thus be in a national position to help implement their mental hygiene vision, using federal funds to do so.[20]

Ewalt, like Felix, had come from a small town in Kansas and had also attended the University of Colorado and trained in psychiatry with Dr. Franklin Ebaugh at the Colorado Psychopathic Hospital. As Ewalt wrote in 1955: "The goal of community mental health services is to prepare people for living, to promote health. It should aid in the development of resilient character among the population, so that the vicissitudes of life can be handled." Its activities should include the early detection of cases but also "consultation with school teachers, guidance counselors, school psychologists, physicians, health nurses, judges, the clergy, and other key persons to promote healthy attitudes in the community, and to improve areas in the community that foster discontent and tensions." Like other members of the mental health lobby, Ewalt believed that the federal government should take financial responsibility for the care of mentally ill persons. In fact, it was said that Ewalt "desired total federal financing for the cost of services for the mentally ill."[21]

Menninger was also from Kansas and had founded, with his father and his older brother, Karl, the Menninger Clinic. As part of the Kansas connection, he was a crucial

Felix ally; their fathers had been friends, and Menninger and Felix had known each other since childhood. Menninger believed that because psychiatrists "have some knowledge of the unconscious dynamics" of human behavior, they are obligated "to participate in community affairs in order to apply our psychiatric knowledge to human problems." Specifically, he urged his colleagues to:

> ...assume citizenship responsibilities for policy forming at whatever level we can—in the Board of Education, City Council, civic clubs, welfare groups, legislative committees, Congressional hearings.... As psychiatrists, we are expected to provide leadership and counsel to the family, the community, the state, welfare workers, educators, industrialists, religious leaders, and others.[22]

The third psychiatrist who was part of Felix's inner circle was Francis Braceland, who had come from Philadelphia and studied psychoanalysis with Carl Jung in Switzerland. Braceland believed that the causes of mental illness lay in interpersonal relations: "Men do not get mentally sick 'out of the blue,' so to speak...their illness or well-being depends upon their relations with other men." The role of the psychiatrist was therefore to teach people how to live together, in the broadest sense. "Modern psychiatry," he said, "no longer focuses entirely upon mental disease, nor the individual as 'mental patient,' but rather it envisages man in the totality of his being and in the totality of his relationships." "Psychiatry," he added, was "an essential part of the overall science of man.... One might even say the ideal goal of the psychiatrist is to achieve wisdom."[23]

Felix, Ewalt, Menninger, and Braceland had lofty visions of using the federal government to create a brave new world, a mentally healthy America. Without Mike Gorman, the fifth member of their group, however, their lobbying would probably have been in vain. The son of Irish immigrant parents, Gorman graduated cum laude from New York University in 1934, then undertook 2 years of graduate work in history but did not receive a degree. Following work with the *New York Post*, he joined the Air Force in 1942 and was assigned as a public relations specialist to Tinker Air Force Base in Oklahoma. After being discharged in 1945, Gorman went to work as a reporter for the *Daily Oklahoman*. Following the publication of *Life* magazine's 1946 exposé of conditions in state mental hospitals, Gorman's editor assigned him to investigate Oklahoma's state hospitals. The result was a sensational newspaper series that, 2 years later, was published as a book: *Oklahoma Attacks Its Snake Pits*. Gorman compared the hospitals to "a witch's brew of jangled minds rattling about in cobwebbed filth and misery." The dining room of one hospital, wrote Gorman, "made Dante's *Inferno* seem like a country club," and the kitchen "was more gruesome than the Black Hole of Calcutta." The patients were described as "groveling about the floors and wards sans the slightest stitch of clothing,"

FIG 2.2 Mike Gorman, a mental health lobbyist who worked for Mary Lasker. He played a major role in getting the community mental health centers program implemented and in shutting down the state psychiatric hospitals. Photo courtesy of Michael Gorman Jr.

and the hospital superintendents as being "more concerned with the animals on the institution farm than with the patients on the crowded wards." Gorman's book was condensed by the *Reader's Digest* in 1948, thus providing him with a national forum. Mary Lasker, a wealthy New York philanthropist who was an advocate for increased research spending on various diseases, subsequently hired him to go to Washington to lobby for increased research spending on mental illnesses (Figure 2.2).[24]

Mike Gorman had two experiences that dominated his thinking on mental illness and ultimately shaped the federal mental health program. First, like many radical students in New York in the 1930s, he was a member of the Communist Party. According to an FBI investigation carried out in 1952, "Gorman was a member and reputed leader of the National Student League," identified as "a front organization of the Communist Party" at New York University. He was said to have been "thoroughly imbued with radical political philosophy,...espoused Communist ideas,...[and] approved a centralized form of government." According to these records, Gorman's mother said that he and his brother both "talked like regular Communists." As late as 1943, while in the Air Force, Gorman was accused of being a Communist and did not deny it.[25]

Second, Gorman had had personal experience with the mental illness treatment system. In 1945 he had been discharged from the Air Force because of psychiatric symptoms, specifically "anxiety...insomnia, emotional outbursts, anorexia and vomiting." The FBI files mention rumors that Gorman had been hospitalized, but this was not verified. Following his discharge, Gorman drank excessively and at some point underwent psychoanalysis, although he later derided psychoanalysts as "the High Priests of the Oedipus Complex and the rampant Id."[26]

Armed with his public relations background, writing skills, and considerable personal charm, Gorman became a consummate Washington insider, one of the most effective lobbyists the nation's capital had ever seen. He claimed to be "on a first-name basis with one hundred fifty, one hundred seventy-five members of the House," including "all the members of the Appropriations committees." On the Senate side, Gorman was on a first-name basis with Senator Lister Hill, chairman of the Committee on Labor and Public Welfare and one of the most powerful men in the Senate. As early as 1955 Gorman was ghostwriting speeches for Hill, and in 1956 Gorman dedicated his book *Every Other Bed* to "Senator Lister Hill, valiant legislator for, and compassionate friend of, the mentally ill of this nation." Gorman's considerable lobbying skills were assisted by Mary Lasker's considerable money; she was known as "one of the nation's more generous campaign contributors." Most of the contributions were publicly targeted to members of the key committees; Bertram S. Brown, former director of NIMH, recalled Gorman showing him $1,200 in hundred-dollar bills to be given to a chairman of a key House subcommittee. Gorman himself described his lobbying activities as a "high class kind of subversion. Very high class. We're not second story burglars. We go right in the front door."[27]

Gorman's mental health agenda coincided perfectly with the agenda of Felix, although the two men did not like each other. No room was large enough for both egos, and on one occasion a friend had to sit them down together to mediate their dispute. Gorman despised state hospitals, referring to them as "secular cloisters of the mad," and he later acknowledged that "my hidden agenda was to break the back of the state mental hospital." The plans of Felix and his psychiatric colleagues to involve psychiatrists in social problems to promote a "mentally healthy" environment would have also resonated with Gorman's socialist beliefs. Gorman wrote: "Mental illness is really a social problem. It is not exclusively a psychological or biological one. We frankly have to help people change their communities if necessary…until the noxious milieu in which the illness festers is tackled." He praised the work of mental health centers that were "involved in housing committees and tenant councils, which force slumlords to improve living conditions." Finally, Gorman strongly agreed with Felix that the federal government should be intimately involved in the care of mentally ill individuals. He wrote: "It was a historic mistake to make the State alone responsible for public care of its mentally ill residents…sparing the Federal Government anything but peripheral involvement in the problem."[28]

## ACTION FOR MENTAL HEALTH

By the mid-1950s, the mental health lobby was fully operational. Felix's psychiatric favors, combined with Lasker's fiscal favors, had persuaded many key members of Congress that supporting mental health was a good thing. The hot war in Korea had given way in 1953 to a more amorphous cold war with Communism, and economic prosperity reigned. Belief in the ability of the federal government to solve all national problems was at an historic high, illustrated by such things as President Harry Truman's Fair Deal and President Dwight Eisenhower's interstate highway system.

To the mental health lobby, it seemed like a propitious time to implement the next phase of the federalization of American mental health. Accordingly, in 1954 the American Psychiatric Association issued a call for a national commission to "study current conditions and develop a national mental health program." This was followed by legislation to create such a commission, introduced in the Senate by Gorman's friend, Senator Hill. First-term Senator John F. Kennedy was a cosponsor; both Felix and Gorman were aware that Kennedy's sister had been mentally ill as well as mentally retarded, and they targeted the new senator to join their cause.[29]

Hearings on the proposed commission were held in the House and Senate during the spring of 1955. Felix described state mental hospitals as warehouses where almost nobody got well or was discharged:

> By the time the patient has been in the hospital for 2 years, his chances of get-ting out alive....I should say, are about 16 to 1. By the time the patient has been in the hospital for 8 years, his chances against getting out alive are poorer than 99 to 1.

Braceland testified that if such statistics were "for any other condition, it would be regarded as a national emergency immediately, but with mental disease peculiarly in many cases we meet with only a sympathetic and respectful apathy." Gorman empha-sized the tremendous cost to the states of caring for mentally ill persons. In New York, he claimed, "the mental health budget for the current year is up to $158 million a year, 35 percent of their operating budget." Nationally, the "annual cost increase" to the states was "exceeding $100 million."[30]

Voting to support a national commission is usually a safe vote for members of Congress, and the bill to establish a Joint Commission on Mental Illness and Health passed both houses without a single dissenting vote. Predictably, Congress then appointed Felix to set up the commission, and Felix promptly appointed Ewalt to be the director and Braceland and Gorman to be commission members.

In setting up the commission, Felix and Ewalt demonstrated their astute under-standing of how Washington works. The intended purpose of the commission was to prepare the ground for a far-reaching national mental health program. To garner public support, a wide range of professional organizations were invited to appoint a member to the commission. By the time Felix and Ewalt finished, they had 45 individual mem-bers representing various organizations and 36 "participating agencies," including the American Academy of Neurology, American Academy of Pediatrics, American College of Chest Physicians, American Medical Association, Catholic Hospital Association, National Education Association, U. S. Department of Defense, and U. S. Department of Justice. Almost everyone, it appeared, was against mental illness and for mental health. But the most inspired move of the organizers was to persuade the politically conservative American Legion to also sign on. As will be described in Chapter 5, many Americans in the 1950s suspected that the mental health movement was a left wing, even Communist, plot. Having the American Legion's imprimatur for the commission blunted such criticism.[31]

The Joint Commission on Mental Illness and Health held a series of public hearings between 1955 and 1960. The purpose of the hearings was to build a consensus and persuade the public, and members of Congress, of the need for a national mental health program. Much of the public education was accomplished, according to historians of the movement, by attracting "broad media coverage over a sustained period of time; from academic journals to Sunday supplements, the whole society had been exposed to an education in mental health." The success of the campaign can be measured by the increases it produced in NIMH's budget. Between 1950 and 1955, the NIMH budget had increased modestly, from $9.2 to $14.0 million ($83.5 to $114.3 million in 2010 dollars). However, between 1955 and 1960, while the Joint Commission was proselytizing the principles of community mental health across the nation, the NIMH budget increased almost fivefold, from $14.0 to $67.5 million ($114.3 to $499.0 million in 2010 dollars). In a 1972 interview, Felix expressed great pride in his success in having increased NIMH's budget, placing the institute in the "top three" institutes at NIH, "along with cancer and heart."[32]

The final report of the commission contained something for everyone. As David Mechanic described in his book *Mental Health and Social Policy*, "the report of the Joint Commission... was largely an ideological document, and, like poetry, it was sufficiently ambiguous to allow various interest groups to read what they wished into it." It included predictable calls for more federal funds for research and mental health manpower training as well as three key recommendations.[33]

First, state mental hospitals were said to be "bankrupt beyond remedy." Second, it said that future psychiatric services should be coordinated by community mental health centers, and the commission recommended one center for each 50,000 population. Third, and most important, the Joint Commission "proposed massive financial participation by the federal government in the care of mental patients who had been the major responsibility of the states." Specifically, the commission report noted:

It is self-evident that the States for the most part have defaulted on adequate care for the mentally ill, and have consistently done so for a century.... As we have seen, it was a historic mistake to make the State alone virtually responsible for public care of its mentally ill residents, relieving the local communities of all further concern and, until recent times, sparing the Federal government anything but peripheral involvement in the problem. Their single source of financial support guaranteed the isolation of State hospitals and the dumping-ground effect that we have stressed.

The proposed recommendation, predictably, was that "Federal aid will be needed, in large sums.... The Federal government should be prepared to assume a major part of the responsibility for the mentally ill insofar as the States are agreeable to surrendering it."[34]

Felix, Gorman, and their colleagues were very pleased with the recommendations of the Joint Commission and well they might be, as they had written them. Many of the ideas had been taken directly from Felix's original national plan. Gorman later claimed that the Joint Commission had merely been a public relations exercise, that he had drafted the legislation creating the Commission for Senator Hill, and that its recommendations had been predetermined:

> I was very happy to be a member of that [Commission] and really made only one contribution although it was a five-year study; I had the good fortune to write my suggested recommendations for Senator Hill in 1956. Old Chinese proverb—"If you appoint a Commission, have all the recommendations finished before you appoint it."

If anyone wished to really understand the recommendations of the Joint Commission, it was not necessary to look further than the title of its final report. Although the commission had been officially baptized by Congress as the Joint Commission on Mental Illness and Health, the final report was titled simply *Action for Mental Health*.[35]

## MENTAL HEALTH: TOWARD THE PROMISED LAND

One of the great ironies of American psychiatric history is that during 1955, at the same time that the Joint Commission on Mental Illness and Health was being charged with finding a solution to the mental illness crisis, a totally unexpected solution was appearing. The solution was chlorpromazine, sold in the United States under the trade name Thorazine. It had been discovered in France in 1952 and reported to dramatically reduce the delusions, hallucinations, and manic symptoms of many patients with severe psychiatric disorders.

By the end of 1952, Thorazine was being used in Canada, and in 1953 it was introduced in several American mental hospitals. The first report of its effectiveness in the

United States was published in the *Journal of the American Medical Association* on May 1, 1954. William Winkelman, a psychiatrist in Philadelphia, reported that for 142 patients with varying psychiatric diagnoses, Thorazine was "especially remarkable in that it can reduce severe anxiety, diminish phobias and obsessions, reverse or modify a paranoid psychosis, quiet mania or extremely agitated patients, and change the hostile, agitated, senile patients into a quiet, easily managed patient." Consistent with the dominant Freudian belief system of that era, however, Winkelman cautioned that Thorazine "should never be given as a substitute for analytically oriented psychotherapy."[36]

Felix and his colleagues were aware of these developments. During his testimony in March 1955 in support of the proposed Commission on Mental Illness and Health, Gorman commented on the "reported remarkable results" brought about by Thorazine. It was, he said, "an important new breakthrough in the fight against mental illness." However, neither Gorman nor anyone else at that time fully appreciated how profound an effect Thorazine and other antipsychotic drugs would have on future psychiatric treatment. This is not to say that the introduction of antipsychotic drugs *caused* deinstitutionalization. The idea that state mental hospitals were therapeutically bankrupt had been growing since the highly publicized exposés of state hospital conditions in the late 1940s, as noted above. In fact, between 1946 and 1955, 17 states decreased the census of their state mental hospitals, although the total census for all 48 states continued to increase. However, 1955 was to be the high-water mark, with 558,922 patients in state mental hospitals; in 1956 there were 7,532 fewer patients, the first such decrease in more than a century. This was the beginning of what would become known as deinstitutionalization. The emptying of state mental hospitals was underway, and although the introduction of antipsychotics had not started the engine, it provided the fuel that initially made it run.[37]

\* \* \*

By early 1959 the deliberations of the Joint Commission had been completed and the report—*Action for Mental Health*—was ready for release. With Dwight Eisenhower in the White House, however, Felix and his colleagues surmised that Republicans would not be enthusiastic about a plan to essentially nationalize mental health. They decided to delay the release of the report to see what would happen in the 1960 elections. They were especially excited about the candidacy of Senator John F. Kennedy, who was fighting Hubert Humphrey, Pat Brown, and Wayne Morse for the Democratic nomination. Felix and others on the Joint Commission had heard the rumors about Rosemary Kennedy's mental retardation and mental illness, and they observed the increased activity of the Kennedy family in its support of mental retardation research. Felix et al. therefore put their report aside to see what would happen in the 1960 election. Following Kennedy's victory, they released their report even before the new president was sworn in.

## MENTAL RETARDATION: TOWARD THE PROMISED LAND

Following Rosemary's lobotomy, tragedy continued to follow the Kennedy family. In 1944 Joe Kennedy Jr. was killed in the war when he was shot down over Belgium on a dangerous mission for which he had volunteered. The victory of Allied Forces in Europe was declared on May 8, 1945; 6 days later, Joe Kennedy incorporated a private foundation, initially named the Mercié Foundation but 5 months later renamed the Joseph P. Kennedy Jr. Foundation. The avowed purpose of the foundation was "the relief, shelter, support, education, protection, and maintenance of the indigent, sick and infirm." Its first grant was to a Catholic group to establish the Joseph P. Kennedy Jr. Convalescent Home for Poor Families.[38]

A major impetus to the formation of the Kennedy Foundation was provided by Richard Cushing, then an auxiliary bishop of Boston. The son of Irish immigrants in South Boston, Cushing had been educated at a Jesuit high school and at Boston College, also a Jesuit institution. It was Cushing who, in 1941, had recommended the permanent placement of Rosemary at the Catholic-run St. Coletta's School in Wisconsin, and thereafter he remained a close friend of the Kennedy family, even officiating at Jack Kennedy's funeral after he had become Cardinal Cushing. Cushing was said to have been "among the first influential Americans to speak out about the plight of the mentally retarded," whom he referred to as "exceptional children." He therefore urged Joe Kennedy to donate to charitable causes, especially mental retardation. As Edward Shorter summarized the relationship in *The Kennedy Family*, "Cushing needed Kennedy as a benefactor, and Kennedy in turn depended upon Cushing for advice, for example, on how to deal with Rosemary."[39]

Thus, from the very beginning, the Kennedy Foundation intended to include support for mental retardation among its charities. In 1947 Joe Kennedy made Eunice one of the trustees of the foundation, and the same year it funded a new St. Coletta School for mentally retarded children in Massachusetts; it would later be named the Cardinal Cushing School and Training Center. The foundation also funded many charities not related to mental retardation, some of which benefited the Kennedy family. For example, according to Shorter, "the Kennedy's Palm Beach house was for many years owned by the foundation."[40]

With the death of Joe Kennedy Jr., the political aspirations of the family fell onto the shoulders of Jack, the second son. Accordingly, in 1946 it was arranged for Jack to run for Congress in a strongly Democratic Massachusetts district, which he easily won, although he was only 29 years old. In 1952 he was elected to the Senate, and in 1956 he narrowly lost out to Estes Kefauver in the bid to become Adlai Stevenson's running mate. Thereafter, it became an all-out push to achieve the 1960 presidential nomination, with the help of many Kennedy family members. Joe Kennedy was determined to make it happen and did whatever was necessary. For example, in December 1957, he gave Henry Luce $75,000 ($611,000 in 2012 dollars) to put Jack on the cover of Luce's *Time* magazine.[41]

Eunice Kennedy, who had married Sargent Shriver, viewed her brother's presidential aspirations as an opportunity to focus research attention on mental retardation and thus salvage some good from her sister's tragedy. In 1957 Joe Kennedy gave Eunice complete control of the Kennedy Foundation funds, and she immediately went to work to ascertain what could be done. One of her first calls was to Dr. Richard Masland, director of the National Institute of Neurological Diseases and Blindness. Significantly, she did not go to Felix, director of the National Institute of Mental Health, which theoretically had responsibility for research on mental retardation but had done almost nothing on it. Dr. Masland directed Eunice to Dr. Robert Cooke, chairman of the Department of Pediatrics at Johns Hopkins University, who himself had two retarded children. Eunice was impressed by Cooke and gave him a research grant, and this was followed by grants for mental retardation research at Massachusetts General Hospital, Stanford University, the University of Chicago, the University of Wisconsin, and Georgetown University. In 1957, when Eunice had taken control of the foundation, only 17% of its budget was spent on mental retardation, but by 1960 this figure had increased to 66%.[42]

Focusing attention of the Kennedy Foundation on mental retardation research, however, carried some risk, because the Kennedys had not yet publicly acknowledged that Rosemary had any problems. In 1957 the family told the *Saturday Evening Post* that Rosemary was "teaching" at St. Coletta's. Two years later, a biography of Jack Kennedy described Rosemary as "a sweet, rather withdrawn girl" who was helping "care for mentally retarded children" at St. Coletta's. Even as late as October 1960, one month before the election, *Look* magazine described Rosemary as "a victim of spinal meningitis, now in a Wisconsin nursing home." Eunice and other Kennedy family members eagerly awaited the opportunity to focus federal attention on mental retardation if Jack won the nomination and election. The question would be how to do so without discussing Rosemary and her problems.[43]

# 3

## THE BIRTH OF THE FEDERAL MENTAL
## HEALTH PROGRAM: 1960–1963

The relationship between Jack Kennedy and his younger sister Rosemary was complex. She was the sibling closest to him in age, and from early childhood he had helped to protect her. Her subsequent mental illness and disastrous lobotomy must have been profoundly painful for him. In addition to Kennedy's interest in mental retardation and mental illness because of Rosemary, he had also developed a special interest in what can go wrong with a growing fetus during pregnancy. Prior to the birth of their daughter in 1957, Jacqueline had experienced a miscarriage and then a stillborn child. One expert on mental retardation recalled a conversation in which the president had expressed an interest in "difficulties of the newborn baby and problems during pregnancy that had some bearing on the development of retardation later," adding that "this seemed to be a particular concern of his." Another colleague claimed that among all the issues Kennedy dealt with during his time in office, the issue of mental retardation "was closest to his heart."[1]

It is not clear whether, at the time Kennedy was running for president in early 1960, he had visited Rosemary since her lobotomy 19 years earlier. Other family members had, especially Eunice and her mother. Because Kennedy was campaigning for the nomination in Wisconsin, "Jack made a campaign stop in a heavily Republican town a few miles from Jefferson [where Rosemary was living at St. Coletta's School] as part of a plan surreptitiously to visit his sister," according to Laurence Leamer's *The Kennedy Women*.[2]

Thus, on Tuesday morning, February 16, 1960, Kennedy arrived in Madison, Wisconsin, for 3 days of campaigning. The state was regarded as crucial for Kennedy's chances of securing the Democratic nomination, and he hoped to defeat Hubert Humphrey there. After briefly campaigning in Madison, Kennedy's entourage drove directly to Fort Atkinson, 8 miles south of St. Coletta's, arriving at 10:40 A.M., "a few minutes ahead of schedule," according to the local newspaper. Because he was campaigning for the Democratic nomination, the choice of Fort Atkinson, described as a "stronghold of Republicanism," was an odd choice for a campaign stop unless there was another reason to be there. Sargent Shriver was directing Kennedy's campaign in Wisconsin, and it seems likely that Eunice had made the arrangements for her brother's visit to Rosemary.[3]

Kennedy proceeded to tour Fort Atkinson for an hour, shaking hands and giving a brief talk. According to the newspaper, "he entered practically every business place, retraced his steps several times to greet persons he missed, and stopped traffic in the streets to shake hands with drivers." And then he left, driving south to briefly stop in Whitewater, Elkhorn, and Lake Geneva, three nearby towns. He was not due in Kenosha (less than 50 miles away) until evening, so he had plenty of time. Leamer, who had access to the Kennedy family archives, simply said: "At the last moment the plans changed and Jack never saw Rosemary." Did Kennedy change his mind? Was Rosemary too agitated? Did the campaign staff become frightened that the press would find out about Rosemary, thus introducing a campaign issue the Kennedys did not want introduced? It is not known. What is known is that Jack Kennedy personally called a local florist on Rosemary's birthday each year to have flowers delivered. Rosemary thus seems to have hovered perpetually over her older brother, an unhappy apparition demanding expiation.[4]

Following Kennedy's election in November 1960, it became impossible to pretend that Rosemary did not exist. Immediately after the election, *Children Limited*, a publication of the National Association for Retarded Children (NARC), noted that "the President-elect has a mentally retarded sister who is in an institution in Wisconsin." Because many leaders in the mental retardation community knew about Rosemary and resented the Kennedys for not acknowledging her, the article may have been an attempt to "out" them. The Kennedys immediately protested to NARC, which then sent a notice to its affiliates saying that "the family preferred not to have this [Rosemary's retardation] mentioned, and we would respect their wishes in this matter as we would any other family's wishes."[5]

By 1962 Rosemary's condition had become common knowledge, and White House efforts to promote research on mental retardation were underway. The Kennedys decided that it was time to acknowledge the obvious, and in September Eunice authored an article, "Hope for Retarded Children," in the *Saturday Evening Post*. She described her sister as having been mildly retarded in childhood. Later, however, Eunice wrote, Rosemary "was becoming increasingly irritable and difficult" and the doctors said that "she would be far happier in an institution." Therefore, they put her in one where "she has found peace." There was no mention of any mental illness and, of course, no mention of the lobotomy. As in all such matters, the ability of the Kennedys to deny inconvenient truths was noteworthy. As late as 1995 Eunice Shriver continued to deny any association between Rosemary's condition and the Kennedy family's interest in mental retardation. In an interview reported by the *New York Times*, Eunice "dismissed out of hand" the idea that her Special Olympics for retarded children "existed because of Rosemary."[6]

## MENTAL HEALTH VERSUS MENTAL RETARDATION

Robert Felix and his colleagues were delighted with Kennedy's election, viewing him as "the right person at the right time." They were aware that "the essential ingredient in the creation of a national mental health program was the interest of the president," and they were aware that he had read in its entirety the report of the Joint Commission on Mental Illness and Health. In July 1960, at the Democratic National Convention, Mike Gorman had even arranged to have a reference to their plan included in the Democratic national platform:

> Mental patients fill more than half the hospital beds in the country today. We will provide greatly increased Federal support for psychiatric research and training, and community mental health programs to help bring back thousands of our hospitalized mentally ill to full and useful lives in the community.

Thus, by the time Kennedy took office on January 20, 1961, Felix et al. were ready to go forward with their national mental health plan.[7]

The White House, however, informed them that mental retardation was going to have first claim on the administration's attention. Eunice Shriver had also read the report of the Joint Commission on Mental Illness and Health and had been appalled. As she later recalled, "I didn't even see the word mental retardation mentioned once. I thought that was awful, and I called up my father and I said to him, 'Dad, would you be willing to let the foundation sponsor a nationwide conference on mental retardation, because this report has obviously nothing to say about the mentally retarded.'" According to Eunice: "My father said we ought to create something like the Hoover Commission, and call it a Presidential Panel." The Hoover Commission had been set up in 1947 by President Truman to recommend administrative changes in the federal government; former president Herbert Hoover had been its chairman.[8]

This was the origin of the President's Panel on Mental Retardation, created in October 1961 with 27 members, including basic brain researchers, educators, and representatives of NARC and other parent organizations. The panel's charge was to create a plan to combat mental retardation within 1 year. Predictably, there was little agreement among the various factions regarding what should be done with "the science-oriented 'researchers' squared off against the education-oriented caregivers." The panel, ultimately divided into six task forces, held a series of public meetings, and visited mental retardation facilities in Europe to gather ideas. In October 1962, it issued a 200-page report with 95 recommendations, including something for everyone.[9]

At the same time that the President's Panel on Mental Retardation was deliberating, plans also proceeded to create a new institute within the National Institutes of Health

(NIH) to focus research attention on mental retardation. The federal Department of Health, Education, and Welfare (DHEW) and James Shannon, the NIH director, both opposed the idea but were overruled by Ted Sorensen, one of Kennedy's key advisors, and by Kennedy himself. The new institute was initially going to be called the National Institute on Mental Retardation, but that was considered to be too narrow a mandate, so it was called the National Institute of Child Health and Human Development. President Kennedy proposed the new institute in a message to Congress on February 27, 1962, and by September the necessary legislation had been passed. The recommendations of the President's Panel were divided into two sets of legislation. The first provided funds from Social Security to provide better care for pregnant women and newborns; the second established 18 university-affiliated clinical facilities for mental retardation. Both pieces of legislation were passed by Congress and signed into law in October 1963.[10]

It should be added that the driving force behind these mental retardation initiatives was Eunice Shriver. In March 1961 her husband became the director of the Peace Corps, and in December 1961 Joe Kennedy had a stroke, effectively disabling him. Eunice, therefore, took command and, using her brother to remove obstacles, made things happen. Crucial to her efforts were Myer "Mike" Feldman and Wilbur Cohen. Feldman worked for Ted Sorensen in the White House, and within the White House he was "the chief force for action on mental retardation." Cohen, who had an undergraduate degree in economics from the University of Wisconsin and had worked on Franklin D. Roosevelt's New Deal programs, was the Assistant Secretary for Legislation at DHEW. As early as May 1961, 5 months before the President's Panel on Mental Retardation had begun discussions, Eunice had begun regular meetings with Feldman, Cohen, and Dr. Robert Cooke to plan the mental retardation legislation. According to Shorter's history of this legislation, Eunice Shriver "acquired the authority to give orders to Mike Feldman, who in turn gave orders to Wilbur Cohen." Eunice's authority came, of course, from the president, whom she pestered persistently. Bobby Kennedy later joked that Jack used to say: "Let's give Eunice whatever she wants so I can get her off the phone and get on with the business of government."[11]

Although Eunice recognized that legislation would ultimately be proposed by the Kennedy administration for both mental health and mental retardation, she was determined to make the latter paramount. As Shorter noted, Eunice "shared the general loathing of the parents' [of mentally retarded children] group for psychiatrists." Eunice's key advisor, Dr. Robert Cooke, similarly remembered that "the feeling [among mental retardation advocates]...against psychiatry was just enormous and that these people had done very little." Dr. Bertram S. Brown, assigned by the National Institute of Mental Health as a liaison to the President's Panel because of his previous writings on mental retardation, also claimed that "there was hatred of psychiatry because mental retardation was more acceptable to them."[12]

Some of the animosity between the mental retardation and mental health advocates arose from the fact that each group felt superior to the other. As described by one historian of these events: "The mental-health groups assumed a superior attitude because mental illness can be a temporary condition from which people recover, while the retarded will always be intellectually inferior." On the other hand, "the mentally retarded group thought, or believed, that mental illness was more of a stigma and didn't want to be identified with it." Their family members may be intellectually slow, they said, but at least they weren't crazy.[13]

Faced with accusations of neglect, Robert Felix and his psychiatric colleagues privately "cried bitterly that they hadn't shortchanged mental retardation." Felix also "protested loudly that he was the first to push for attention for the area of mental retardation," although he had difficulty citing specific examples. The psychiatrists felt that the Kennedys were being disingenuous in giving priority to mental retardation, as Rosemary was both mentally retarded and mentally ill. Bertram Brown later characterized this Kennedy lack of candor "the biggest mental health cover-up in history."[14]

Nevertheless, the mental health advocates said little publicly, because they did not want to offend the Kennedys or the mental retardation advocates. Mike Gorman had tested the waters in Congress and found that joint legislation, covering both mental health and mental retardation, stood a better chance of being enacted than legislation on mental health alone. Thus, Gorman proposed an alliance with the mental retardation group. However, "the retardation groups not only did not want such a coalition, they also wanted any new appropriations to be directed primarily to mental retardation programs."[15]

The real battle, like most Washington fights, was about budgets. Presidential interest in a program inevitably means more money, the ambrosia of the Potomac. Felix correctly perceived that Eunice Shriver was not going to allow the National Institute of Mental Health to keep the mental retardation program. In exchange for giving up the program, Felix and his colleagues attempted to extract more concessions for their national mental health program.

## SHAPING A NATIONAL MENTAL HEALTH PLAN

Once President Kennedy had gotten the mental retardation planning efforts underway, he turned his attention to mental illness. Unlike with mental retardation, however, no Kennedy family member offered to take a leadership role as Eunice had done, and the president was uncertain what to do. He therefore did what most American presidents have done in similar circumstances, and on December 1, 1961, he appointed a committee to make recommendations.

To chair his Interagency Committee on Mental Health, Kennedy asked Anthony Celebrezze, the Secretary of the Department of Health, Education, and Welfare (DHEW). Celebrezze in turn asked Boisfeuillet Jones, a lawyer who was his special assistant, to do the actual work and chair the committee. Jones had been a dean and vice president at Emory University and had previously served on the National Advisory Mental Health Council, so he had a special interest in these issues. Other members of the Interagency Committee were Daniel P. Moynihan, a sociologist, representing the Department of Labor; Robert Atwell, an economist, representing the Bureau of the Budget; Rashi Fein, an economist, representing the Council of Economic Advisers; and Robert Manley, an administrator representing the Veterans Administration. Dr. Felix, representing NIMH, was, of course, a member, and in a 1972 interview Felix claimed that he had had input on the selection of the other committee members. The committee was asked to make recommendations on future mental illness services in state hospitals versus community mental health centers, on federal versus state funding for the enhanced services, and on possible ways to increase the pool of mental health professionals to staff the enhanced services. What was clear to everyone was that President Kennedy was committed to some kind of new mental illness program. Jones recalled in a 1972 interview that Kennedy made it clear that he wanted a new program but did not specify the details of such a program.[16]

As the only mental health professional on the Interagency Committee, Felix inevitably dominated the proceedings. In later interviews, both Jones and Moynihan verbalized great deference to Felix. Fein recalled that "a lot of time was spent hearing Felix extol the medical approach." Felix was assisted in his committee efforts by two other NIMH psychiatrists: Stanley F. Yolles and Bertram S. Brown. Brown was especially well placed to be useful to Felix, as he was also serving as the NIMH liaison to the President's Panel on Mental Retardation. Yolles would succeed Felix as director of NIMH in 1964, and Brown would succeed Yolles in 1970. Thus, from 1946, when NIMH was created, until 1977, when Brown left NIMH, the official mental health policies of the U. S. government were dominated by these three men.[17]

Yolles, age 41 years, had a master's degree in parasitology and had worked during World War II on the prevention of insect-borne diseases. Following the war he obtained a medical degree and a master's degree in public health, then took a psychiatric residency at the federal narcotics treatment center in Lexington, Kentucky— the same hospital where Felix had worked. Yolles was a highly intelligent but dour, unfriendly man, said to be "obsessed with organization and the model trains he kept in his basement" (Figure 3.1).[18]

Brown, just 31 years old at the time, had originally been interested in infectious diseases and pediatrics. After getting his medical degree, he took a residency in psychiatry at the Boston Psychopathic Hospital under Dr. Jack Ewalt. While there he also

FIG 3.1  Stanley F. Yolles, M.D., who operationalized the federal mental health program and was NIMH director from 1962 to 1970. In 1977, he admitted that the assumption on which the program had been founded "has not proven to be correct." Photo courtesy of the National Library of Medicine.

got a master's degree in public health and moonlighted by working in state prisons. His public health interest caught the attention of Ewalt, who encouraged him to go to work with Felix after he finished. In contrast to Yolles, Brown was gregarious, politically astute, and did not take himself seriously, sometimes introducing himself by saying, "My parents didn't name me B. S. Brown for no reason." He was also a concert pianist who had studied at the Julliard School of Music for 3 years (Figure 3.2).[19]

Felix, Yolles, and Brown shared several traits in addition to being psychiatrists. All three were career officers in the U. S. Public health Service and had obtained master's degrees in public health. Thus, they viewed intended targets of their policies as entire populations, not just individual patients, as public health officials are inclined to do.

FIG 3.2  Bertram S. Brown, M.D., who was the first director of the Community Mental Health Centers program and NIMH director from 1970 to 1977. In 2010, he assessed the federal program as "a grand experiment" but added: "I just feel saddened by it." Photo courtesy of the National Library of Medicine.

Brown, for example, sometimes facetiously claimed that his real patient was the United States. As public health specialists, all three men also viewed prevention as the ultimate goal of psychiatry.[20]

## THE DEATH OF THE ASYLUM

The first issue addressed by the Interagency Committee on Mental Health was whether state mental hospitals should continue to be the primary locus of treatment for mentally ill individuals or whether the primary locus of treatment should be shifted to the proposed community mental health centers. The report of the Joint Commission on Mental Illness and Health had called state hospitals "bankrupt beyond remedy" but had recommended that federal funds be invested in improving them. The president of the American Psychiatric Association in 1958 had recommended that state mental hospitals should all be "liquidated as rapidly as can be done in an orderly and progressive fashion."[21]

In addressing the future of the state mental hospitals, it is important to note that nobody on the Interagency Committee had had any significant experience with them. Felix and Brown had been trained in special state research hospitals, called Psychopathic Hospitals, which were not representative of most state hospitals. Felix had worked for one summer in a Colorado state hospital, and Brown had briefly visited several state hospitals in Massachusetts. Yolles had been trained at a narcotics treatment hospital, and there is no evidence that he had even visited state hospitals. The three psychiatrists providing professional input on the future of state hospitals had thus had very little experience with these hospitals or the patients in them. Not surprisingly, none of the psychiatrists was willing to defend the hospitals. Felix envisioned "a new role for the state hospital.... [It] will become a psychiatric institute, linked with research centers and medical schools, where techniques for treating chronic patients can be tested." This was a model similar to the state psychopathic hospital in which Felix had trained. Yolles said that "we all devoutly wish to see the reduction in the size and eventual disappearance of the State hospital as we know it today" and later said that he had truly believed that the hospitals would no longer be needed because community mental health centers would take over their function. Brown recalled that "the power structure of mental health was the state hospital superintendents and the state commissioners.... That was the system we had to break in order to have a community mental health system."[22]

One other member of the Interagency Committee emerged as an outspoken opponent of state mental hospitals. Robert Atwell, just 29 years old, had been appointed to the committee as a representative of the Bureau of the Budget because he was the budget examiner for the National Institute of Mental Health. Atwell had a bachelor's degree in political science and a master's degree in public administration. His only experience with mental illness or state psychiatric hospitals was a single visit to a state hospital in Pennsylvania where his grandmother worked as a cleaning woman. He acknowledged in a recent interview that, in retrospect, "I did have some pretty strong views," some of which were derived from Brown, who became his close friend. In Interagency Committee discussions, Atwell was adamant that federal funds should not be used to improve state hospitals. "He had read the joint commission's complete studies [and] in his judgment, those studies totally discredited the system of state mental hospitals." In the end, the committee "agreed to support a federal initiative that would eliminate the State mental institution as it now exists in a generation."[23]

In rejecting in 1962 any significant role for state mental hospitals in the national mental health plan, the Interagency Committee on Mental Health was reflecting ideas circulating at that time in the mental health community. Thomas Szasz's *The Myth of Mental Illness* and Erving Goffman's *Asylums* had both been published in 1961. Szasz claimed that mental illnesses did not exist, while Goffman argued that most of the disabilities seen in hospitalized mental patients were a consequence of their having been institutionalized. In 1962 Ken Kesey's *One Flew over the Cuckoo's Nest* was published and immediately developed cult status among opponents of state hospitals. Like Goffman, Kesey portrayed mental patients as fundamentally sane and implied that if they were simply allowed to leave the hospital, they would live happily ever after. Given the popularity of these books and the interest of the Interagency Committee members in the state hospital issue, it seems likely that these books may have influenced them.

The rejection of state hospitals by the Interagency Committee would have profound effects on the subsequent failure of the emerging system. Because no Committee member really understood what the hospitals were doing, there was nobody who could explain to the committee that large numbers of the patients in those hospitals had no families to go to if they were released; that large numbers of the patients had a brain impairment that precluded their understanding of their illness and need for medication; and that a small number of the patients had a history of dangerousness and required confinement and treatment. Nobody could explain to the committee that the state hospitals were playing a role in protecting the public, and in protecting mentally ill individuals from being victimized or becoming homeless. Whatever their other shortcomings, state mental hospitals were still functioning as asylums in the original sense of the term.

## THE BIRTH OF THE COMMUNITY
## MENTAL HEALTH CENTER

Because state hospitals were no longer going to be the primary locus of treatment for mentally ill individuals in the emerging national mental health program, that role would be assumed by the community mental health centers (CMHCs) being proposed by Felix and his colleagues. According to interviews, Jones, Moynihan, and Fein all "accepted the idea that NIMH knew what programs were needed and, in their own minds, 'The CMHC program was reasonable.'" Fein also acknowledged that committee members "were captive of the leadership of NIMH" on this issue. Moynihan had a special interest in making services more available to poor people and keeping families intact, so community treatment, closer to their homes, appealed to him. Robert Manley, the Veterans Administration representative on the committee, thought the CMHC idea "was very good, the best thing so far" and expressed the hope that "it all comes about." Atwell also found the CMHC idea to be "exciting, different, innovative...this was the new frontier," but he expressed the need for standards of some sort to evaluate the new mental health program.[24]

By the time of the Interagency Committee meetings in 1962, Robert Felix had been planning his national mental health program for 20 years and had become an articulate spokesman for it. The community mental health centers, he maintained, would not only treat existing cases of mental illness without the need to send patients to distant state hospitals but, more important, the centers would prevent future cases. This would be accomplished in two ways. First, the CMHCs would identify cases of mental illness in their earliest stages and, by treating them, prevent the full-blown emergence of serious illness. Second, the mental health center staff would work with community leaders to alter social, economic, and cultural factors that were thought to be causing mental illness. As articulated by Felix, the plan presented an attractive if overly optimistic scenario.

The efforts of Felix to promote his national plan for community mental health centers received an important boost in 1961 with the publication of Gerald Caplan's book *An Approach to Community Mental Health*. Caplan was an English-trained psychoanalyst who was an associate professor at the Harvard School of Public Health, where Brown had studied under him. Caplan's ideas about mental health coincided closely with those of Felix, Yolles, and Brown. Caplan denigrated state hospitals, saying that "the best of treatment-minded state hospitals perform a disabling custodial function." He called the idea of early case finding and treatment "secondary prevention" and believed, following classical Freudian teachings, that most mental illnesses are caused by a failure of individuals to resolve early developmental problems. Small problems, if untreated, became neuroses, and these, in turn, became psychoses:

> In other words, in order to avoid facing the tensions that his unified, integrated personality would face if dealing with this unsolved problem, he [the patient] just smashes up his personality, as it were. This gives him a psychosis. One of the most typical of these is schizophrenia....If your personality is fragmented you cease to exist from a certain point of view, and cease to feel

then the tensions of the unsolved problem. This is a way to escape, and is a quite primitive way. Sometimes there is a complete and absolute disorganization of the personality.[25]

Felix was an enthusiastic advocate for prevention and a promoter of Caplan's ideas. In a Foreword to Caplan's 1964 book *Principles of Preventive Psychiatry*, Felix extolled the book as "not only a primer for the community mental health worker—it is a Bible." To prevent future problems, Felix urged mental health professionals to become involved in all of life's major decisions:

Essential to the effective operation of a preventive mental health program are, first, a population which knows what to do and is prepared to act at the first sign of trouble and, next, services that can give the requested help. People need to know what services are available, and the reasons for utilizing such services, before they find themselves in serious difficulty. They must know why they should seek advice when they plan for retirement, when they consider having a relative live with them, when they prepare a child for hospitalization. All these situations can lead to emotional problems if people are not prepared to cope with them adequately. Most people, however, do not consider seeking professional help until a problem becomes too large for them to handle. They will consult their insurance agents before embarking upon a new insurance program, they will consult their clergyman before getting married, they will do a great deal of research before buying a new car. But very few will consult an appropriately trained person before major problems in their lives get out of hand.[26]

Felix's other method of preventing mental illnesses, as he explained to the Interagency Committee, was to alter social, economic, and cultural factors that were thought to be causing the illnesses. As early as 1948, he had written that "the content and the orientation of personality are powerfully influenced by the social setting," including factors such as a "disorganized community life." Caplan called the alteration of such factors "primary prevention," which included "inducing community change by administrative action." Felix agreed that social action should be part of the job description for a community psychiatrist:

To be fully effective, a good mental health program must include some provision for social action so that the total community environment is a mentally healthy one. This is particularly important for those areas, such as family life and school experience, which affect the individual most closely.

By the use of such preventive measures, mental illness would be reduced and fewer individuals would require hospitalization.[27]

It is unknown whether any member of the Interagency Committee questioned Felix's plan to use community mental health centers to prevent mental illness. How did he know it would work? If they had, Felix would almost certainly have described the pilot mental health clinic he had set up in 1948 in Prince George's County, Maryland, on the outskirts of Washington. In congressional testimony, both Felix and Yolles sometimes alluded to this clinic as an "operational model" for community mental health centers.[28]

When Felix had set up the clinic in 1948, he had described its goals as developing "case finding techniques" to achieve the "goals of early diagnosis and treatment." Ultimately, he said, the clinic should play a role in "supplementing and unifying all community forces working toward better mental health." Yolles had worked at the clinic for 6 years, after which he had been appointed deputy director of NIMH by Felix. Brown had also begun his NIMH career at the Prince George's clinic.[29]

However, by 1962, although the clinic had been in existence for 14 years, there is no evidence that it had prevented a single case of mental illness. Clinic personnel had provided traditional outpatient psychotherapy, mostly to children and adolescents, and had undertaken studies on such things as the mother–child relationship, the number of children in schools with reading disabilities, and how many adults join community voluntary organizations. Yolles, for example, had been the senior author on a paper on the "epidemiology of reading disabilities." No study had been done to demonstrate that the early treatment of minor problems would prevent the later emergence of major problems. And virtually no efforts had been made to provide services to individuals with schizophrenia or other major psychiatric disorders. According to Dr. Alan Miller, an NIMH psychiatrist who worked at the Prince George's County clinic for 6 years: "We even tried to work with one of the Maryland State Hospitals, with the idea of providing what was called Aftercare to discharged patients. But I think the hospitals were not ready for us; I know we were not ready for them." After 14 years as an "operational model" for community mental health centers, there was no evidence whatsoever that the mental health of Prince George's County had been improved in any way.[30]

In fact, by 1962 there had been only one published study assessing whether the early treatment of minor problems prevents the later development of major problems. Given the findings of this study, it was not likely to have been discussed by Felix with the Interagency Committee. The study started in the 1930s as the Cambridge-Somerville Delinquency Prevention Project and involved more than 600 Boston-area boys judged likely to become delinquent. The boys were randomly assigned either to a "no-treatment" control group or to a "treatment" group that consisted of ongoing psychotherapy with a social worker. The social workers met with the boys an average of twice a month for 5.5 years. The social workers were said to use both traditional psychoanalytic techniques and also nondirective, psychotherapeutic techniques based on the theory of Carl Rogers. In addition to the therapy, more than half the boys in the treatment group were tutored in academic subjects, half were sent to summer camps, and one-third were referred for "medical or psychiatric help." The boys averaged 10 years of age at the start of the treatment program and almost 16 years at the end.

In 1948, 3 years after the project ended, an initial evaluation of the results revealed that "the boys who had received treatment were not less likely to have been brought to criminal court; nor were they committing fewer crimes." It was predicted, however, that the effectiveness of the treatment would become evident over longer time. "The evaluation of the program in the 1950s…again revealed no benefits from the program." In 1975 a 30-year follow-up was undertaken during which 95% of the study group was located. It was found that "as adults, equal numbers [of the treatment and no-treatment groups] had been convicted for some crime.…Unexpectedly, however, a higher proportion of criminals from the treatment group than of criminals from the control groups committed more than one crime," and the difference was statistically significant. Further analysis of the study revealed that longer treatment had increased the chances of later criminal behavior and more intensive treatment, in which the social workers had focused on personal or family problems, had also increased the chances of later criminal behavior. Therefore, the one study that had attempted to prevent major problems by early identification and treatment of minor problems had been a resounding failure.[31]

## THE FEDERAL ROLE

Another major issue on which the Interagency Committee was asked to make recommendations was what the federal role should be in regard to the new mental health programs. Should federal funds be used to construct the mental health centers? Should federal funds be used for staffing the centers? And where should control of the centers lie along the spectrum of federal, state, and local government?

Regarding the first question, there was unanimous agreement on the committee that federal funds should be used to cover some of the construction costs. The Hill-Burton program, which was cited as a precedent, had provided federal funds to help construct general hospitals since 1946. The federal government contributed between 33% and 67% of the construction costs, depending on the state, with state and local governments picking up the remainder. In the end, the federal contribution for the mental health center construction program was recommended to be between 45% and 75%, thus somewhat more generous than the Hill-Burton program.

The possible use of federal funds for staffing the mental health centers proved to be a highly contentious issue. Staffing of mental health facilities had been a state and local responsibility for more than a century, and there was virtually no precedent for using federal funds for this purpose. Publicly, Felix argued that federal funds should be used for staffing for only the first 4 years of the centers' operation, to help centers get started. He referred to this in congressional testimony as "grub-stake money." Following the withdrawal of federal funds, the centers' staffing would then be funded by the state and local governments and "by the traditional financing patterns of the care of physically ill in the community. In other words, the individuals who would be served at the center would pay the costs of their care just as they pay a hospital bill." Privately, however, Felix and his colleagues were in favor of permanent federal financing for the mental health centers. They reasoned that once federal financing had been established, it would be difficult to cut it off. In a 1972 interview, Atwell confirmed that the "seed money" concept being promoted by Felix was just "for effect—seed money was the way you had to go for political reasons." The federal training also had political implications for the future power of NIMH. According to Henry Foley's history of this period, *Community Mental Health Legislation*, "a federally financially-assisted system of approximately two thousand centers would provide NIMH with the same type of political power that the postal system possessed. A center located in every congressman's district would increase the patronage power of Congress and enhance the political viability of NIMH as coordinating agency of this new system."[32]

The Interagency Committee was, in fact, divided on the staff funding issue. According to Foley, "Fein argued that the states were not in the position adequately to support the care of mental patients...[and] had no objection to the position that financing mental health care should become a permanent federal subsidy." In contrast, Jones represented the opinion of his boss, HEW Secretary Celebrezze, who was unalterably opposed to the use of federal funds for staffing the centers, arguing that it was a state responsibility. In the end, the issue of initial staffing was resolved by President Kennedy, who ordered Celebrezze "in November 1962 to put provisions for operating costs into the proposed legislation."[33]

The issue of long-term financing for the mental health centers was, however, never resolved. Proponents of the program cited self-pay by users as one source, despite the fact that the purported target population of users would be mostly unable to pay. Local funds were suggested, without any evidence that cities or counties would be willing to put up funds. State funds were also suggested, especially the funds that would theoretically be saved as state hospitals discharged more patients and downsized. However, proponents of the centers' program were simultaneously telling states officials that the states were going to be able to spend less money as the hospitals were downsized. In internal documents, NIMH officials acknowledged that "it is true that the assumption [of state funds for long-term CMHC staffing] is an optimistic one."[34]

Of all the issues debated by the Interagency Committee, the most contentious was the relative roles of federal and state governments in control of the mental health centers. Felix and his colleagues viewed the centers as a national program and thus expected that NIMH would retain ultimate authority over the centers. State mental health directors, by contrast, assumed that the ultimate control of the centers would rest with them. To maintain state support for their program, this assumption was encouraged by NIMH, which awarded them planning grants and projected optimistic scenarios about the money that the centers program would save them.

The members of the Interagency Committee debated the issue *in extenso*. Felix wanted NIMH to retain the ultimate control but believed that the state mental health authorities should also be involved; this opinion was shared by Jones and Moynihan, who were sensitive to the political implications of federal–state relations. Atwell, by contrast, was convinced that states had abdicated their responsibilities for the treatment of mentally ill individuals and "argued that the states should be bypassed because they were an obstruction." "Why get involved with state bureaucracy," he argued. "It would just mean more red tape and involvement with state politics." Manley, whose experience was in the federal Veterans Administration program, also had no problem with bypassing the states, and Fein concurred. This later position ultimately prevailed, and it was decided that NIMH would award CMHC grants directly to cities, counties, and other local entities without the approval of state authorities. According to Yolles, when the state authorities "realized that they would not get the funds, they started screaming bloody murder."[35]

It should be added that the assumption of partial federal authority for the problems of mental retardation and mental illness was consistent with other initiatives of the Kennedy administration. There was a belief that Washington could, and should, solve a host of problems that previously had been the primary responsibility of state and local governments. Thus, Kennedy proposed to solve the problem of juvenile delinquency through the Juvenile Delinquency and Youth Offenses Control Act; the loss of jobs in depressed areas through the Area Redevelopment Agency; unemployment through the Manpower Development and Training Act; housing problems through the Omnibus Housing Act; and education problems by giving "federal aid to every school district in America." The Kennedy administration also "favored a strong federal role in stimulating and managing the economy." Washington, in short, was going to be the source of solutions for many of the nation's problems, including mental retardation and mental illness.[36]

## STATE PROGRAMS ALREADY UNDERWAY

Given the fact that states had been responsible for the treatment of mentally ill individuals for more than a century, the decision of the Interagency Committee to bypass them in setting up a new mental health treatment program was a major mistake. In fact, by the time the committee was debating the details of the new mental health centers program in 1962, many states were already developing innovative community treatment programs in response to deinstitutionalization, which was well underway.

As noted previously, the census of the state mental hospitals had shown its first downturn in 1956. For the 4 years from 1955 to 1959, the decrease in hospitalized patients was modest, averaging 4,259 per year. From 1959 to 1963, the average decrease was 9,320 patients, and from 1963 to 1967 it was 19,514 patients. Thus, the emptying of state mental hospitals was well underway before the first community mental health center was ever opened, and the rate of deinstitutionalization was accelerating. One of the most prominent promises made by advocates for the community mental health centers program was that the centers would result in the halving of the state hospital population in 10 or 20 years. This claim was even included in President Kennedy's 1963 message to Congress: "If we launch a broad new mental health program now," Kennedy asserted, "it will be possible within a decade or two to reduce the number of patients now under custodial care by 50 percent or more." In fact, given the rate of accelerating deinstitutionalization already in progress, the state hospital population would have been halved in 10 years without any community mental health centers having ever been built.[37]

As patients were discharged from state hospitals in the late 1950s, states began experimenting with various aftercare programs. Most such programs were funded by state and local governments, with a few funded by NIMH grant funds or private foundations such as the Milbank Memorial Fund. What should be stressed is that there was a lot of activity and experimentation with mental illness services taking place at the state and county levels at the same time that Felix and his colleagues were attempting to implement a national plan. Indeed, according to medical historian Gerald Grob, "by 1959 there were more than 1,400 clinics" providing outpatient psychiatric services to approximately 294,000 adults.[38]

An example of such activity was documented in the "First National Report on Patients of Mental Health Clinics," which identified 1,294 existing outpatient psychiatric clinics in 1955 in the United States. Two-thirds of the clinics received state funds, and one-third were funded locally or privately. A diagnostic breakdown of the patients being seen in 1956 reported that 20% had serious mental illnesses ("psychotic disorders"). Another report in 1959 noted that there had been a 32% increase in patients seen at the outpatient psychiatric clinics in the previous 4 years, from 379,000 to 502,000 patients, and that 15% of the patients were diagnosed with a "psychotic disorder." Thus, even as the Joint Commission on Mental Illness and Health had been meeting between 1955 and 1959, the states on their own initiative had been rapidly expanding the psychiatric outpatient clinics, with almost no assistance from the federal government. And the percentage of seriously mentally ill patients seen in the state-funded clinics was 15% to 20%, whereas the percentage in the federally funded community mental health centers would never rise above 5%. Thus, in the 1950s, state-funded psychiatric outpatient clinics were doing a significantly better job of providing care for the sickest patients than the federally funded CMHCs would do later.[39]

By 1960, as patients were being discharged from the state hospitals, many states had accelerated their aftercare activities. Starting with New York in 1954, 7 states had passed community mental health legislation, and 13 more would do so by 1964. In 1957 the Joint Commission on Mental Illness and Health began a project that identified 234 psychiatric programs that were said to have "certain of the elements of a community mental health program." Among the programs were the Massachusetts Mental Health Center (1950), California's San Mateo County Mental Health Services (1958), Colorado's Fort Logan Mental Health Center (1961), and the Prairie View Hospital in Newton, Kansas (1961). All of these were regarded as model psychiatric centers well before they received federal funds as community mental health centers.[40]

All of this information was, of course, known to Drs. Felix, Yolles, and Brown. The data on the state clinics were, in fact, being collected by the Biometrics Branch of NIMH, and the agency's files contain extensive reports of attempts by states to improve psychiatric services prior to the implementation of the federal CMHC program. The following are selected samples:

- In *California*, the first Fairweather Lodge, a model rehabilitation program for released state hospital patients, was begun in the late 1950s.
- In *Georgia*, four psychiatric units in general hospitals were opened.
- In *Illinois*, a pilot program showed that patients could be treated in psychiatric units in general hospitals for half the cost of state hospitals.
- In *Kansas*, the first American day hospital had opened at the Menninger Clinic in 1949. By 1964 the effectiveness of such facilities, as alternatives to full-time hospitalization, had been clearly established.
- In *Kentucky*, the Louisville Homecare Project was started in 1961 and demonstrated that many individuals with schizophrenia could be treated at home using daily visits by public health nurses and guaranteed medication compliance.
- In *Maine*, eight mental health clinics were funded with equal shares state and local money.
- In *Massachusetts*, a Psychiatric Home Treatment Service was established at Boston State Hospital in 1957.
- In *Minnesota*, 16 community mental health clinics were established by the state. Services included outpatient clinics and rehabilitation programs primarily for discharged state mental hospital patients.

- In *New Jersey*, there had been an increase in state-funded community psychiatric clinics from 17 to 43.
- In *New York*, Fountain House, the first clubhouse, had been established in 1948 for patients discharged from Rockland State Hospital. Also in New York, in a pilot program half the psychotic patients who would have been admitted to a state hospital were referred to a clinic for treatment, instead.
- In *Oregon*, a special intensive treatment hospital had opened and reported that it could treat patients at less than one-third the cost of the state hospitals.
- In *Vermont*, mental health programs had been established in 7 of the state's 11 areas, using matching state and local funds.
- In *Wyoming*, six community mental health centers had been established.[41]

Although these psychiatric programs were all underway in 1962, at the same time that the Interagency Committee was discussing the new federal mental health program, the new state programs were almost certainly not brought up for discussion by Felix and his colleagues. To do so would have invited unwanted questions. For example, wouldn't it be prudent to assess the outcome of the state experiments and model programs before implementing a massive new federal program? This was not the kind of question Felix wanted to hear. He had a president who needed a new mental illness program, and he had a program ready to go. This was his moment, and he was determined to seize it.

## THE FEDERAL MENTAL HEALTH PLAN IS PASSED

By late 1962 all the pieces were finally in place. The President's Panel on Mental Retardation had completed its list of recommendations, and the Interagency Committee on Mental Health had accepted Felix's national plan for community mental health centers. In October, President Kennedy had stared down Nikita Khrushchev in the Cuban Missile Crisis. Then, in November, the Democrats had retained their majority in both the House and Senate in the midterm elections.

Kennedy was at the height of his power and popularity and determined to push his new programs through Congress. The mental retardation proposals were expected to pass easily. However, problems were anticipated for the mental health centers proposal, because it "represented a major departure in the national approach to mental illness and would involve considerable input of federal resources in the years to come." Despite this, Kennedy personally instructed HEW secretary Celebrezze to include in the proposed legislation the provision for federal funds for staffing the centers, to which Celebrezze was strongly opposed. When it was pointed out to Kennedy that the 5-year cost of the program was estimated to be $850 million ($6.1 billion in 2010 dollars), Kennedy simply responded that the 5-year cost of the defense budget was $250 billion ($1.8 trillion in 2010 dollars). According to one observer, "this sort of stunned Celebrezze."[42]

On December 11, the major players from both programs met at the White House to coordinate their plans and outline the president's message. According to notes from that meeting, the definition of community mental health centers and the role of the states were still under discussion. Predictably, Eunice Shriver did everything she could to favor the mental retardation programs. When the president's message had been finally drafted, Eunice sat with the president's aides and "for six hours straight she went over every word, every nuance, struggling to advance her cause."[43]

On February 5, 1963, President Kennedy delivered his historic speech to Congress. Significantly, it was titled "Mental Illness and Mental Retardation," because everyone acknowledged that "mental illness" would be a much easier sell to Congress than "mental health." With his own family almost certainly in mind, Kennedy said that mental illness and mental retardation "cause more suffering by the families of the afflicted...than any other single condition." He called for the use of federal funds to increase research, increase the training of mental health professionals, and create community mental health centers to replace the "shamefully understaffed, overcrowded, unpleasant institutions from which death too often provided the only firm hope of release." The mental health centers would be "a bold new approach.... When carried out, reliance on the cold mercy of custodial isolation will be supplanted by the open warmth of community concern and capability."[44]

One month after the president's special message to Congress, hearings on the proposed legislation opened before the Senate Committee on Labor and Public Welfare; Lister Hill—Felix and Gorman's old friend—was chairman of the committee. Passage of the legislation seemed likely, but as insurance Edward Kennedy, who had been elected as a senator from Massachusetts 4 months earlier, was given a seat on the committee. As in previous congressional hearings on mental health issues, state mental hospitals were excoriated. Gorman even claimed to have had "a fantasy of borrowing a bulldozer and running it...right smack through the walls of the State institution." By contrast, community mental health centers were depicted as the great hope for the future. Felix assured the committee "as certain as I am that I am sitting here that within a decade or two we will see...the population of these mental hospitals cut in half."[45]

Hearings on the House side before the Committee on Interstate and Foreign Commerce began 3 weeks later. The chairman of the committee was Oren Harris, a Democrat from Arkansas. He was known to be less enthusiastic than Senator Hill about the proposed legislation, so President Kennedy asked his brother Robert, who was the U.S. Attorney General, to visit Harris and personally let him know that "the new [community mental health] concept originated with the Kennedys."[46]

Several members of Harris's committee strongly opposed the use of federal funds to staff the proposed mental health centers, arguing that it would "set a new federal precedent." There was also a concern that the funds would become a permanent federal subsidy. Anchor Nelson, a Republican from Minnesota, expressed these doubts most forcefully:

> I think it is very difficult to assume that your plan will work, because I have never seen a temporary government program that didn't become permanent and I see no way that you can terminate this financing of staffing in the future. It seems to me the very reason that you propose it be terminated at a future date is an admission of the fact that it shouldn't continue, and if it shouldn't continue, why start?

Ultimately, the House committee voted against the inclusion of federal staffing funds but approved the use of construction funds, although in a reduced amount.[47]

At the same time that some members of Congress were raising doubts about the proposed federal mental health plan, several state mental health officials were also doing so. Representative of such doubts was a letter from Dr. Paul Hoch, commissioner of the New York State Department of Mental Hygiene, to New York senator Jacob Javits, who was a member of Senator Hill's committee. "On the basis of first-hand experience in New York State," said Hoch, "I maintain that it will not be feasible to treat all the mentally ill or even most of the mentally ill in community mental health centers." Hoch had hard data to support his position, as a paper had been published the previous year reporting a 50% increase in readmissions to the New York state mental hospitals. This suggested that some discharged patients were more liable to "recirculation," and for such patients "drugs may have to be maintained indefinitely afterward."[48]

Hoch also criticized the proposed funding of the mental health centers' program for bypassing the states and not taking state differences into account. "It is essential," he said, "that all federal funds be channeled through state government to insure integration and coordination of services within the state." Further, "each state has its own problems and its own level of development...[yet] so unalterable is the federal concept of a state program that its chief feature is incorporated into the proposed legislation." Finally, Hoch questioned whether "families would be willing to tolerate these patients in the home," especially because "the behavior of many schizophrenics can be trying and disruptive."[49]

Felix and his NIMH colleagues were asked to respond to the criticisms being raised by Hoch. As had become their custom in such circumstances, they referred to the recent research of Dr. John Wing et al. in England, implying that such research had already established the validity of their mental health center concept. In fact, Wing in 1960 had published a study in which 20 young males with non-severe schizophrenia

had been placed in an industrial workshop, and at the end of 1 year, 40% of them had been discharged. Wing et al. had also studied 113 patients with schizophrenia who had been discharged from hospitals in 1959; within 1 year, 56% had deteriorated and 43% had been readmitted. In still another study, published in 1962, the same research group reported that 44% of patients with schizophrenia did not take their medication after discharge, and most required readmission. When the administration of medication was supervised by a relative, however, most patients took their medications and remained well. In 1961 Ewalt had also written about problem patients who refused to take medication once discharged from the hospital. "Not simple is the problem of how one obtains a medical certificate when the patient is disturbed and stubborn in his refusal of help," wrote Ewalt.[50]

Thus, by 1963, when the community mental health centers legislation was being debated by Congress, there was evidence that a significant number of patients being discharged from mental hospitals required ongoing supervision, especially in regard to their medication, to stay well. By this time, almost 50,000 more patients had been discharged from state hospitals than had been admitted, so many state authorities had become aware of the readmission problem. In addition, according to medical historian Gerald Grob, "data collected by the NIMH's own Biometric Branch ... raised troubling questions" regarding whether the patients being discharged had homes to go to or, if they did, whether their families accepted them. "The assumption that patients would be able to reside with their families while undergoing rehabilitation was hardly supported by these data."[51]

In response to criticism of the mental health centers proposal, Felix and his colleagues again invoked the promise of prevention. The centers, they said, would detect cases of mental illness early in development and, by treating them, prevent more severe cases from developing. Thus, there would ultimately be fewer chronic cases and less need for beds in state hospitals. There was, of course, no evidence to support this claim.

* * *

Ultimately, none of the criticisms of the community mental health centers program received serious consideration. Felix's 1941 dream of a federal mental health program had met the needs of the Kennedy family for "a bold new approach," a tacit tribute to Rosemary. Shorn of federal money for staffing, Public Law 88-164, the Mental Retardation Facilities and Community Mental Health Centers Construction Act of 1963, passed Congress easily and was signed by the president on October 31, 1963 (Figure 3.3). Would it be a treat or a trick?

Felix was ecstatic, saying, "We have come further than I ever dreamed that in my life we would come.... This has been my blood, it has [been] my life, it has all the energy I have been able to muster." He envisioned the future:

The frontier of community psychiatry has been won, and the time has come when the colonists and organizers can begin to function effectively....We are now concerned with a framework of service which admits to no separation of prevention, treatment, and rehabilitation. This is the crux of the new concept of community medicine which focuses on the social functions of medicine as well as on the specific actions intended to prevent or cure disease in the individual patient....We have passed the point of no return in our long journey from a helter-skelter system of mental health services divorced from community life, without real grass roots support, crippling to the patient, and self-defeating in terms of the state of our medical and scientific knowledge. Whatever difficulties we shall face in the future cannot be more difficult than those of the past—and the seeds of the future which we have sown and are now nurturing give every promise of bearing good fruit.[52]

Unfortunately, the mental health centers legislation passed by Congress was fatally flawed. It encouraged the closing of state mental hospitals without any realistic plan regarding what would happen to the discharged patients, especially those who refused to take medication they needed to remain well. It included no plan for the future funding of the mental health centers. It focused resources on prevention when nobody understood enough about mental illnesses to know how to prevent them. And by

FIG 3.3  President Kennedy, after signing the federal mental retardation and mental health legislation in October, 1963, handing the pen to his sister, Eunice Shriver, who had championed federal funding for mental retardation. Vice-President Lyndon Johnson can be seen on the left. This was the last piece of major legislation signed by Kennedy before his assassination. (AP Photo)

bypassing the states, it guaranteed that future services would not be coordinated. "The seeds of the future" had indeed been sown, but they would not bear good fruit.

President Kennedy's signing of the mental retardation and mental health bill on October 31 was to be the last public bill-signing ceremony in which he would participate. Twenty-two days later in Dallas, he was assassinated.

# 4

## THE SHORT, UNHAPPY LIFE OF THE FEDERAL
## MENTAL HEALTH PROGRAM: 1964–1970

When it was signed on October 31, 1963, the legislation creating federally funded community mental health centers was a reliquary for Rosemary Kennedy. One month later, the legislation had also become a memorial for Jack Kennedy, a cairn that marked his concern for individuals who are mentally ill or mentally retarded. Like the Peace Corps program, the community mental health centers represented the spirit of Jack Kennedy and merged with his persona. To disavow, or even criticize, the program was a repudiation of Kennedy and all that he stood for.

One of the effects of Kennedy's death was the purchase of five politically halcyon years for the mental health centers program. President Lyndon Johnson, always looking for ways to capture some of Kennedy's magic dust, vowed to fully support the centers program. "We must step up the fight on mental health and mental retardation," Johnson announced. "I intend to ask for increased funds for research centers, for special teacher training, and for helping coordinate state and local programs." Following Johnson's demolition of Barry Goldwater in the 1964 presidential election, with the largest plurality in American history, Kennedy's mental health programs were incorporated into Johnson's Great Society legislative agenda, alongside job training, low-income housing, community action programs, civil rights, and Medicare and Medicaid. As historian Alonzo Hamby noted, Johnson "transformed a feeling of national mourning into a feeling of national unity directed toward enactment of the Kennedy legislative program as a memorial to a national martyr."[1]

National Institute of Mental Health officials saw their opportunity. They persuaded White House officials to reintroduce the piece of the original CMHC legislation that Congress had failed to pass—the use of federal funds for staffing the first 5 years of community mental health centers. In contrast to 1963, the legislation passed Congress relatively easily in 1965. Three years later, Congress increased the duration of federal staffing funds to 8 years. Philip Sirotkin, then deputy director of NIMH, later recalled: "We weren't kidding ourselves about this. At the end of eight years, we'd renew." The 1965 amendments also "authorized considerable regulatory and rule-making discretion to NIMH." As summarized in Foley and Sharfstein's *Madness and Government*: "Indeed, the cup of NIMH runneth over." The federal CMHC express had left the station and was headed for a mentally healthy new land. During the 1965 hearings, Congressman Horace Kornegay, Democrat from North Carolina, appeared to be one of the few members of Congress who understood where the train was really going: "I also recognize the tendency on the part of State and local officials that if someone in Washington will pay the bill, it is the easy way out for them."[2]

## THE CMHC PROGRAM GETS UNDERWAY

The first federally funded community mental health center opened in 1966, followed by 53 others in 1967. Altogether, 789 centers would be funded in the following 13 years, with a total of $2.7 billion ($13.3 billion in 2010 dollars) in federal outlays. The majority of centers received both construction and staffing grants and were legally obligated for a period of 20 years to provide five essential services: inpatient beds, partial hospitalization beds, 24-hour emergency evaluations, outpatient services, and consultation/education. The last was the community outreach the centers were supposed to do to detect early cases of illness and alter community stressors, theoretically preventing mental illnesses.

The five essential services had been selected by Drs. Felix, Yolles, and Brown, with input from other NIMH staff. Felix retired shortly after the CMHC legislation passed, thereby elevating Yolles to be NIMH director, supervising Brown, who became CMHC's first program director. Yolles was thus the "key architect of the centers program" implementation. As part of the CMHC regulations, NIMH also mandated that the centers serve catchment areas (a term borrowed from public health engineers) of between 75,000 and 200,000 people. This federal regulation led to numerous problems. As described by one CMHC director: "The boundaries of centers are seldom congruent with those of other public services, voluntary agencies, and the formal and informal political power structure. At times, there is almost a complete incongruity between the area and the location of important activities of its residents." Thus, the catchment area regulation was to become one more impediment to the CMHC program, which was already severely conceptually challenged.[3]

In the regulations written for community mental health centers, there was one glaring omission. Despite the abundant rhetoric of NIMH officials regarding how CMHCs would reduce the population of state mental hospitals, the CMHC regulations did not even mention the hospitals. This omission was highlighted by a 1974 evaluation of CMHCs:

> Perhaps the most striking aspect of the regulations is what they omit. They describe no plans, mechanisms, nor procedures to guide centers in determining

their relationship to state hospitals; no methods to divert potential state hospital admissions to community mental health centers; and no procedures whereby patients released from state hospitals could be rehabilitated and assisted back into the community. Indeed, the regulations contain not a single reference to the goal of supplanting state hospitals!

Medical historian Gerald Grob also commented on this deficiency: "The absence of any links between new, free-standing centers and the existing mental hospital system was striking. If centers were designed to provide comprehensive services and continuity of care, how could they function in isolation from a state system that provided care and treatment for most of the nation's severely and chronically mentally ill population?"[4]

The omission of state mental hospitals from the CMHC regulations was intentional. The hospitals were the past, CMHCs were the future. The hospitals were a state program, CMHCs were a federal program. As described by Brown in a 1972 interview, "Yolles hated the state hospitals and wanted to shut down those goddamn warehouses." He "did not want the control of the [CMHC] operating costs to shift to the states by means of the regulations," so he simply ignored the hospitals. Besides, Yolles argued, state hospitals would no longer be needed once CMHCs managed to prevent future cases of mental illness. Dr. Alan Miller, a special assistant to Yolles, recalled the intellectual ambiance of the period:

There was an optimism in the air, perhaps a carry-over from WWII, that we knew how to help people with such problems, especially if they were reached early. There was even a belief that serious problems could be prevented that way.... It was an exhilarating time for many of us who were caught up in this project. One of the most powerful intoxicants is the feeling that you are making history.[5]

## PREVENTING MENTAL ILLNESS

Stanley Yolles was 45 years old when he replaced the retiring Robert Felix as NIMH director in 1964. He was less capable and charismatic than his predecessor and tried to compensate by carrying Felix's programs to extremes. Thus, said Yolles, "psychiatry is no longer concerned only with patients and only with illness...we have altered our professional horizons.... we are increasingly becoming involved in social planning and the contemporary issues of the day."[6]

Yolles was especially interested in the effects of poverty on mental health. This echoed President Johnson's concurrent call for a war on poverty, a popular theme at the time reflected in books such as Michael Harrington's *The Other America* (1962) and Harry Caudhill's *Night Comes to the Cumberlands* (1962). In 1965 Yolles wrote:

> The psychiatrist is aware that a man's mind, assaulted by poverty in either its acute or chronic form, is susceptible to mental disturbance, disorder or disease.... The conditions of poverty, since they constitute a breeding ground for mental disease, require the professional involvement of the modern psychiatrist. Working with community leaders and specialists in other professions, we, as specialists in the art of psychiatry, have skills and knowledge which can help the statesman, the politician, and the poor man himself to intervene in this condition of poverty before it creeps into the fiber and style of a man's thoughts and behavior.

And 1 year later:

> Through community planning on a comprehensive basis, through crisis intervention and other methods, mental health professionals can share with other community leaders in environmental manipulation to eliminate known producers of stress as well as loci of stress such as urban slums and rural depressed areas—potential breeding grounds of mental disease. All of these are perfectly legitimate methods of treatment and no longer have the overtones of quackery which have in the past been attributed to them.

Therefore, added Yolles, the primary responsibility of psychiatrists is "to improve the lives of the people by bettering their physical environment, their educational and cultural opportunities, and other social and environmental conditions. In accepting such a responsibility, mental health professionals do not claim omnipotence.... Our first priority must be to expand our newly established policy of treating the mentally ill into a policy of enhancing mental health." Yolles was thus trying to follow in the footsteps of his predecessor, Robert Felix, who, as he retired from NIMH, had urged that CMHCs be used to provide "a climate in which each citizen has optimum opportunities for sustained creative and responsible participation in the life of the community, and for the development of his particular potentialities as a human being."[7]

Consistent with his rhetoric, Yolles encouraged the newly emerging mental health centers to focus their resources on social problems as a means of preventing mental illness. Because NIMH was the source of their federal funding, the center directors got the message. In an NIMH-sponsored survey of 198 CMHCs carried out between 1970 and 1972, center directors were asked to rank by priority six activities. The activity ranked most important by the center directors was "the reduction of the incidence of mental disorders (prevention)." Ranked second was to "increase the rate of recovery from mental disorders." Ranked third was to "raise the level of mental health and improve the quality of community." Ranked last was "the reduction of the level of disability associated with chronic mental disorders."[8]

Despite paying lip service to the importance of prevention, few community mental health centers actually did much in this regard. A 1970 NIMH survey reported that the average CMHC spent between 3% and 4% of staff time on preventive activities, mostly teaching classes on parent and teacher effectiveness. A few centers took on more ambitious agendas. Woodlawn CMHC in Chicago hired noted community organizer and activist Saul Alinsky to help plan their program. Sound View CMHC in New York "helped establish a mini-park, assisted a church in receiving funds for a nursery program,...helped form a few block associations,...[and] organized picketing at a difficult [street] crossing which eventually led to the installation of a traffic light." Central City CMHC in Los Angeles also organized parents to get a traffic light installed at a busy crossing; the center's staff led a group "down to the city councilman's office and from there to the Division of Traffic." Temple CMHC in Philadelphia "became significantly involved in such work as rent strikes with escrow accounts, stimulation of voter registration, and other political activism." The community board of Temple CMHC defined the center's mission as working "to resolve the underlying causes of mental health problems such as unequal distribution of opportunity, income, and benefits of technical progress."[9]

Yolles and the NIMH staff praised such prevention efforts as carrying out the vision of Felix and the true mission of the CMHC program. In a 1969 paper, Yolles wrote:

> Besides treating the classic range of mental illnesses, the center staffs are helping clients with such matters as housing, finances, reading difficulties, and the misuse of marijuana, LSD, and other drugs. Such problems seem to be side effects of affluence as well as of deprivation.

Those on the CMHC front lines who were actually doing the work, however, quickly realized the absurdity of their task. Jack Wilder, director of the Sound View CMHC, noted that his center's resources "had to be allocated to treating those who had an 'existing illness' and clamored for help." Similarly, Anthony Panzetta, director of the Temple CMHC, observed that "doing a good job of comprehensive and continuous care of the psychotic and mental retardates of the base population group of from 75,000 to 200,000, may very likely absorb every available manhour of resource and then some." Moreover, added Panzetta, the prevention of mental illnesses depends on knowing the causes, and "we are at a level of understanding of most human events which rivals the level of cosmic understanding enjoyed by the amoeba." Panzetta then summarized the task of a preventive psychiatrist as follows:

> The preventive psychiatrist is a bits and pieces practitioner with built-in chutzpah. He takes this piece and that, fills the gap with maybe, packages his war on evil so that it will be funded, and sets out...When we in psychiatry wave our preventive banners, we must look ridiculous to even the gods on Mount Olympus who once held the key to the causal mysteries of human events.[10]

## THE NATION'S MENTAL HEALTH CENTER

It is important to note that these experiments in preventive psychiatry were taking place during an especially turbulent time in American history. Between April 1963, when Martin Luther King Jr. was arrested in Birmingham, and April 1968, when he was assassinated in Memphis, a continuous series of racial confrontations rocked the nation—Selma, Watts, Newark, Chicago, Atlanta, Detroit, New York. Simultaneously, antiwar demonstrations were taking place, and Johnson's War on Poverty was highlighting conditions in Appalachia and elsewhere. One might have been excused for thinking that the nation itself needed psychiatric help.

Yolles and his NIMH staff were eager to try to provide such help, essentially transforming the institute into a mental health center for the nation. For the "mass violence on the streets of our cities and student demonstrations on the campuses of our colleges," Yolles claimed that "behavioral science research does provide a framework for effective *preventive* action."[11]

Yolles's chief of planning at NIMH was Leonard Duhl, a psychiatrist and psychoanalyst. Duhl viewed whole cities as potential patients:

> The city...is in pain. It has symptoms that cry out for relief. They are the symptoms of anger, violence, poverty, and hopelessness. If the city were a patient, it would seek help....The totality of urban life is the only rational focus for concern with mental illness....our problem now embraces all of society and we must examine every aspect of it to determine what is conducive to mental health.

As a preventive psychiatrist, Duhl consulted with city mayors and urged other psychiatrists to do likewise:

> If we can reach the mayors and the people concerned about the cities in their crises with assistance in the acute problems they are facing, they will begin to

use us and we can help bring about change. I suggest that we begin to take them on as clients. We cannot wait for them to request our services, because they are not going to ask us. We must begin right now to fill in and be of assistance to them with the issues they are facing.

Duhl recognized that the role of psychiatrist as change agent meant that he would become involved in community politics: "Such a role requires that he undertake action to persuade a majority to support his decision, and to involve people in implementing his ideas. This, by any definition, is political action."[12]

Another member of Yolles's staff at this time was Matthew Dumont, also a psychiatrist and psychoanalyst, who was assistant chief of the NIMH Center for Studies of Metropolitan Mental Health Problems. Dumont also viewed the city "as an ecological unit, as an organism capable of health or suffering." For Dumont, there was "little doubt that the urban organism is indeed distressed; it is feeling symptoms." Like Duhl's, Dumont's solution involved political action in which psychiatrists should play a prominent role: "In short, the changes I am talking about, the treatment for the ailing organism, involves a redistribution of wealth and resources of this country on a scale that has never been imagined. We should be constructing a society for the urban poor of such beauty and richness, with so many options for behavior, that it becomes nothing less than a privilege to be called poor."[13]

In retrospect, such statements appear fatuous, but they should be considered in their historical context. American psychiatry in general was grandiose at this time. For example, Howard Rome, a past president of the American Psychiatric Association, in 1968 urged psychiatrists to become involved in foreign affairs, poverty, violence, and unemployment. "If psychiatry is to move into the avant-garde of meaningful social reform," wrote Rome, "it will have to greatly extend the boundaries of its present community operations. Actually no less than the entire world is a proper catchment area for present-day psychiatry, and psychiatry need not be appalled by the magnitude of this task." Such thinking was also consistent with many social scientists working in the Kennedy and Johnson administrations. For example, the federal program to combat juvenile delinquency, a favorite of Attorney General Robert Kennedy, was run by two sociologists who viewed such delinquency "not as individual pathology but as community pathology":

For delinquency is not, in the final analysis, a property of individuals or even of subcultures; it is a property of social systems in which these individuals and groups are enmeshed.... The target for preventive action, then, should be defined, not as the individual or group that exhibits the delinquent pattern, but as the social setting that gives rise to delinquency.

Presidents Kennedy and Johnson were going to lead Americans to a brave new world, of which the community mental health centers were merely one part.[14]

During the 1960s, NIMH thus viewed itself and its federally funded community mental health centers as important players in the war on racism and poverty. NIMH provided special funding to CMHCs set up in poverty areas and at one point explored a "mental health tie-in" between NIMH and "both the Appalachia and poverty programs." Political action, such as that advocated by Drs. Duhl and Dumont, was consistent with the mission of community psychiatry to change social systems to promote mental health.[15]

By 1969 NIMH had virtually abandoned the treatment of mental illness as its primary mission in favor of promoting mental health. Consistent with its self-perceived calling, NIMH left the aegis of the disease-oriented National Institutes of Health and became an independent institute under the Alcohol, Drug Abuse, and Mental Health Administration. At the time, Yolles even explored the possibility of building a new campus in Columbia, Maryland, to accommodate his expanding mental health institute as part of a collection of institutes for the behavioral sciences. It was to become a behavioral sciences rival to the National Institutes of Health. NIMH, wrote Yolles, "has long and successfully argued the necessity of viewing its programmatic efforts on a total and comprehensive basis with an emphasis on mental health rather than mental illness. What is needed now is an even greater effort and utilization of the behavioral sciences in achieving that goal of mental health."[16]

## THE PASSING OF PREVENTION

The attempts of Yolles and the NIMH to prevent mental illnesses by intervening in social and political issues were criticized even in their earliest stages. In 1965, prior to the opening of the first federally funded CMHC, sociologist Warren Dunham labeled community psychiatry "the newest therapeutic bandwagon" and said it was attracting "those who jump on any bandwagon as long as it is moving." He noted:

> There is no doubt that the word "prevention" falling on the ears of well-intentioned Americans is just what the doctor ordered....But, of course, there is a catch. How are we going to take the first preventive actions if we are still uncertain about the causes of mental disorders?

Dunham reminded his readers that the Cambridge-Somerville Delinquency Prevention Project, the only major study in which psychiatry had been used to try to prevent future criminal behavior, had produced "mainly negative" results.[17]

Other skeptical voices followed. Psychiatrist Bernard Rubin noted that "the concept of prevention in psychiatry is limited by little knowledge of etiology.... there is no evidence that any particular interventive activity with individuals or groups of individuals reduces or has reduced the incidence of any mental illness.... A move to the social fields within the community implies an unlimited expansion of the boundaries of psychiatry to encompass all social ills." Sociologist Morton Wagenfold could find no evidence to support "the notion that mental illness is etiologically or sequentially associated with social conditions such as poverty and racism." Psychiatrist William Davidson wondered whether "the ultimate goal of community psychiatry... will be to produce a psychiatrist who never sees a patient." And sociologist Dale DeWild asked perhaps the most embarrassing question of all: "If mental health professionals are given some control over how social systems are organized, who is going to control the mental health professionals?"[18]

Such criticisms did not deter NIMH, which continued encouraging CMHCs to become involved in social issues to prevent mental illnesses. Lincoln CMHC in the South Bronx was cited by NIMH in 1968 as one of eight model centers, and the center received a prestigious award from the American Psychiatric Association. The center's directors, Drs. Harris Peck, Seymour Kaplan, and Melvin Roman, were strongly committed to the NIMH goal of using CMHCs to improve the lives of "the relatively neglected—the disadvantaged urban community with predominantly minority ethnic populations." Accordingly, the Lincoln CMHC staff became involved in such problems as garbage collection services, rat control, housing code enforcement, and organizing tenant councils to force absentee landlords to make improvements to their buildings. The ultimate goal of the Lincoln program was to improve the mental health of residents by teaching "the dispossessed how to use the political process to ameliorate their own conditions." This was exactly what Yolles was encouraging.[19]

On March 4, 1969, a few residents of the South Bronx improved their own mental health dramatically by taking over the offices of Drs. Peck, Kaplan, and Roman and locking them out. Almost 200 local residents, including 70% of the Lincoln CMHC staff, declared a strike and installed a nonprofessional mental health worker as the new CMHC director. The event was widely covered by the media, including the *New York Times*, which headlined "Community Takes over Control of Bronx Mental Health Services." Because the Lincoln CMHC directors had encouraged community control, the logic of the takeover was inescapable and emphasized by the news accounts:

Dr. Harris B. Peck of the Lincoln Hospital Mental Health Service, used to pound the table at staff meetings and call for a "revolution." He urged community workers, one of them recalled, to wrest control of their South Bronx mental health project from him and other professional administrators and put him out of a job.

Yesterday, they did.

The strike continued for 3 weeks and became increasingly contentious as the Black Panthers, the Students for a Democratic Society, and other radical political action groups became involved. Finally, police were sent in and arrested 23 strikers.[20]

The Lincoln CMHC strike almost instantaneously discredited the idea of using CMHCs to prevent mental illness. To be locked out of your office by your own employees was humiliating enough, but to be hoisted on the petard of your own rhetoric and ridiculed by the *New York Times* went beyond the pale. The Lincoln CMHC directors summarily resigned. NIMH, which had watched the events with growing horror, tried to disassociate itself from its model CMHC as quickly as possible. Elsewhere, CMHC directors who had been moving toward increasing preventive services made a rapid about-face.

The Lincoln CMHC fiasco in 1969 was a major setback for the idea of using CMHCs to prevent mental illnesses. Events of 1970 extinguished any remaining coals of prevention that were still aglow at that time. Dr. Leopold Bellak was one of the leaders of the CMHC movement. His 1964 book, *Community Psychiatry and Community Mental Health,* had claimed that "community psychiatry is designed to guarantee and safeguard, to a degree previously undreamed of, a basic human right—the privilege of mental health." Bellak proposed that a national psychiatric case register be created:

There the social, emotional, and medical histories of every citizen who had come to attention in any way because of emotional difficulties would be tabulated by computer. When these persons were divorced or widowed or encountered other difficulties, they could be offered guidance and treatment.

Bellak acknowledged that his proposals "may arouse violent reactions" and "invoke the image of Big Brother....But I am reminded that income taxes were once considered basic violations of personal freedom and fluoridation of water was held to be a subversive plot." Why shouldn't there be a "Sound Mind Bill?"[21]

Given the assumptions of preventive psychiatry as propounded by NIMH, the logic of Bellak's proposal was as compelling as its potential consequences were chilling. Richard Nixon had assumed the presidency in January 1969 and thus would theoretically be the ultimate authority overseeing a national psychiatric case register. This fact became salient a few months later when Nixon's former personal physician, Dr. Arnold A. Hutschnecker, proposed that all high school students in the United States be psychologically tested. Those who were found to be deviant would be "weeded out." Hutschnecker also suggested that a "mental health certificate" be required for all adults before being allowed to assume "any job of political responsibility."[22]

Yolles and the staff of the NIMH suddenly questioned whether preventing mental illnesses was such a good idea after all. It had seemed to be, under a predictably liberal president like Lyndon Johnson, who presumably would have appointed psychiatrists like Yolles to oversee the program. But with a conservative president like Nixon in charge, who could predict what conditions might be labeled as needing treatment? The cumulative effect of the demise of the Lincoln CMHC program and the proposals by Nixon's former personal physician effectively terminated the prevention dreams of the NIMH psychiatrists. Their federal attempts to prevent mental illnesses would become a mere footnote in history but would have profound and long-lasting effects on the nation's mental illness treatment system.

## COURT RULINGS AND MEDICAID

During the decade of the 1960s, therefore, public psychiatric care in the United States changed markedly. At the beginning of the decade, states and counties had been actively developing programs to provide follow-up care for patients already being discharged from the state hospitals. By the end of the decade, state and local efforts had largely ceased, usurped by the federal community mental health centers program. States and counties had been told that they no longer needed to worry about such matters because Superman, disguised as NIMH, had arrived and would prevent these psychiatric conditions from developing. By 1969, however, it had become clear that prevention, the centerpiece of the federal mental health program, was without substance.

Meanwhile, patients with serious mental illnesses were progressively being discharged from state mental hospitals to live in the community, despite the fact that there had been virtually no planning for meeting their needs. The census of the hospitals decreased by 165,571 patients between 1960 and 1969. Each year, the exodus increased, and even accelerated, because of two unrelated events.

The first of these events was a series of court rulings. In 1966 a 60-year-old woman, Mrs. Lake, was found wandering around Washington, D.C., in a confused manner. A court ruled that she was a danger to herself and ordered her committed to St. Elizabeths Hospital, the local public psychiatric hospital. Mrs. Lake appealed the decision, and the case was reviewed by David Bazelon, the chief judge of the U. S. Court of Appeals for the District of Columbia. In a landmark decision, Bazelon ruled that Mrs. Lake was entitled to be released if a less restrictive alternative to the hospital could be found. Unfortunately for Mrs. Lake, one was not, and she died in the hospital 5 years later. However, the concept of least restrictive alternative had been introduced into the court system and would become a stimulus to the emptying of public mental hospitals. In a complementary decision, also issued in 1966 by Judge Bazelon, it was ruled that Mr. Rouse, another patient who had been committed to St. Elizabeths Hospital, must either be treated for his mental illness by the hospital or be released. This became part of the legal right-to-treatment concept that encouraged hospitals to release many patients, especially those who were difficult to treat.

At the same time that some courts were setting legal precedents facilitating the release of patients from mental hospitals, other courts were handing down decisions making it more difficult to get patients into the hospitals. One of the first of these decisions was also in the District of Columbia, where in 1964 the grounds for the involuntary commitment of psychiatric patients was changed from a need-for-treatment standard to a danger-to-self-or-others standard. Being in need of treatment is a more liberal standard and allows a person to be involuntarily hospitalized and treated before that person has demonstrated dangerousness. By contrast, danger-to-self-or-others is more restrictive, especially if it is interpreted strictly, which has happened in many states.

The second event that increased the discharge of patients from state hospitals was a fiscal one. In 1965 President Johnson persuaded Congress to enact, as centerpieces for his Great Society programs, Medicare and Medicaid—both being modifications of the existing Social Security Act. Medicare provides hospital insurance for individuals age 65 years and older and is completely funded by the federal government. Medicaid was designed to provide medical care for poor people and is funded jointly by the federal and state governments, utilizing a formula by which the federal government contributes a greater share to fiscally poorer states. At the time they were passed, almost all the attention was paid to Medicare, which American medicine opposed as being socialized medicine. Medicaid, by contrast, was not even included in the original legislation but, rather, tacked on to the bill by Wilbur Mills, chairman of the House Ways and Means Committee. Mills viewed it as a fiscal mechanism for getting additional federal funds to his poor constituents in Arkansas. A history of Medicaid claimed that "a legislative draftsman said that he doubted that more than half a day was devoted to consideration of its provision" and that "Medicaid seems to have received almost no consideration in the [congressional] Committees deliberations nor in floor debates in the House." It was "a low profile item," "a casual add-on" to the Medicare bill.[23]

Neither Medicare nor Medicaid was conceived of as a program for mentally ill individuals. Both programs, in fact, sought to exclude the mentally ill to avoid having the federal government usurp state fiscal responsibility. For Medicaid, this was done by decreeing that Medicaid funds could not be used for individuals in mental institutions, which became known as the Institutions for Mental Diseases (IMD) exclusion.

The fact that Medicare and Medicaid ultimately became two of the most important forces driving the emptying of state mental hospitals, although completely unintended, is a telling commentary on the lack of coordination and planning for human services at the federal level. According to Brown, who was the deputy director of the NIMH at the time, there was no discussion about the proposed Medicare and Medicaid programs between the Social Security Administration and the NIMH, despite the fact that both agencies were under the Department of Health, Education, and Welfare. This lack of consultation was confirmed in a 1977 report by the General Accounting Office in which another NIMH official described the lack of input by his agency on a proposed change to the Social Security Act:

> While we were reviewing and commenting on issue papers we found out there were already draft regulations. When we were reviewing and commenting on draft regulations, we found out that regulations had already been published in the Federal Register.[24]

In addition to the absence of internal federal communication regarding possible effects of the proposed Medicare and Medicaid programs on individuals with mental illness, there was also apparently no discussion with state departments of mental health. The federal government was acting independently, seemingly unaware of the profound impact these new programs would ultimately have on state mental health programs.

* * *

By 1970, the federally funded community mental health centers program was well underway, with 270 centers in operation. However, the program was saddled with multiple conceptual flaws, and its most important component—the prevention of mental illnesses—had already been proven to be unfeasible. In addition, courts had issued rulings that would facilitate the exit of patients from state mental hospitals, and Medicare and Medicaid had created additional fiscal incentives to discharge patients. Local communities were about to be inundated with released state hospital patients—the very patients the federally funded mental health centers had the least interest in serving.

Officials in the Department of Health, Education, and Welfare (DHEW) were aware that there were problems and proposed transferring some authority for the federally funded mental health centers from the NIMH to the 10 DHEW regional offices. Yolles and other NIMH officials, aware that the regional offices were sympathetic to state needs, strongly resisted the change. The CMHC program had been conceived as a federal program, they argued, and it should remain as a federal program. Shortly thereafter, when Yolles made an indiscreet public comment regarding federal drug policies, DHEW officials used the occasion to summarily fire him.[25]

# 5

## THE DEATH OF THE FEDERAL MENTAL
## HEALTH PROGRAM: 1971–1980

It is possible that the federal program of community mental health centers might have survived in some modified form if Richard Nixon had not been elected president. Nixon disliked the program, and to repel assaults from the White House, the National Institute of Mental Health (NIMH) erected bulwarks of fictional success. For 8 years, fortress NIMH continued doing business as usual, unable to acknowledge that its programs were not working, lest that allow the White House barbarians into the breach. By the time Nixon's successor, Gerald Ford, left office in January 1977, the community mental health centers (CMCHs) program was, in effect, undergoing rigor mortis.

Nixon's suspicion of psychiatry had deep roots. The Southern California district from which he had been elected to the House of Representatives in 1946 became the nidus for a national anti–mental health movement that attempted to link psychiatry and communism. A large billboard in Los Angeles carried the following message in the 1950s:

> It is amazing and appalling how many supposedly intelligent people have been duped by such COMMUNIST SCHEMES as FLUORIDATION and "Mental Health" especially since both the AMERICAN LEGION and the D.A.R. have publicly branded "Mental Health" as a COMMUNIST PLOT to take over our country.

The John Birch Society and the Daughters of the American Revolution (DAR) led the anti-psychiatry troops, the latter with a series in its magazine describing mental health as a "Marxist weapon" and claiming that 80% of American psychiatrists were foreigners, "most of them educated in Russia." The alleged link between mental health and Communism resonated with Nixon, who in 1948 had been a member of the House Un-American Activities Committee, which had investigated Alger Hiss as a Communist agent.[1]

Nixon's suspicion of psychiatrists, especially psychoanalysts, was further reinforced by their pattern of voting. In 1956, only 15% of psychoanalysts cast votes for Dwight Eisenhower, the Republican presidential candidate. In 1960 Nixon received only 6% of their vote, and in 1964 Barry Goldwater received only 5%. Even more damning for Nixon was a survey published by *Fact* magazine in 1964. The magazine had sent a questionnaire to psychiatrists asking whether they thought Goldwater, the Republican candidate, was psychologically fit to become president. Among the respondents, 657 psychiatrists said that he was psychologically fit, but 2,417 said that he was not. Some of the published responses labeled Goldwater "immature," "narcissistic," "paranoid," and "megalomaniac," and a few offered a diagnosis of schizophrenia. This blatant attempt by psychiatrists to discredit a political candidate was widely condemned by the media.[2]

Thus, when Nixon assumed the reins of government in January 1969, he arrived with an enduring suspicion of psychiatrists. This became further magnified as Nixon became aware of the activities of the NIMH and its federally funded CMHCs. The government's chief psychiatrist, Stanley Yolles, was openly encouraging centers to become involved in social and political issues, even advocating voter registration among poor people who, Nixon knew, were not likely to vote Republican. Among Yolles's staff was Matthew Dumont, the psychiatrist who was advocating "a redistribution of wealth and resources of this country on a scale that has never been imagined." Here indeed was proof of a Communist conspiracy among those left-leaning, federally funded mental health subversives.[3]

## COMMUNITY MENTAL HEALTH CENTERS

As the battle between Nixon and NIMH got underway, the discharge of seriously mentally ill patients from the state hospitals was accelerating. In January 1969, when Nixon took office, there were 399,152 mentally ill patients remaining in state hospitals. By the end of the Nixon and Ford administrations in late 1976, only 170,619 patients remained. First, individual wards closed, then whole buildings, and finally entire hospitals; between 1970 and 1973, at least 12 state hospitals were shuttered. Hospitals that had been cities unto themselves, such as New York's Pilgrim State Hospital with 14,000 patients, were progressively depopulated, and abandoned buildings began outnumbering those being used. In the two decades since deinstitutionalization had begun in 1956, almost 400,000 state hospital beds had been closed; it was an ongoing exodus of biblical proportions.[4]

Meanwhile, CMHCs continued to open despite efforts of Nixon administration officials to phase out the program. By the end of 1976, 548 centers were in business and almost 200 more had been funded but were not yet operational. If any federal or state official at that time had asked who was supposed to provide treatment for the patients being discharged from the state hospitals, the reflex reply would have been the CMHCs. Yet both federal and state officials were well aware that this was not happening.

Data collected by NIMH were especially damning. It showed that between 1968 and 1978 patients who had been discharged from state mental hospitals who then were followed up in CMHCs made up only 3.6% to 6.5% of all CMHC patients. Moreover, the longer a CMHC was in business, the fewer state hospital patients it saw. In 1976, for example, CMHCs that had been operational for 1 to 2 years had 5.5% of their admissions referred from state hospitals, whereas CMHCs that had been operational for 6 to 7 years had only 2.6% of their admissions referred from these hospitals. Other NIMH studies also documented the failure of the federally funded centers to provide care for patients being released from the state hospitals. A 1972 study concluded that "relationships between community mental health centers and public mental hospitals serving the same catchment area exist only at a relatively minimal level between the majority of the two types of organizations." A 1979 assessment stated this even more strongly: "*The relationships between CMHCs and public psychiatric hospitals are difficult at best, adversarial at worst*," with the emphasis in the original.[5]

The fact that the federally funded mental health centers were not working cooperatively with state mental hospitals surprised no one. NIMH had failed to mandate any relationship between the two in its original guidelines. Its message to the centers was to prevent new cases of mental illness, not worry about existing cases. CMHCs received praise from NIMH officials when they became involved in a community's social problems, not when they provided follow-up care for patients released from state hospitals. State hospitals, likewise, had no incentive to cooperate with the CMHCs, which, state hospital officials were told, were being built to replace them. Thus, state hospitals largely ignored the CMHCs, and the latter were happy to reciprocate. An extreme example of the behavior that inevitably ensued was a state hospital in Kansas that, when ordered to inform the local CMHC each time it discharged a patient, dutifully did so by sending to the CMHC the patient's discharge sheets but with the patient's name, address, and all other identifying information blacked out. Surveying the scene in 1972, Harry Schnibbe, head of the organization representing state mental health directors, called it "a disaster situation.... follow-up service [for discharged patients] is our number one headache."[6]

If community mental health centers were not taking care of the thousands of patients being discharged from state mental hospitals, who were they seeing? According to NIMH records, the largest numbers of CMHC patients were diagnosed with "social maladjustment or no mental disorder" (22%) or "neuroses and personality disorder" (21%). Childhood disorders, mostly behavioral problems (13%) and depressive disorders (13%) followed, with substance abuse (10%) and schizophrenia (10%) at the bottom. A catchall category of "all other diagnoses" comprised the others.

Probably representative of the largest group of CMHC patients was "a middle class clergyman...recently divorced and having trouble with his children....He told us that he came to the center looking for some 'sound perspective and advice.'" Such patients, often referred to as the "worried well," fit the original vision of Robert Felix, who believed that by treating small problems early you would prevent large problems later.[7]

The skewing of CMHC patients toward those with less severe diagnoses became more pronounced the longer CMHCs were in existence. According to the 1978 report of President Carter's Commission on Mental Health, "the major trend in the diagnostic composition of the centers' clients has been the decreasing percent of those diagnosed with depressive disorders and schizophrenia, counterbalanced by an increase of those classified as socially maladjusted, no mental disorder, deferred diagnosis, or nonspecific disorder." One psychiatrist described the process as follows:

> In some instances mental health centers tended to select attractive, easy patients to treat, and referred to the state hospital patients that the staff and community wanted to reject.

A 1977 study of CMHCs in Washington, D.C., confirmed that 90% of the patients being sent to St. Elizabeths Hospital "could have been treated at a CMHC or other alternative" to the hospital. Most CMHCs saw very few patients with serious mental illnesses. Anthony Lehman, chairman of the Department of Psychiatry at the University of Maryland, recalled his disappointment in the mid-1970s when, as a resident at UCLA, he asked to work in a CMHC to gain experience. He was assigned to a CMHC in Santa Monica that was said to be highly regarded:

> The experience was quite disappointing. The CMHC was seeing very few individuals with serious mental illnesses. I'm not sure I even saw one. Instead, the patients were people from the community with various personal crises—marital, job-related, housing, etc. The staff was using a crisis consultation model in which it was believed that most such crises could be resolved with twelve sessions of psychotherapy.[8]

Among the 789 community mental health centers ultimately funded by the federal government, a few actually did provide significant care for patients being discharged from state hospitals, despite NIMH's lack of encouragement to do so. Most such centers were run by directors who had a special interest in providing services for individuals with serious mental illnesses; examples included the Sacramento County and Santa Barbara County CMHCs in California, Salt Lake Valley CMHC in Utah, and Range CMHC in Minnesota. Several other centers that did good work had been started with state or private funds prior to the beginning of the federal CMHC program, as described in Chapter 3; they took the federal money and continued doing what they had previously been doing. Examples of such centers were Prairie View CMHC, which had been founded by Mennonites in 1954 in Newton, Kansas; San Mateo County CMHC in California; Fort Logan CMHC in Colorado; and Massachusetts CMHC in Boston. Overall, however, probably no more than 5% of the federally funded CMHCs made any significant contributions to the care of patients being released from state mental hospitals.

By contrast, there is a long list of federally funded CMHCs that delivered almost no public psychiatric services and were grossly out of compliance with federal regulations to deliver the five essential services they had agreed to provide. Many of these received CMHC construction money and built the buildings but then used them for other purposes. For example, in Michigan the Battle Creek Adventist hospital received $709,988 ($4.0 million in 2010 dollars) to build a CMHC; it instead used the building as a private psychiatric hospital, and the CMHC, in federal parlance, "never materialized." In Minneapolis, the Metropolitan CMHC received $1.8 million ($10.1 million in 2010 dollars) for the construction and staffing of a CMHC. The facility was instead used as a private psychiatric hospital, complete with swimming pool and gymnasium; in 1969, only 11% of its patients even lived in its catchment area. In New Orleans, the DePaul Hospital CMHC received $474,484 ($2.7 million in 2010 dollars) in federal construction funds, built the building, and a year later sold it to a for-profit hospital chain. Hospitals in Philadelphia used CMHC construction money to build a business office, data processing room, operating room, and inhalation therapy room.[9]

Such abuses of CMHC funds were widespread and well known. In 1968 Lawrence Kubie, a professor of psychiatry at Johns Hopkins University School of Medicine, publicly commended what he called this "benevolent profiteering" on the CMHC "fad":

> Several department heads have stated frankly that they are glad to take federal money…To get this money, they are forced to call their new facilities "community mental health centers." They do not hesitate to add that within a dozen years the words will have dropped into innocuous desuetude.[10]

In this laissez-faire atmosphere, almost everything appeared to be acceptable to NIMH as long as it labeled itself a CMHC. The Orlando Regional Medical Center in Florida demonstrated how far the funds could be abused. With more than $2.8 million ($15.7 million in 2010 dollars) of CMHC construction and staffing funds, it built space for what was essentially a private psychiatric hospital as well as a swimming pool, tennis court, and volleyball court. With its federal staffing funds it hired four surgical technicians, a cosmetic and fashion counselor, six maids, six porters, a gardener, a pool lifeguard, and a swimming instructor. NIMH records and site visit reports suggest that at least 10%, and probably 20%, of all federally funded CMHCs were similar to these centers and grossly out of compliance with federal regulations.[11]

Because the federally funded CMHCs were seeing neither the patients being discharged from the state hospitals nor many of the patients being admitted to the hospitals, there was essentially no relationship between the opening of CMHCs and the decreasing state hospital population. From the late 1960s onward, the exodus of state hospital patients was on autopilot, driven by the availability of antipsychotic drugs, which got the patients well enough to be discharged; the availability of federal Medicaid and Medicare funds, which effectively saved state funds; and court rulings, which encouraged patient discharge. NIMH's own studies verified the lack of any effect of CMHCs on the census of the state hospitals. A 16-state study published in 1976 reported "no consistent relationship between the openings of centers and changes in state hospital resident rates." The following year, a report from the Government Accounting Office similarly concluded that "the CMHC program was having only a limited impact on reducing public mental hospital populations." NIMH was so desperate for any data suggesting the CMHCs were responsible for decreasing state hospital populations that a 1975 study suggesting a possible relationship in a single state was titled "Is NIMH's Dream Coming True?" Perhaps most damning was a survey of 175 CMHC directors who were asked to rank order 10 CMHC goals and objectives. The goal of reducing the utilization of state mental hospitals was ranked next to last.[12]

## NATIONAL INSTITUTE OF MENTAL HEALTH PUTS UP THE BARRICADES

In early 1970, when Bertram Brown was appointed director of NIMH following the firing of Stanley Yolles, he knew the Nixon years were likely to be problematic. Like Yolles, Brown regarded Robert Felix as a father figure and shared Felix's vision of a federally funded network of CMHCs. Brown was intrigued by the fact that a network of two thousand CMHCs, with their community boards, might develop into "a powerful political organization." Like both Felix and Yolles, Brown had been impressed by "the horrendous conditions in state mental hospitals" and believed that "employment, family interactions, mobility, environment and other conditions...were...central to the mission of the CMHC." Psychiatrists, said Brown, had a "special position" to provide insight into social problems, and "it *is* our responsibility to interpret these matters." Brown viewed the CMHC movement as "a grand experiment" and "a test of American democracy."[13]

Brown did not have to wait long to hear Nixon's White House operatives knocking on his door. The CMHC program should be terminated, they said, and "states and localities should assume total responsibility for these programs." The previous year, Yolles had told

Congress that federal funds from the 5-year staffing grants were running out for many centers and other funds had not materialized; thus, he said, the federal funding should be extended for an additional 3 years. Using his imagination, Yolles added that "largely because of the impetus of community mental health centers we have seen a startling reduction of patients in mental hospitals in the United States." If that is the case, replied Nixon officials, why haven't the states picked up the costs of staffing the centers? This was not a discussion that Brown, or anyone else at NIMH, wished to have. Politically astute, Brown simply went to Congress, which was controlled by the Democrats, behind the administration's back and arranged to extend the staffing grant for an additional 3 years, also increasing the maximum federal share of the CMHC grants.[14]

Thus began a 6-year siege. In what became an annual ritual, first Nixon's, and then Ford's, administrators recommended terminating the CMHC program. Each year NIMH persuaded the Democratic Congress to restore Nixon's proposed cuts. Nixon then impounded the appropriated CMHC funds, leading to court suits forcing their release. Brown continued to publicly extol the merits of the CMHCs, annually telling Congress that they were primarily responsible for the reduction in the state hospital patient population. In 1973, for example, Brown asserted that "where a center has been operational three years or longer, the possibility of a person being a mental patient in that area is reduced by a third." A decade later, one of Brown's staff acknowledged that the number had been the product of "a special analysis." "You know," he added, "we were all good soldiers then."[15]

Each year the CMHC program became more heavily politicized and the discussion in Congress more heated. The CMHC standard bearer in the Senate was Ted Kennedy, who represented Jack Kennedy's legacy. In 1973, Caspar Weinberger, secretary of the Department of Health, Education, and Welfare, again advocated a phase out of the CMHC program because "the Federal Government is ill equipped and the wrong agency to provide health care treatment and services":

Kennedy: "It appears quite clear that you have made up your own mind, and the Congress be damned... "
Weinberger: "If you wish to misquote me continually, of course you are free to do so."[16]

Within such an atmosphere, a constructive analysis of the CMHC program was impossible. Saul Feldman, who was the NIMH deputy director of the CMHC program at that time, recalled:

During the early 70s, a common enemy in the form of the Nixon administration caused many in the community mental health movement to become even more strident and perhaps defensive in their advocacy of the program. As the efforts to discontinue federal support for the centers increased, so did the claims for them, and the interest in critical self-examination seemed to diminish substantially. In the struggle for survival the virtues of the community mental health centers were magnified, the defects were overlooked, and there was a tendency to perceive the environment in two simple dimensions—the "good guys" who supported them and the "bad guys" who opposed them.

Similarly, in 1976 Frank Ochberg, then director of the CMHC program, wrote: "We are virtually in a state of siege." Everyone at NIMH associated with the centers program had abundant evidence that the program was not working and that abuse of the federal CMHC funds was widespread. But nothing was done.[17]

NIMH was not, in fact, interested in evaluating its premier program. Until 1969, when Congress mandated that evaluation be done and earmarked 1% of the CMHC appropriations for such studies, NIMH had done nothing. In *The Madness Establishment*, Franklin Chu and Sharland Trotter explained why:

> Perhaps the fundamental reason that NIMH did not begin evaluation efforts on its own initiative is that evaluation does not serve the Institute's bureaucratic self-interests. Like any government agency, NIMH is primarily concerned with the maintenance and expansion of its programs. Because the Institute has from the start claimed great success for the center's program, evaluation is a great liability, since any negative findings can be used by opponents of the program as evidence of ineffectiveness and failure. Moreover, as Bertram Brown has confessed, there is an inherent embarrassment in asking Congress for more money to evaluate a program whose success was all but guaranteed in order to obtain congressional approval in the first place.

Between 1969 and 1973, NIMH spent $2.9 million in congressionally mandated dollars ($15.6 million in 2010 dollars) on contracts related to evaluation efforts. In 1974 the General Accounting Office issued a scathing assessment of NIMH's evaluation efforts, citing examples such as the following:

> A contract was awarded for $356,650 to develop a program for evaluating patient care. After almost 3 years of work and expenditures of over $330,000, the contractor did not succeed in developing a manual useful for conducting patient care reviews. NIMH said that the contractor did not set a goal of developing a specific product useful to NIMH but rather was inclined to treat the project as a grant for basic research.[18]

If NIMH was uninterested in seriously evaluating the effectiveness of its CMHCs, it was even more averse to doing anything about the abuse of the federal construction and staffing grants. As early as 1972, an internal NIMH report that I coauthored as an NIMH employee documented egregious abuse at several centers, including an estimate of the funds the centers should be required to repay to the federal government for being out of compliance. The report concluded:

> The main point of this report is not how ineffective these particular Centers are, but that because of the present system of non-accountability *all Centers could be this ineffective.* Those Centers which are doing a better job are doing so because of their leadership, not because NIMH has required them to do so. The lack of accountability of the Centers means that all Centers, no matter what they are doing, continue to receive public money from NIMH. If a Center is not doing what it said it would, NIMH is not really interested in knowing. This is the heart of the problem—the slow, sad steps which lead to a minuet of mutual deception.

In fact, no funds were recovered from the out-of-compliance centers until 1982, when a new employee, Paul Curtis, assumed responsibility for monitoring CMHC funds and initiated legal action against 10 centers. Although he recovered $3.8 million ($8.6 million in 2010 dollars), Curtis said he "met with very determined resistance from the NIMH....I was actively discouraged from seeking recoveries." After Curtis retired in 1986, all efforts to recover federal funds ceased. NIMH viewed its role as giving away federal money, not monitoring how it was being spent.[19]

The CMHC program survived the early 1970s for only two reasons: Nixon's other problems and the Democratic Congress. Nixon's problems began in November 1969 with the largest antiwar rally in American history. This was followed by the My Lai massacre and the sending of U. S. troops into Cambodia; by this time, the Vietnam War had become Nixon's war. In 1972, five Republican operatives were arrested while breaking into the Democratic National Headquarters in the Watergate. In what would become a political soap opera, this was followed by Vice President Spiro Agnew's resignation after being charged with income tax evasion; the firing of Special Prosecutor Archibald Cox; the resignation of Attorney General Elliot Richardson; the indictment of seven White House aides for obstructing the Watergate investigation; and finally, on August 8, 1974, the resignation of Nixon himself. Although Nixon disliked psychiatrists and the community mental health program, his ongoing personal crises precluded giving sustained attention to these issues.

In Congress, both the House and Senate were solidly Democratic throughout the 1960s and 1970s. Nixon was unpopular, so whatever he recommended, Congress often did the opposite. All NIMH had to do to keep the CMHC program going was to remind Congress that the program was Jack Kennedy's legacy and that Nixon opposed it; this combination virtually guaranteed congressional approval. Presidents Nixon and Ford could veto CMHC appropriation bills all they wanted; Congress simply overrode the vetoes.

Even in Congress, however, increasing questions were being raised about the effectiveness of the CMHC program. By the mid-1970s, homeless mentally ill persons were becoming more obvious in the nation's cities, and people began asking why. In 1974 the General Accounting Office published a highly critical report on CMHCs, and in late 1974 and 1975 congressional hearings were held. The outcome reaffirmed the support of Congress for the program but also mandated seven more services to be added to the original five: screening of patients prior to admission to state hospitals; follow-up care for those released from the hospitals; development of transitional living facilities for released patients; and specialized services for children, the elderly, drug abusers, and alcohol abusers. Because the CMHC program was failing abjectly to deliver its original five mandated services, adding seven more was a feat of illogic remarkable even by Washington standards. Saul Feldman described the 1975 CMHC amendments as "a good example of... overpromise and self-defeating behavior":

> Whatever short-term political advantage the Amendments may have served is of little consequence compared with the frustration and disillusionment already becoming visible.... It seems clear that community mental health centers cannot now and will not in the near future be able to do what the legislature requires, that failure is inevitable, and that the cost of this failure may be severe.[20]

## A MERCIFUL DEATH

The election of Jimmy Carter as president in November 1976 provided the CMHC program with a temporary reprieve, even if it was by then on life support. Rosalynn Carter had a special interest in mental health issues, and one of the president's first official acts was to sign an executive order creating a President's Commission on Mental Health. Thirty-five task panels met over the following year and in April 1978 the commission delivered a 2,139-page report with 117 recommendations.

Like the Joint Commission on Mental Illness and Health two decades earlier, the Carter Commission report included something for everyone. Two of the 35 task panels assessed services for people with severe psychiatric disorders: "Community Mental Health Centers Assessment" and "Deinstitutionalization, Rehabilitation, and Long-Term Care." The other 33 task panels covered everything from "Rural Mental Health" and "Migrant and Seasonal Farmworkers" to "Americans of Euro-Ethnic Origin" and "Arts in Therapy and Environment." The CMHC panel acknowledged that the program had failed in many ways but attributed the failure to the fact that "previous administrations had sought to end the program" and to "a failure of Federal oversight, technical assistance, evaluation and leadership." Incredibly, the task panel even concluded that "to criticize the centers themselves for many (but not all) of their failings is to 'blame the victim!'"[21]

Despite its criticism of past federal leadership, the Carter Commission's recommendations focused mostly on creating new federal mental health programs and making federal support permanent. The commission proposed the funding of additional CMHCs and even included a new federal grant program to prevent mental illness by reducing "societal stresses produced by racism, poverty, sexism, ageism and urban blight." Most remarkable, however, was its recommendation that "states receiving Federal funds for the care of the chronically mentally disabled must, in conjunction with local authorities, designate an agency in each geographic area to assume responsibility for ensuring that every chronically mentally disabled person's needs are adequately met." This, of course, was what the CMHC program should have been doing all along. It was as if the CMHCs did not even exist.[22]

Even as the Carter Commission was deliberating, evidence continued to accumulate that the CMHC program was failing to provide care for the masses of patients being discharged from state hospitals. Increasingly, psychiatric leaders publicly repudiated the program. One called it a "sham":

> Many centers pay little attention to former state hospital patients and hard-to-treat and seriously disturbed patients.... Some critics have suggested...that the recipients of services would do better if they were given the money that the services cost instead of the services.

Another critic castigated the CMHC program "for embodying the arrogance of social engineering by euphoric experts...[and] for being primarily an ambitious power play by federal mental health bureaucrats." The National Institute of Mental Health, realizing that its prize program was in trouble, invoked a classic governmental ploy. Rather than trying to correct the existing program, it instead started a new program in 1977. It was called the Community Support Program (CSP) and initially made available $3.5 million ($12.6 million in 2010 dollars) in grants to states to coordinate services "for one particularly vulnerable population—adult psychiatric patients whose disabilities are severe and persistent." The tasks designated under the CSP grants were precisely those things the CMHCs should have been doing.[23]

For the leadership of NIMH, however, it was too little, too late. In December 1977, Brown was fired by DHEW Secretary Joseph Califano. The firing was the result of accumulated minor departmental grievances combined with Brown's having alienated leaders of American psychiatry, some of whom wanted his job. Brown had, ironically, survived 8 years under Presidents Nixon and Ford, who disliked mental health, but he could not survive under President Carter, who was a strong mental health advocate. With the departure of Brown, the last of the architects of the CMHC program was gone, bringing to an end more than 30 years of an attempted federal solution to the nation's mental illness problems.

## ADDITIONAL LEGAL ACTIONS AND FISCAL INCENTIVES

During the 1970s, as the CMHC program spiraled slowly toward its inevitable demise, legal actions and fiscal incentives further complicated the nation's mental illness treatment system. Both would play important roles in determining the fate of the patients who were being released from the state mental hospitals.

Legally, additional court cases reinforced earlier decisions promoting the discharge of patients from state hospitals and making it increasingly difficult to get patients admitted to the hospitals. In the 1971 *Wyatt v. Stickney* ruling in Alabama, the court ruled that involuntarily hospitalized mental patients had a legal right to adequate treatment. The court also established standards for such treatment, including a minimum staff-to-patient ratio. The decision was hailed by many as an important step toward better care for the seriously mentally ill; in fact, it simply led to the discharge of many more patients, because a better staff-patient ratio could be achieved less expensively by discharging patients than by hiring more staff. A further impetus to deinstitutionalization came in 1975 from the *O'Connor v. Donaldson* case in Florida in which a court awarded $20,000 in compensatory damages to a patient who had been kept in a hospital for nearly 15 years without proper treatment. Making a state monetarily liable for inadequate hospital care was a strong incentive to discharge more patients. The most important court decision that made it much more difficult to get patients admitted to mental hospitals was the 1972 *Lessard v. Schmidt* decision in Wisconsin. The judge ruled that being a danger to self or others was the only justification for involuntary hospitalization.

Most of these court cases were orchestrated by the American Civil Liberties Union (ACLU). Bruce J. Ennis, a leading ACLU lawyer and subsequent chair of the American Bar Association's Commission on the Mentally Disabled, wrote at the time that "the goal [of legal efforts] should be nothing less than the abolition of involuntary hospitalization." Lawyers such as Ennis viewed any involuntary psychiatric hospitalization as inherently bad. The popularity of Kesey's 1961 book *One Flew over the Cuckoo's Nest* had been reinforced by the 1967 movie *King of Hearts*, which featured psychiatric inmates in France released from their asylum by departing German soldiers at the end of World War II. The inmates were depicted as living happily ever after and being more sane than the departing soldiers. The movie ran for 5 consecutive years in Cambridge, Massachusetts, a bastion of civil liberties support.[24]

The major fiscal change related to mentally ill individuals during the 1970s was the federalization of the Supplemental Security Income (SSI) program for the aged, blind, and disabled. For many years, there had been state-operated welfare and disability programs, with federal supplements, in which states determined who would be eligible and what state payments would be. This resulted in eligibility standards and payment levels that varied considerably among states. In 1972 President Nixon decided to reform and standardize the welfare and disability system. SSI was created, which established standard federal eligibility requirements and a standard federal payment that states could supplement if they wished. SSI essentially reversed the historic state and federal roles for welfare. SSI was not targeted for mentally ill individuals and, in fact, specifically sought to exclude most of them by making ineligible any resident of a state mental hospital or other public institution. Nor is there evidence that any consultations took place between the Social Security Administration and the NIMH regarding what effect the SSI program might have on mentally ill individuals.

Following the implementation of the SSI program in January 1974, it soon became clear that SSI would be an enormous fiscal incentive for states to empty their state hospitals. In New York, for example, the annual state cost for a person in a state mental hospital was $13,835. If the person was discharged to live in a group home or boarding house, according to the calculations of social work expert Stephen Rose, then the maximum state costs, including all services, would be $4,600, because federal SSI would be paying the person's living costs. Thus, for every person discharged from the hospital, the state saved more than $9,000 per year and also decreased state costs for running the hospitals. It would not take the states long to figure out the rules of the game.[25]

## A QUIET DEATH AND BURIAL

In November 1980, Republican Ronald Reagan overwhelmingly defeated Jimmy Carter, who received less than 42% of the popular vote, for president. Republicans took control of the Senate (53 to 46), the first time they had dominated either chamber since 1954. Although the House remained under Democratic control (243 to 192), their margin was actually much slimmer, because many southern "boll weevil" Democrats voted with the Republicans.

One month prior to the election, President Carter had signed the Mental Health Systems Act, which had proposed to continue the federal community mental health centers program, although with some additional state involvement. Consistent with the report of the Carter Commission, the act also included a provision for federal grants "for projects for the prevention of mental illness and the promotion of positive mental health," an indication of how little learning had taken place among the Carter Commission members and professionals at NIMH. With President Reagan and the

Republicans taking over, the Mental Health Systems Act was discarded before the ink had dried and the CMHC funds were simply block granted to the states. The CMHC program had not only died but been buried as well. An autopsy could have listed the cause of death as naiveté complicated by grandiosity.[26]

President Reagan never understood mental illness. Like Nixon, he was a product of the Southern California culture that associated psychiatry with Communism. Two months after taking office, Reagan was shot by John Hinckley, a young man with untreated schizophrenia. Two years later, Reagan called Dr. Roger Peele, then director of St. Elizabeths Hospital, where Hinckley was being treated, and tried to arrange to meet with Hinckley, so that Reagan could forgive him. Peele tactfully told the president that this was not a good idea. Reagan was also exposed to the consequences of untreated mental illness through the two sons of Roy Miller, his personal tax advisor. Both sons developed schizophrenia; one committed suicide in 1981, and the other killed his mother in 1983. Despite such personal exposure, Reagan never exhibited any interest in the need for research or better treatment for serious mental illness. [27]

Thus, by 1981, the CMHC movement had come and gone. In its brief existence, it had profoundly changed the treatment of mentally ill persons in the United States, although not in the direction Felix had envisioned. Felix had written that "mental hygiene must be concerned with more than the psychoses and with more than hospitalized mental illness." He had created a program that, in fact, had been concerned with almost everything except psychoses and hospitalized mental illness.[28]

In 1963, when the Community Mental Health Centers Act had been signed, there had been a coherent, if flawed, mental illness treatment system, which had been run by the states for over a century. It consisted of state hospitals that were in poor shape but slowly improving, thanks to the availability of new medications. Deinstitutionalization was underway, with 10% of the 1955 peak patient census having already been placed in the community. Most states were opening state-funded outpatient treatment clinics, and according to a 1959 report, 20% of the clinic patients were diagnosed with "psychotic disorders." States controlled the eligibility and payments for the state disability programs, more generous in some states, less generous in others. Most important, there was an established level of authority and accountability: the state legislature, the state department of mental health, and the governor were ultimately responsible even in states that passed along some program responsibility to the counties.[29]

Eighteen years later, when the CMHC program was effectively buried, the landscape for the treatment of mental illness had changed profoundly. States had been told that state hospitals would no longer be needed, because they would be replaced by the federally funded community mental health centers. According to Brian O'Connell, executive director of the National Mental Health Association, "the state hospitals were downsized or closed and the states in many cases just washed their hands of the treatment of mental illness." In setting up the CMHC program, federal officials had bypassed the state mental health authorities and sent the federal funds directly to local organizations. As Robert Rich noted in 1985: "There was no precedent for this new model of intergovernmental relations: bypassing the states and working directly with the localities. The federal government was going into the business of competing with [an] already established public sector program."[30]

Whereas the original state treatment programs had been funded almost exclusively with state and local funds, the emerging treatment system included funding by federal Medicaid, Medicare, SSI, SSDI, block grants, food stamps, employment programs, housing, etc. In 1981, Murray Levine noted:

> At present, 11 major federal departments and agencies are responsible for 135 programs that could provide service to the mentally disabled. The agencies control funds for direct clinical care, education, rehabilitation, employment, housing, and income support. There are federal programs to cover just about any need a mentally disabled individual might have. However, the agencies do not coordinate, do not cooperate, and tend to pursue their own priorities for program development.

State governors watched this proliferation of uncoordinated federal programs with increasing concern. At their annual meeting in 1977, they voted to express concern about the "lack of continuity of care caused by fragmented federal programs and compounded by complex and irrational federal regulations and guidelines."[31]

The federal support of mental health programs was, of course, attractive to fiscally conservative state officials. The more patients who were discharged and the more state hospital beds that were shut down, the more state money was saved and the happier such conservative officials were. Simultaneously, civil rights lawyers were instituting lawsuits to further encourage states to empty the hospitals. The more patients who were discharged and the more state hospital beds shut down, the more state money was saved and the happier the civil rights lawyers were as well. This malformed marriage of fiscally conservative state officials and politically liberal civil rights lawyers produced a strong advocacy coalition guaranteeing that the existing deinstitutionalization policies would be continued into the future.

Of major concern, however, was that by 1981, all authority and responsibility for the mental illness treatment system had essentially disappeared. Authority that had been previously vested in the state legislatures, departments of mental health, and governors had become so diffused that it seemed to evaporate altogether. As noted in many reports, the mental illness treatment system had been essentially beheaded.

*1974*: No state or local agency has sole responsibility for discharged patients; the agency, like the patient, is bewildered.

*1977*: Responsibility for the mentally disabled in communities was generally fragmented and unclear....Responsibility for their care and support frequently becomes diffused among several agencies and levels of government....The roles and responsibilities of these agencies and specific actions to be taken by them for deinstitutionalization, however, have frequently not been clearly defined, understood, or accepted.

*1978*: Perhaps the most critical factor contributing to inadequacies in community-based care is fragmentation and confusion of responsibility among the many Federal, State, and local agencies whose programs have an impact on services to the mentally disabled in the community....No one agency at any level has been clearly charged with responsibility for comprehensive assessments of mental health and community support needs of the mentally disabled....What has been particularly lacking, however, is clarity about who should provide the necessary leadership at Federal, State, or local levels to move things forward. The need for such leadership has been a recurring theme.

*1978*: Today no agency of government—local, state, or federal—is taking comprehensive responsibility for providing psychiatric and social services for chronically mentally ill patients.

This lack of coordination was evident at the federal as well as the state level, because "no single agency has power or authority to coordinate policies and programs cutting across agency and cabinet lines." Even for the CMHCs, it had been unclear whether authority over them ultimately resided at the NIMH level or within the DHEW regional offices. When there is no authority, there is also no responsibility, and no one can be blamed. [32]

It should be added that the failure of the federal CMHC program was just one of many failures of Great Society programs initiated by the Johnson administration. As Allen Matusow noted in *The Unraveling of America*, "the War on Poverty was destined to be one of the great failures of twentieth-century liberalism." Other programs, such as the Mobilization for Youth, produced "little real change" in job training, while the Community Action Program was a fiasco. In the latter, for example, $20 million that went into it in New York City "disappeared without a trace." This does not excuse the failure of CMHCs or their misuse of federal funds but merely illustrates that the poorly conceived CMHC program had plenty of federal company.[33]

\* \* \*

Thus, in 1981, as the last remnants of the federal mental health centers program were being block-granted to the states, its failure was complete. The life of the program was reflected by Dr. Horace G. Whittington, director of psychiatry for the Denver Department of Health and Hospitals. Whittington had been one of the earliest enthusiasts for CMHCs and in 1969, in congressional testimony, had described them as "the most effective mental health service delivery system that has existed in the United States." A decade later, bitterly disillusioned, Whittington described the CMHCs as follows:

> I was already beginning to feel very much like a parent must feel who has a badly handicapped child. Should I smother it in its sleep, or should I help the poor little deformed bastard grow up to do the best it can in life? The deformed creature that has developed from the original community mental health center movement does not arouse much enthusiasm in any of us, I am sure, who had some more grandiose visions.

Dr. Donald Langsley, who had been the director of the highly regarded Sacramento County CMHC, similarly reflected: "Those of us who were once so enthusiastic now weep a little as we look backwards at what has happened to the promising child of the 1960s and early 1970s."[34]

# 6

## THE PERFECT STORM: 1981–1999

In 1981, as the last vestige of the federal community mental health centers (CMHCs) program was being block-granted to the states, ominous clouds hung over the future. A total of 432,633 beds in state psychiatric hospitals had been closed since 1955, entire hospitals having closed their doors. In the intervening years, the nation's population had increased by 39%, from 165 to 230 million. Thus, there was an additional cohort of seriously mentally ill individuals, many of whom had been hospitalized briefly or not at all, living in the community. The true number of effectively deinstitutionalized individuals at that time was thus approximately 650,000; 30 years earlier they would have been hospitalized, but in 1981 they were living in the community and dependent on public mental health services for their psychiatric care.

Given the effectiveness of medications that had become available to treat serious psychiatric disorders starting in the 1950s, discharging hundreds of thousands of mentally ill individuals from state mental hospitals was both logical and humane. Thus, deinstitutionalization per se was not the mistake. The mistake, rather, was our failure to provide continuing treatment and rehabilitation for these individuals once they left the hospitals.

In 1981 a coordinated plan for aftercare did not exist. States had essentially been told that they were no longer responsible for mentally ill individuals once they had left the state hospital, a suggestion to which most states had readily acquiesced. Most federal CMHCs, which had been supposed to assume that responsibility, had not done so. What the federal government *had* provided, however, was federal dollars under Medicaid, Medicare, SSI, and SSDI for seriously mentally ill individuals living in the community; this provided enormous incentives for states to continue emptying the state hospitals, thereby shifting most of the costs for mentally ill individuals from states to the federal government. Available psychiatric medications made it possible to get patients well enough for discharge, but for most there were few plans for aftercare, without which many quickly relapsed. Civil rights lawyers further accelerated the outpouring of patients and then defended the patients' rights to refuse further treatment once in the community. For the most massive movement of medical care in twentieth-century America, there was no master plan, no coordination, no corrective mechanism, no authority, no one in charge. By aborting the development of the states' own programs for aftercare, the federal government effectively decapitated the existing public mental health system, leaving a bureaucratic creature with neither eyes nor a brain.

## THE GOOD NEWS AND THE "CONSUMER" MOVEMENT

Despite the lack of a coordinated aftercare system, some mentally ill individuals did reasonably well in the earlier years of deinstitutionalization. Such individuals tended to be those with less severe symptoms, an awareness of their own illness and need for medication, and an existing family support system. They were also more likely to have become sick at an older age, after they had completed their education and thus had acquired some vocational and interpersonal skills. Such individuals also did better if they were geographically fortunate enough to live near one of the few good rehabilitation programs. An example of such a program was the Eden Express, a restaurant in Hayward, California, run by Barbara Lawson, a restaurant owner who had a mentally disabled daughter. Using state rehabilitation funds, she created a 15-week training program for mentally disabled individuals to teach them food preparation, catering, cooking, waiting on tables, hosting, and cashiering. Between 1980 and 1990, Ms. Lawson trained 700 individuals, 80% of whom completed the training and 94% of whom then obtained employment.[1]

It was also during the 1980s and 1990s that the organization of mentally ill "consumers" took place. The use of the term "consumer" indicated that such mentally ill individuals no longer viewed themselves as passive recipients of mental health services but, rather, wished to play an active role in determining and selecting such services. They organized self-help groups under such names as Depressive and Manic-Depressive Association (DMDA), Recovery Inc., GROW, Schizophrenics Anonymous, On Our Own, and Psychosis Free. Such groups provided support, education, and a sense of hope as mentally ill individuals sought to put their lives together while living in the community.

It was at the time that some mentally ill individuals also began to be employed as ancillary mental health workers. One of the first programs began in Denver in 1986, when mentally ill individuals were enrolled in a 6-month training program to become consumer case management aides in mental health centers. Within 5 years, similar programs had been started in Texas, Massachusetts, and Washington, with such individuals being employed in a variety of roles. In San Mateo County in California, for example, consumer "peer counselors" were employed to assist other mentally ill individuals who were being moved from psychiatric hospitals to community living facilities and also to do AIDS education for mentally ill individuals. The employment of stable mentally ill individuals to help deliver mental health services has become much more widespread in recent years, as will be described in the following chapter.

## TRANSINSTITUTIONALIZATION

The number of seriously mentally ill individuals who did reasonably well in the community during the 1980s and 1990s was a minority. The majority of lives were little different than they had had while hospitalized, and a significant number were considerably worse off. Many of these individuals had more severe psychiatric symptoms, often exacerbated by substance abuse problems, and had little or no family support. Many had also become sick at a younger age and thus had limited vocational and interpersonal skills. Most important, many of them had no awareness of their own illness or need to take medication. This condition, called anosognosia by neurologists, occurs when specific areas of the brain are damaged, as also occurs in Alzheimer's disease and some individuals with strokes. Individuals with serious mental illnesses who are unaware of their own illness usually do not take medication voluntarily and thus have a high relapse rate when living in the community.

One group of mentally ill patients who were no better off in the 1980s than they had been in the 1960s were elderly mentally ill individuals who were transferred directly from state mental hospitals to nursing homes. Medicare and Medicaid had come into existence in 1965, just as the exodus of patients from state hospitals was increasing. Nursing homes had traditionally been used for demented and physically disabled elderly patients who required 24-hour care; such homes were called skilled nursing facilities (SNFs). In 1967 Congress, led by Senator Frank Moss, with strong support from Senator Ted Kennedy, passed amendments to the Social Security Act, creating a second type of nursing home called an Intermediate care facility (ICF). Intermediate care facilities were intended for elderly disabled individuals who did not need full-time care yet were not capable of living on their own.

Intermediate care facilities had not been created for individuals with psychiatric disorders but were immediately appropriated for them. The attraction for states was irresistible; an elderly patient in a state hospital in 1977 cost the state approximately $1,000 per month, but if the patient was transferred to an ICF, the state paid only approximately $120 per month in Medicaid matching funds. Without intention or planning, the federal government rapidly became the primary funding source for elderly mental patients. By 1968 a New York nursing home survey found that "about 36 per cent" of patients were seriously mentally ill. A federal survey reported that "between 1969 and 1974 there was a 44% decline in the state hospital population [of elderly patients] and a 48% increase in the number of nursing home residents with mental disorders." Some states were very aggressive in transferring their elderly mentally ill patients to nursing homes during this period; California (86%), Massachusetts (87%), and Wisconsin (98%) were the leaders. Thus, in Wisconsin in 1969 there were 4,616 patients aged 65 years and older in the state hospitals, and in 1974 only 96 of them remained.[2]

The massive transfer of elderly mentally ill individuals from state hospitals to nursing homes was a fiscal win for the states and a fiscal win for the owners of the nursing homes. The proliferation of Medicaid-funded ICFs was a major impetus to the subsequent incorporation of for-profit nursing home chains, followed by intermittent exposés of Medicaid fraud, kickbacks from pharmacies, and allegations of gross profiteering. Everyone appeared to win except the patients themselves, who, according to a 1977 report, had "fewer opportunities for socialization and recreation, less sophisticated use of medication, [and] a possible increase in mortality." The last was confirmed by a California study that reported a nine-fold increase in deaths among patients who had been transferred from a state hospital to a nursing home, compared to a matched group of patients who remained at the state hospital. Many of the nursing home patients were, in fact, worse off than they had been in the state hospitals. They had not been deinstitutionalized, merely transinstitutionalized.[3]

## A CANARY IN THE COAL MINE

California has traditionally been on the cutting edge of American cultural developments, with Anaheim and Modesto experiencing changes before Atlanta and Moline. This was also true in the exodus of patients from state psychiatric hospitals. Beginning in the late 1950s, California became the national leader in aggressively moving patients from state hospitals to nursing homes and board-and-care homes, known in other states by names such as group homes, boarding homes, adult care homes, family care homes, assisted living facilities, community residential facilities, adult foster homes, transitional living facilities, and residential care facilities. Hospital wards closed as the patients left. By the time Ronald Reagan assumed the governorship in 1967, California had already deinstitutionalized more than half of its state hospital patients. That same year, California passed the landmark Lanterman-Petris-Short (LPS) Act, which virtually abolished involuntary hospitalization except in extreme cases. Thus, by the early 1970s California had moved most mentally ill patients out of its state hospitals and, by passing LPS, had made it very difficult to get them back into a hospital if they relapsed and needed additional care. California thus became a canary in the coal mine of deinstitutionalization.

The results were quickly apparent. As early as 1969, a study of California board-and-care homes described them as follows:

These facilities are in most respects like small long-term state hospital wards isolated from the community. One is overcome by the depressing atmosphere.... They maximize the state-hospital-like atmosphere.... The operator is being paid by the head, rather than being rewarded for rehabilitation efforts for her "guests."

The study was done by Richard Lamb, a young psychiatrist working for San Mateo County; in the intervening years, he has continued to be the leading American psychiatrist pointing out the failures of deinstitutionalization.[4]

By 1975 board-and-care homes had become big business in California. In Los Angeles alone, there were "approximately 11,000 ex-state-hospital patients living in board-and-care facilities." Many of these homes were owned by for-profit chains, such as Beverly Enterprises, which owned 38 homes. Many homes were regarded by their owners "solely as a business, squeezing excessive profits out of it at the expense of residents." Five members of Beverly Enterprises' board of directors had ties to Governor Reagan; the chairman was vice chairman of a Reagan fundraising dinner, and "four others were either politically active in one or both of the Reagan [gubernatorial] campaigns and/or contributed large or undisclosed sums of money to the campaign." Financial ties between the governor, who was emptying state hospitals, and business persons who were profiting from the process would also soon become apparent in other states.[5]

Many of the board-and-care homes in California, as elsewhere, were clustered in city areas that were rundown and thus had low rents. In San Jose, for example, approximately 1,800 patients discharged from nearby Agnews State Hospital were placed in homes clustered near the campus of San Jose State University. As early as 1971 the local newspaper decried this "mass invasion of mental patients." Some patients left their board-and-care homes because of the poor living conditions, whereas others were evicted when the symptoms of their illness recurred because they were not receiving medication, but both scenarios resulted in homelessness. By 1973 the San Jose area was described as having "discharged patients...living in skid row...wandering aimlessly in the streets...a ghetto for the mentally ill and mentally retarded."[6]

Similar communities were becoming visible in other California cities as well as in New York. In Long Beach on Long Island, old motels and hotels were filled with patients discharged from nearly Creedmore and Pilgrim State Hospitals. By 1973, community residents were complaining that their town was becoming a psychiatric ghetto; at the local Catholic church, patients were said to "have urinated on the floor during Mass and eaten the altar flowers." The Long Beach City Council therefore passed an ordinance requiring patients to take their prescribed medication as a condition for living there. Predictably, the New York Civil Liberties Union immediately challenged the ordinance as being unconstitutional, and it was so ruled. By this time, there were about 5,000 board-and-care homes in New York City, some with as many as 285 beds and with up to 85% of their residents having been discharged from the state hospitals. As one New York psychiatrist summarized the situation: "The chronic mentally ill patient has had his locus of living and care transferred from a single lousy institution to multiple wretched ones."[7]

California was the first state to witness not only an increase in homelessness associated with deinstitutionalization but also an increase in incarceration and episodes of violence. In 1972 Marc Abramson, another young psychiatrist working for San Mateo County, published a landmark paper entitled "The Criminalization of Mentally Disordered Behavior." Abramson claimed that because the new LPS statute made it difficult to get patients admitted to a psychiatric hospital, police "regard arrest and booking into jail as a more reliable way of securing involuntary detention of mentally disordered persons." Abramson quoted a California prison psychiatrist who claimed to be "literally drowning in patients.... Many more men are being sent to prison who have serious mental problems." Abramson's paper was the first clear description of the increase of mentally ill persons in jails and prisons, an increase that would grow markedly in subsequent years.[8]

By the mid-1970s, studies in some states suggested that about 5% of jail inmates were seriously mentally ill. A study of five California county jails reported that 6.7% of the inmates were psychotic. A study of the Denver County Jail reported that 5% of prisoners had a "functional psychosis." Such figures contrasted with studies from the 1930s that had reported less than 2% of jail inmates as being seriously mentally ill. In 1973 the jail in Santa Clara County, which included San Jose, "created a special ward...to house just the individuals who have such a mental condition"; this was apparently the first county jail to create a special mental illness unit.[9]

Given the increasing number of seriously mentally ill individuals living in the community in California by the mid-1970s, it is not surprising to find that they were impacting the tasks of police officers. A study of 301 patients discharged from Napa State Hospital between 1972 and 1975 found that 41% of them had been arrested. According to the study, "patients who entered the hospital without a criminal record were subsequently arrested about three times as often as the average citizen." Significantly, the majority of these patients had received no aftercare following their hospital discharge. By this time, police in other states were also beginning to feel the burden of the discharged, but often untreated, mentally ill individuals. In suburban Philadelphia, for example, "mental-illness-related incidents increased 227.6% from 1975 to 1979, whereas felonies increased only 5.6%."[10]

Of all the omens of deinstitutionalization's failure on exhibit in 1970s California, the most frightening were homicides and other episodes of violence committed by mentally ill individuals who were not being treated.

1970: John Frazier, responding to the voice of God, killed a prominent surgeon and his wife, two young sons, and secretary. Frazier's mother and wife had sought unsuccessfully to have him hospitalized.

1972: Herbert Mullin, responding to auditory hallucinations, killed 13 people over 3 months. He had been hospitalized three times but released without further treatment.

1973: Charles Soper killed his wife, three children, and himself 2 weeks after having been discharged from a state hospital.

1973: Edmund Kemper killed his mother and her friend and was charged with killing six others. Eight years earlier, he had killed his grandparents because "he tired of their company," but at age 21 years had been released from the state hospital without further treatment.

1977: Edward Allaway, believing that people were trying to hurt him, killed seven people at Cal State Fullerton. Five years earlier, he had been hospitalized for paranoid schizophrenia but released without further treatment.

Such homicides were widely publicized. Many people perceived the tragedies as being linked to California's efforts to shut its state hospitals and to the new LPS law, which made involuntary treatment virtually impossible. The foreman of the jury that convicted Herbert Mullin of the murders for which he was charged reflected the sentiments of many when he publicly stated:

> I hold the state executive and state legislative offices as responsible for these ten lives as I do the defendant himself—none of this need ever have happened. . . . In recent years, mental hospitals all over this state have been closed down in an economy move by the Reagan administration. Where do you think these . . . patients went after their release? . . . The closing of our mental hospitals is, in my opinion, insanity itself.[11]

In response to queries about the homicides, the California Department of Mental Health had its deputy director, Dr. Andrew Robertson, testify before a state legislative inquiry in 1973. His testimony must rank among the all-time least successful attempts by a public official to reassure the public:

> It [LPS] has exposed us as a society to some dangerous people; no need to argue about that. People whom we have released have gone out and killed other people, maimed other people, destroyed property; they have done many things of an evil nature without their ability to stop and many of them have immediately thereafter killed themselves. That sounds bad, but let's qualify it. . . . the odds are still in society's favor, even if it doesn't make patients innocent or the guy who is hurt or killed feel any better.[12]

## 1980S: THE PROBLEMS BECOME NATIONAL

Until the 1980s, most people in the United States were unaware that the deinstitution-alization of patients from state mental hospitals was going terribly wrong. Some were aware that homicides and other untoward things were happening in California, but such things were to be expected, because it was, after all, California. President Carter's Commission on Mental Health issued its 1978 report and recommended doing more of the same things—more CMHCs, more prevention of mental illness, and more federal spending. The report gave no indication of a pending crisis. The majority of patients who had been discharged from state hospitals in the 1960s and 1970s had gone to their own homes, nursing homes, or board-and-care homes; they were, therefore, out of sight and out of mind.

In the 1980s, this all changed. Deinstitutionalization became, for the first time, a topic of national concern. The beginning of the discussion was heralded by a 1981 editorial in the *New York Times* that labeled deinstitutionalization "a cruel embarrass-ment, a reform gone terribly wrong." Three years later, the paper added: "The policy that led to the release of most of the nation's mentally ill patients from the hospital to the community is now widely regarded as a major failure." During the following decade, there were increasing concerns publicly expressed about mentally ill indi-viduals in nursing homes, board-and-care homes, and jails and prisons. There were also periodic headlines announcing additional high-profile homicides committed by individuals who were clearly psychotic. But the one issue that took center stage in the 1980s, and directed public attention to deinstitutionalization, was the problem of mentally ill homeless persons.[13]

During the 1980s, an additional 40,000 beds in state mental hospitals were shut down. The patients being sent to community facilities were no longer those who were moderately well-functioning or elderly; rather, they included the more difficult, chronic patients from the hospitals' back wards. These patients were often younger than patients previously discharged, less likely to respond to medication, and less likely to be aware of their need for medication. In 1988 the National Institute of Mental Health (NIMH) issued estimates of where patients with chronic mental illness were living. Approximately 120,000 were said to be still hospitalized; 381,000 were in nurs-ing homes; between 175,000 and 300,000 were living in board-and-care homes; and between 125,000 and 300,000 were thought to be homeless. These broad estimates for those living in board-and-care homes and on the streets suggested that neither NIMH nor anyone else really knew how many there were.[14]

Abuse of mentally ill persons in nursing homes had originally come to public atten-tion during 1974 hearings of the Senate Committee on Aging. Those hearings had described nursing homes actually bidding on patients in attempts to get those who were most easily managed; bounties of $100 paid by nursing homes to hospital psychiatrists for every patient sent to them; and exorbitant profits for the nursing homes. As a consequence of such hearings and a 1986 study of nursing homes by the Institute of Medicine, Congress passed legislation in 1987 requiring all Medicaid-funded nursing homes to screen new admissions to keep out patients who did not qualify for admission because they did not require skilled nursing care. Follow-up studies indicated that the screening mandate had little effect on admission policies or abuses.[15]

Abuse of mentally ill persons in board-and-care homes also periodically surfaced at this time:

1982: "Nine ragged, emaciated adults" were found in an unlicensed home for mentally ill individuals in Jackson, Mississippi. They were living in a 10-by-10 foot building with "no toilet or running water, only a plastic bucket to collect body wastes. A hose and faucet outside the building were used for washing. There were two mattresses on the concrete floor and a single cot in the room." There were also "two vicious dogs chained outside the room."

1984: Seven "former patients" died in a fire in a "rooming house" in Worcester, Massachusetts. "The report released this week said officials of Worcester State Hospital who referred the former patients to the rooming house had been warned by community health workers that the privately owned house was not safe."

Sociologist Andrew Scull in 1981 summarized the economics of the board-and-care industry: "The logic of the marketplace suffices to ensure that the operators have every incentive to warehouse their charges as cheaply as possible, since the volume of profit is inversely proportional to the amount expended on the inmates." In addition, because many board-and-care homes were in crime-ridden neighborhoods, mentally ill individuals living in them were often victimized when they went outside. A 1984 study of 278 patients living in board-and-care homes in Los Angeles reported that one-third "reported being robbed and/or assaulted during the preceding year."[16]

The problems of mentally ill individuals in nursing homes and board-and-care homes rarely elicited media attention in the 1980s. By contrast, the problem of homeless persons, including the mentally ill homeless, became a major story. In Washington, Mitch Snyder and the National Coalition for the Homeless burst onto the national scene by staging hunger strikes and sleep-ins on sidewalk grates. Their message was that homeless persons are just like you and me and all they need is a house and a job. Snyder challenged President Reagan, accusing him of being the main cause of homelessness, and the media extensively covered the controversy. By the time Snyder committed suicide in 1990, homelessness had become a major topic of national discussion.

Despite the claims of homeless advocates, media attention directed to homeless persons made it increasingly clear that many of them were, in fact, seriously mentally ill. In 1981, *Life* magazine ran a story titled "Emptying the Madhouse: The Mentally Ill Have Become Our Cities' Lost Souls." In 1982, Rebecca Smith froze to death in a cardboard box on the streets of New York; the media focused on her death because it was said that she had been valedictorian of her college class before becoming mentally ill. In 1983, the media covered the story of Lionel Aldridge, the former all-pro linebacker for the Green Bay Packers; after developing schizophrenia, he had been homeless for several years on the streets of Milwaukee. In 1984, a study from Boston reported that 38% of homeless persons in Boston were seriously mentally ill. The report was titled "Is Homelessness a Mental Health Problem?" and confirmed what people were increasingly beginning to suspect—that many homeless persons had previously been patients in the state mental hospitals.[17]

By the mid-1980s, a consensus had emerged that the total number of homeless persons was increasing. The possible reasons for this increase became a political football, but the failure of the mental health system was one option widely discussed. A 1985 report from Los Angeles estimated that 30% to 50% of homeless persons were seriously mentally ill and were being seen in "ever increasing numbers." The study concluded that this was "in part the product of the deinstitutionalization movement....The 'Streets' have become 'The Asylums' of the 80s."[18]

The appearance of Joyce Brown on the streets of New York in 1986 added a new dimension to the national dialogue. Prior to taking up residence on a steam grate at the corner of East 65th Street and Second Avenue, Brown had worked for 10 years as a secretary. She had then become mentally ill, was hospitalized, and discharged. While living on the street, Brown was observed urinating on the sidewalk, defecating in the gutter, tearing up money given to her by passersby, and running into traffic. New York mayor Ed Koch ordered her to be involuntarily hospitalized, well aware that the Civil Liberties Union's lawyers would contest the case. Koch's statement reflected the sentiments of many: "If the crazies want to sue me, they have every right to sue, and by crazies I'm...talking about those who say, 'No, you have no right to intervene to help.'" The civil liberty lawyers prevailed, and the civil right to be both psychotic and homeless thus added another legal wrinkle to the ongoing homeless debate.[19]

By the end of the 1980s, the origins of the increasing number of mentally ill homeless persons had become abundantly clear. A study of 187 patients discharged from Metropolitan State Hospital in Massachusetts reported that 27% had become homeless. A study of 132 patients discharged from Columbus State Hospital in Ohio reported that 36% had become homeless. In 1989, when a San Francisco television station wished to advertise its series on homelessness, it put up posters around the city saying, "You are now walking though America's newest mental institution." Psychiatrist Richard Lamb

added: "Probably nothing more graphically illustrates the problems of deinstitutionalization than the shameful and incredible phenomenon of the homeless mentally ill."[20]

* * *

At the same time that mentally ill homeless persons were becoming an object of national
concern during the 1980s, the number of mentally ill persons in jails and prisons was
also increasing. A 1989 review of available studies concluded that "the prevalence
rates for major psychiatric disorders... [in jails and prisons] have increased slowly and
gradually in the last 20 years and will probably continue to increase." Various studies
reported rates ranging from 6% (Virginia) and 8% (New York) to 10% (Oklahoma
and California) and 11% (Michigan and Pennsylvania). By 1990, a national survey
concluded:

> Given all the data, it seems reasonable to conclude that approximately 10 per-
> cent of inmates in prisons and jails, or approximately 100,000 individuals, suffer
> from schizophrenia or manic-depressive psychosis [bipolar disorder].

This 10% estimate contrasted with the 5% prevalence rate that had been widely cited
a decade earlier.[21]

Amid the various studies, disturbing trends were evident. Among 132 patients discharged from Columbus State Hospital in Ohio, 17% were arrested within 6 months. In
California, seriously mentally ill individuals with a history of past violence, including
armed robbery and murder, were being discharged from mental hospitals without any
planned aftercare. In Colorado in 1984, George Wooton, diagnosed with schizophrenia, was booked into the Denver County Jail for the hundredth time; he would be the
first prominent member of a group that would become widely known as "frequent
flyers." In several states the bizarre behavior of mentally ill inmates was also becoming
problematic for jail personnel; in Montana a man "tried to drown himself in the jail
toilet," and in California inmates tried to escape "by smearing themselves with their
own feces and flushing themselves down the toilet." To make matters worse, civil liberties lawyers frequently defended the rights of mentally ill prisoners to refuse medication and remain psychotic. At a 1985 commitment hearing in Wisconsin, for example,
a public defender argued that his jailed mentally ill client, who had been observed
eating his feces, "was in no imminent danger of physical injury or dying" and should
therefore be released; the judge agreed.[22]

As more and more mentally ill individuals entered the criminal justice system
in the 1980s, local police and sheriffs' departments were increasingly affected. In
New York City, calls associated with "emotionally disturbed persons," referred to as
"EDPs," increased from 20,843 in 1980 to 46,845 in 1988, and "experts say similar

increases have occurred in other large cities." Many such calls required major deployments of police resources. The rescue of a mentally ill man from the top of a tower on Staten Island, for example, "required at least 20 police officers and supervisors, half a dozen emergency vehicles, several highway units and a helicopter." In an attempt to deal with these psychiatric emergencies, the police department in Memphis, Tennessee, in 1988 created the first specially trained police Crisis Intervention Team, or CIT, as it would become known as it was replicated in other cities.[23]

\* \* \*

Finally, the 1980s witnessed increasing episodes of violence, including homicides, committed by mentally ill individuals who were not receiving treatment. The decade began ominously with three high-profile shootings between March 1980 and March 1981. Former congressman Allard Lowenstein was killed by Dennis Sweeney, John Lennon was killed by Mark David Chapman, and President Ronald Reagan was shot by John Hinckley. All three perpetrators had untreated schizophrenia. Sweeney, for example, believed that Lowenstein, his former mentor, had implanted a transmitter in his teeth through which he was sending harassing voices.

As the decade progressed, such widely publicized homicides became more common:

1985: Sylvia Seegrist, diagnosed with schizophrenia and with 12 past hospitalizations, killed three and wounded seven in a Pennsylvania shopping mall.

Bryan Stanley, diagnosed with schizophrenia and with seven past hospitalizations, killed a priest and two others in a Wisconsin Catholic church.

Lois Lang, diagnosed with schizophrenia and discharged from a mental hospital 3 months earlier, killed the chairman of a foreign exchange firm and his receptionist in New York.

1986: Juan Gonzalez, diagnosed with schizophrenia and psychiatrically evaluated 4 days earlier, killed two and injured nine others with a sword on New York's Staten Island Ferry.

1987: David Hassan, discharged 2 days earlier from a mental hospital, killed four people by running them over with his car in California.

1988: Laurie Dann, who was known to both the police and FBI because of her threatening and psychotic behavior, killed a boy and injured five of his classmates in an Illinois elementary school.

Dorothy Montalvo, diagnosed with schizophrenia, was accused of murdering at least seven elderly individuals and burying them in her backyard in California.

Aaron Lindh, known to be mentally ill and threatening, killed the Dane County coroner in Madison, Wisconsin. This was one of six incidents in that county during 1988 "involving mentally ill individuals...[that] resulted in four homicides, three suicides, seven victims wounded by gunshots, and one victim mauled by a polar bear" when a mentally ill man climbed into its pen at the local zoo.[24]

1989: Joseph Wesbecker, diagnosed with bipolar disorder, killed 7 and wounded 13 at a printing plant in Kentucky.

Another indication that such episodes of violence were increasing was a study that compared admissions to a New York state psychiatric hospital in 1975 and 1982. It reported that "the percentage of patients who had committed violence toward persons while living in the community in the 1982 cohort was nearly double the percentage in the 1975 cohort." In addition, "the percentage of patients who had had encounters with the criminal justice system in the 1982 cohort was more than quadruple the percentage in the 1975 cohort."[25]

Is there any way to estimate the frequency of these episodes of violence committed by mentally ill person who were not being treated? There was then, and continues to be, no national database that tracks homicides committed by mentally ill persons. However, a small study published in 1988 provided a clue. In Contra Costa County, California, all 71 homicides committed between 1978 and 1980 were examined. Seven of the 71 homicides were found to have been done by individuals with schizophrenia, all of whom had been previously hospitalized at some point before the crime. The 10% rate was also consistent with the findings of another small study in Albany County, New York. Therefore, by the late 1980s, it appeared that violent acts committed by untreated mentally ill persons was one of the consequences of the deinstitutionalization movement, and the problem appeared to be a growing one.[26]

## 1990S: FROM BAD TO WORSE

The decade of the 1990s witnessed the advanced stages of deinstitutionalization with the closure of 44 more state hospitals and loss of an additional 40,000 beds. The patients being discharged to live in the community by this stage were the sickest and most difficult to manage. They were the patients who were most in need of well-organized community mental health services that could ensure that patients receive the treatment needed to remain well. With rare exceptions, such services did not exist. The primary concern of most state mental health agencies was to continue emptying their hospitals as quickly as possible, thereby shifting the cost to the federal government and saving state funds. Where the patients went was of lesser concern.[27]

Nursing homes, once used exclusively for elderly patients, increasingly became dumping grounds for younger mentally ill patients. This was especially true in Illinois, which, by the late 1990s, had 12,000 mentally ill patients in 562 nursing homes. The consequences of such placements were dramatically described in a 1998 series in the *Chicago Tribune*.[28]

One patient described in the series was Victor Reyes, a 20-year-old, 190-pound young man with fetal alcohol syndrome and an extensive history of violent behavior. At age 17 years, it was recommended that he be placed "in a highly structured environment with a significant amount of supervision." At age 19 years, he was expelled from a board-and-care home because of violent episodes. He was therefore placed in a nursing home that included many elderly residents. Within 2 days of arriving, Reyes had threatened to kill his roommate and "dumped an elderly man from a wheelchair." Over the following 4 months, he sexually harassed patients and staff and ran away several times, until May 6, 1997, when he brutally beat to death a 69-year-old woman with dementia who had denied him sex. He then ran away, stole a car, and intentionally drove it head-on into a group of bicyclists, killing one.

As the *Chicago Tribune* series made clear, Reyes was not an isolated aberration. At another nursing home, "state inspectors discovered that a 34-year-old blind, schizophrenic woman had been sitting naked on a toilet for up to 14 hours a day....Her meals were frequently delivered and consumed in the bathroom." In another home, "a man diagnosed with mental disorders had fondled the private parts or was found naked with at least three female residents, two with Alzheimer's disease," and there were 13 such incidents in 1 month. The response of the staff was to tell the man that he could be involved in no more than three incidents monthly; his official treatment plan thus read: "Decrease fondling to 3x monthly by 4/15/98."

The state of Illinois not only encouraged the placement of severely mentally ill individuals in nursing homes but also abetted the process by intentionally misdiagnosing patients so that they would be eligible for federal Medicaid. Nursing homes in which more than half the patients had diagnoses of mental illnesses are officially categorized as "institutions for mental diseases" (IMDs) and ineligible for Medicaid. State-employed nurses in Illinois therefore went to nursing homes and reclassified many patients. For example, a 65-year-old woman who had had schizophrenia for decades was no longer diagnosed with schizophrenia; instead, her diagnoses were arthritis, ovarian dysfunction, and dandruff. According to the 1998 *Chicago Tribune* report, "the state has modified at least 1,000 psychiatric patient files at 20 other nursing homes, collecting an extra $30 million from Medicaid since 1995."

States reaped rich Medicaid rewards by using such arrangements, and nursing home owners did as well. In Illinois, this included multimillionaire Morris Esformes, an ordained rabbi, who owned 18 nursing homes, and his business partner, Leon

Shlofrock, a former union leader who owned 7 other homes. Shlofrock described his business success in an interview with the Chicago newspaper:

> It's like falling off a log. If you knew at all what you were doing, you had to be successful. It's almost impossible not to make money—unless you're a total and complete idiot.

To facilitate his business interests, Shlofrock founded a lobbying group, the Illinois Council for Longterm Care, which in 1998 was headed by a former state legislator. State records showed that the Council "contributed hundreds of thousands of dollars to legislators of both parties, while successfully lobbying for higher state and federal subsidies.... The nursing home industry, based on total contributions, ranks among the top five most powerful political action groups in Illinois." Shlofrock acknowledged that he had "successfully crafted state regulations that favor him, such as limiting the training requirements of nurses aides." He also acknowledged being on a first-name basis with those wielding political power. "It's nice when you walk into a room and the governor says, 'How are you, Leon?' ... You have to have access. It's as simple as that."

* * *

Illinois was not the only—merely the most publicized—state in which nursing home abuse of mentally ill individuals became news during the 1990s. At a nursing home in Florida, it was alleged that "aggressive mentally ill residents...have killed, injured, fought and committed sexual battery upon other residents." There were also occasional exposés of board-and-care homes during the 1990s, including one home in New York described as "filthy, an overpowering stench...rampant roach problem.... Two [residents] wore pajamas all day." In one board-and-care home in California, a mentally ill woman was found in a "room with no windows, an open bucket for a toilet, and a padlock securing the door." In response to such publicity, authorities pointed to the total lack of coordination between agencies at the federal, state, and county levels: "There are too many agencies here. There is a mishmash between these agencies, and the board-and-care operators are dodging everyone."[29]

It was also during the 1990s that the ghettoization of board-and-care homes, previously an urban phenomenon, also reached smaller towns. For example, Devine, Texas, a town of 4,100 residents south of San Antonio, had more than 500 patients discharged from San Antonio state hospitals living in mostly rundown board-and-care homes. Ocean Grove, New Jersey, a historic town of 5,600 residents founded by the Methodist Church, had at least 600 patients, most of who had been discharged from nearby Marlboro State Hospital. One street became known as "Thorazine Alley" because of its accumulated trash. Ocean Pathway, a street once labeled by the *National Geographic* as the "shortest, prettiest street in America" had to have all its hedges removed because they were regularly being used as a bathroom. Ocean Grove mothers could no longer let their children play outside alone. As one said: "All the pleasures of visiting friends, playing together in the parks, and bike riding are not permitted unless I escort them." Despite the concentration of discharged patients, New Jersey set up no outpatient clinic, day program, or vocational or rehabilitation program in Ocean Grove.[30]

Mentally ill homeless persons continued to be the most visible manifestation of the nation's failed mental health policies during the 1990s. When Yetta Adams, diagnosed with schizophrenia and alcoholism, froze to death in 1993 on a Washington bench across the street from the headquarters of the Department of Housing and Urban Development (HUD), the Secretary of HUD joined the crowd to find out what had happened. He later wrote: "Yetta Adams' death jarred me and all my colleagues at HUD." A study of 99 mentally ill homeless women—like Yetta Adams—done at that time in Washington reported that two-thirds of them had been raped and that "violent victimization was so high as to amount to normative experience for this population."[31]

In San Francisco, by 1998 the city's homeless population had increased to 16,000, of which an estimated 6,000 were thought to be mentally ill. Mayor Willie Brown called it "the most complex problem" he faced, and the local paper described it as "a cancer on This City's soul." Included among the homeless were a Cornell University graduate who was trained as a physician and a Stanford University graduate who was trained as a lawyer, both diagnosed with schizophrenia. The father of the latter said: "He needs hospitalization and custodial care, but we can't seem to get any help for him without violating his civil rights. It is very painful for all of us."[32]

In 1992, Larry Hogue achieved celebrity status as a homeless person in New York City when he was publicly labeled "The Wild Man of West 96th Street." Diagnosed with bipolar disorder and cocaine addiction, Hogue set fires beneath cars, broke stained-glass church windows, masturbated in front of children, threatened to eat the dog of one resident, and on one occasion tried to push a schoolgirl into the path of an oncoming truck. Such behavior continued for almost a decade; the media became fascinated with Hogue because, despite multiple brief psychiatric admissions, officials claimed that state commitment laws prohibited his long-term involuntary hospitalization. During these same years, Hogue continued to received $3,000 each month in disability benefits from the Veteran's Administration, most of which was used to buy cocaine.[33]

Hogue's terrorization of an upscale, West Side New York neighborhood helped focus attention on the effects homeless mentally ill individuals were having on public spaces. Writing in the *Wall Street Journal* at this time, a woman said that "a simple visit to the local elementary school, post office or grocery store…can be a Dantean journey through the dark underside of our society." Another woman described "a deranged man" who tried to bite her husband's leg: "We have, sadly, grown accustomed to the images of madness on our streets and the menacing life that lives on them and now owns them." Approximately 20 homeless men were described living in the men's room at Pennsylvania Station:

> One man was trying to bathe in the cold trickle at the sink. Another was building a fire in a corner to heat the remnants of some abandoned food. A third was curled at the base of a toilet, asleep. They hunkered or leaned or sat or sprawled in total silence.

At New York's Kennedy International Airport, approximately 12 homeless people were living permanently, including a 33-year-old woman who had been "sent to the airport by Jesus Christ after a short-lived dalliance with a man named Joseph from Queens." George Will reflected on this problem in an editorial:

> We are focusing exclusively on the individual, and in terms of his or her rights. But the community, too, has rights, needs and responsibilities that, if attended to, will leave the homeless better off.... Society needs order and hence has a right to a minimally civilized ambience in public spaces."[34]

* * *

Finally, the 1990s witnessed a continuing increase in mentally ill persons in jails and prisons as well as an apparent increase in mentally ill–related homicides. Problems in jails and prisons were reported from virtually every state:

> 1992, California: The use of the Santa Clara County jail's psychiatric unit had "more than doubled" since 1986, and "there are 16 times as many outpatient psychiatric visits in the jail as there were five years ago."
> 1993, Texas: Travis County jail officials reported "a dramatic increase in prisoners with mental and emotional disorders." The jail psychiatrist said: "We've become the state hospital."
> 1994, Ohio: The Cleveland Plain Dealer described "an explosion in the number of mentally ill inmates" in Ohio prisons.
> 1997, Michigan: The Detroit News headlined: "Mentally ill flood prisons: critics say state is dumping patients out of psychiatric hospitals."
> 1999, Utah: The police chief of Salt Lake City said that "never in his 40 years in law enforcement has he seen so many psychologically disturbed people on the streets and in jails."

2001, Georgia: Between 1992 and 2001, the number of seriously mentally ill individuals in Georgia's prisons quadrupled, from 1,251 to almost 6,000. The annual spending for mental health services increased from $2.6 million to $24.1 million.[35]

Estimates of the percentage of jail and prison inmates who were seriously mentally ill varied geographically but ranged from 8% to 12% (Florida) and 12% (Texas) to 16% (California) and 33% (Tennessee). A federal Department of Justice survey in 1998 reported that "16% of State prison inmates" and "16% of those in local jails reported either a mental condition or an overnight stay in a mental hospital." These estimates contrasted with estimates from the 1970s averaging around 5% and estimates from the 1980s of around 10%.[36]

Given the numbers of seriously mentally ill persons ending up in jails and prisons, the process of getting them there increasingly involved the police. In Los Angeles between 1987 and 1993, annual calls to the Police Mental Evaluation Unit more than quadrupled, from 12,613 to 54,737. In New York the number of mentally ill persons taken to hospital emergency rooms for evaluation increased from 18,500 in 1986 to 24,787 in 1998, and the police department was said to be "the world's largest psychiatric outreach team." Many of the arrests involved repeat offenders, including Gloria Rodgers, a mentally ill woman in Tennessee who in 1999, after 259 arrests, was finally "committed indefinitely... to a state mental hospital."[37]

Despite an increasing number of training programs to teach law enforcement officials how to respond to mentally ill individuals, tragedies continued. In California's Ventura County, police killed 32 individuals between 1992 and 2001; 18 of these were mentally ill. In New York and Seattle, studies reported that one-third of the people killed by police were mentally ill. Conversely, untreated seriously mentally ill individuals were also increasingly reported as having killed law enforcement officers. Between 1998 and 2002, in the Washington, D.C. metropolitan area alone, six law enforcement officers were killed by individuals diagnosed with schizophrenia.[38]

Violent behavior by individuals with serious mental illnesses, most of whom were not being treated, became increasingly visible in the 1990s. Interviews with 1,401 members of the National Alliance for the Mentally Ill in 1990 revealed that in 11% of families the severely mentally ill family member had physically harmed another person during the previous year. A study of mentally ill patients living in New York reported that they had committed three times more violent acts (e.g., used a weapon, hurt someone badly) compared to nonmentally ill persons in the same community. By this time, the association of untreated mental illness and violence had become so clear that even those who had previously been skeptical were persuaded. John

Monahan, a professor of law at the University of Virginia, concluded his 1992 litera-ture review as follows:

> The data that have recently become available, fairly read, suggest the one con-clusion I did not want to reach: Whether the measure is the prevalence of vio-lence among the disordered or the prevalence of disorder among the violent, whether the sample is people who are selected for treatment as inmates or patients in institutions or people randomly chosen from the open community, and no matter how many social or demographic factors are statistically taken into account, there appears to be a relationship between mental disorder and violent behavior.[39]

Throughout the 1990s, the public was constantly reminded of this association by high-profile homicides committed by mentally ill individuals. The names of the perpetrators flashed across the evening news with predictable regularity, each story different and yet each remarkably the same. If the individuals had been receiving treatment for their mental illness, such tragedies would probably not have occurred. As the decade progressed, the pace seemed to quicken: James Brady in Atlanta; Gary Rimert in South Carolina; John Kappler in Boston; Betty Madeira in Los Angeles; Kevin McKiever in New York; Gary Rosenberg in Rochester; Jeanette Harper in Virginia; Debra Jackson in Minnesota; Gian Ferri in San Francisco; James Swann in Washington, DC; Colin Ferguson in New York; Linda Scates in California; William Tager in New York; Michael Laudor in New York; John Salvi in Massachusetts; Wendell Williamson in North Carolina; Michael Vernon in New York; Reuben Harris in New York; Mark Bechard in Maine; John DuPont in Pennsylvania; Alfred Head in Virginia; Daniel Ellis in Iowa; Jorge Delgado in New York; Steven Abrams in California; Julie Rodriguez in Sacramento; Larry Ashbrook in Fort Worth; Russell Weston in Washington; Lisa Duy in Salt Lake City; Michael Ouellette in Connecticut; Paul Harrington in Michigan; Salvatore Garrasi in New York; Andrew Goldstein in New York—the list seemed to stretch endlessly. After each headline, people inevitably asked why it had happened; no answers were forthcoming, and then the story was gone. The only tragedy that generated sustained attention was the Weston case because he killed two guards as he stormed the U. S. Capitol, try-ing to reach a machine he believed could reverse time. Because several members of Congress were nearby when this happened, it did get the attention of Congress, at least briefly.

Perhaps most discouraging of all at this time was evidence that no learning was occurring among public officials. Violent acts and homicides committed by mentally ill individuals were simply written off as random asteroids, events that just happen from time to time and over which nobody has any control. This failure to learn from experience was demonstrated most dramatically by mentally ill individuals who had committed a violent crime and then were released without ongoing treatment, only to commit another violent crime.

1990: John Kappler, diagnosed with bipolar disorder, killed a random bicyclist in Massachusetts with his car. As a physician who practiced anesthesiology, he had tried to kill patients in 1975, 1980, and 1985. Although he responded well to antipsychotic medication, he was not mandated to take it.

1993: Jeanette Harper, diagnosed with psychosis, stabbed to death a 71-year-old woman in Virginia. In 1986 she had killed a man and had been found not guilty by reason of insanity. She was released from the hospital in 1990 and allowed to stop taking medication a year later.

1995: Gerald Barcella, diagnosed with bipolar disorder, bludgeoned to death his landlord in Washington State. Barcella had 47 previous arrests for violent offenses.

1997: Eugene Devor, diagnosed with schizophrenia, severely beat a female university student with a large stapler in Wisconsin. In 1979 he had beaten another female student with an ax, causing severe head injuries.

1998: Daniel Ellis, diagnosed with bipolar disorder, ran his car through a stop sign at 70 miles per hour in Iowa, killing a man. In 1993 Ellis had been convicted of kidnapping and attempting to kill a 3-year-old boy. Ellis was not taking his medication.

1999: Salvatore Garrasi, diagnosed with schizophrenia and not taking his medication, killed his wife in New York. In 1983 Garrasi, also not taking his medication, had killed his 10-year-old son "out of love."[40]

There is an additional suggestion that homicides committed by mentally ill persons were increasing in the 1980s and 1990s. In 2000, the *New York Times* published a series on "rampage killers," homicides in which multiple people had been killed but that were not associated with a domestic dispute or robbery. The articles identified 102 such incidents that had taken place between 1949 and 1999. Six such incidents occurred in the 1970s, 17 in the 1980s, and 73 in the 1990s. Many, but not all, of the "rampage killers" were known to be seriously mentally ill.[41]

And that was how the century ended. In 1900, there had been almost 2,000 seriously mentally ill individuals per million population in state mental hospitals. In 2000, there were just under 200 seriously mentally ill individuals per million population in state mental hospitals. In the intervening years, the hospitals had overflowed with patients, reaching 3,388 per million in 1955. At that point, a new plan was adopted: Move the patients out of the hospitals and treat them in the community. Federal CMHCs were created and tried but failed. As Andrew Scull aptly noted, the federal plans for treating patients in the community turned out to be "castles in the air, figments of their planners' imagination." In one sense, deinstitutionalization was never really tried; rather, what had happened had merely been depopulation of the hospitals. John Talbott, one of the few American psychiatrists to focus on this disaster, summarized it as follows:

> With the knowledge that state hospitals required 100 years to achieve their maximum size, the precipitous attempt to move large numbers of their charges into settings that in fact did not exist must be seen as incompetent at best and criminal at worst.[42]

# 7

## DIMENSIONS OF THE PRESENT
## DISASTER: 2000–2013

In the fall of 1941, Joseph Kennedy arranged for his daughter Rosemary to have a lobotomy. He did so because she had become psychotic, was behaviorally out of control, and was in danger of becoming pregnant. The operation was a disaster, leaving Rosemary profoundly brain damaged. Twenty years later, Jack Kennedy assumed the presidency and authorized a new mental health and retardation program to honor his sister, although he never publicly acknowledged her connection to these programs. The program involved closing state psychiatric hospitals, shifting outpatient care to federally funded community mental health centers, and preventing mental illnesses. As implemented, the new federal program effectively lobotomized both the existing and the emerging state mental health programs. The federal program has been a disaster, and the current chaotic, dysfunctional mental health system is, in one sense, Rosemary's baby.

It is important to recognize that this failed federal mental health program was not merely a one-time disaster. By aborting the development of emerging state systems and replacing them with a potpourri of uncoordinated federal programs, it set in motion an ongoing disaster that continues today. With each passing decade, the situation has become progressively worse, and it will continue to do so until corrective action is taken.

### THE GOOD NEWS

As described in the previous chapter, the federally initiated mental health disaster has not affected all individuals with mental illnesses. Many of those with less severe symptoms and with awareness of their need for medication have done reasonably well, especially if they live in areas where rehabilitative programs are available. The employment of mentally ill individuals by state or county mental health agencies has been especially successful. In approximately one-third of the states, there are active programs to train and employ mentally ill individuals as "peer counselors" in outpatient treatment teams, substance abuse programs, and housing programs. Studies of the effectiveness of these "peer counselors" have been positive, and it is a promising line of employment for mentally ill individuals who are stable.[1]

Another generally positive development for mentally ill individuals has been the recent "recovery movement." This movement focuses first on the needs and treatment goals of the patient, so that treatment becomes a shared endeavor between the patient and the treatment team. As characterized by one summary, "recovery requires reframing the treatment enterprise from the professional's perspective to the person's perspective." The major problem, of course, is that many people with serious psychiatric disorders have anosognosia, meaning that they are not aware they are sick, because of their brain disorder. The concept of "recovery" is meaningless to them, because they believe they have nothing to recover from. The "recovery movement" thus is useful for some individuals with mental illnesses but not for many others. In large measure, "recovery" is simply a restatement of what should be the optimal relationship between a patient and doctor, and it is unclear at this point whether the movement is merely an anodyne of hope or a fad.[2]

Unfortunately, both the employment of mentally ill individuals as peer counselors and the "recovery movement" have been partially discredited by the parallel "psychiatric survivor" movement. This consists of a small but vocal group of individuals who have more or less recovered from their previous mental illness and who profess four beliefs (although, of course, not every "survivor" agrees with all four): (1) psychiatric medications are extremely dangerous and best not taken at all; (2) no mentally ill person should ever be treated involuntarily; (3) electroconvulsive therapy (ECT) should never be used; and (4) serious psychiatric disorders are not physiological brain disorders but, rather, merely states of "emotional distress." The "survivors" had their philosophical origin in their own experiences of having been mentally ill as well as in the writings of Thomas Szasz (*The Myth of Mental Illness*) and R. D. Laing; a few were also influenced by the antipsychiatry teachings of Scientology. They have organized themselves over the years into groups such as the Insane Liberation Front, the Network Against Psychiatric Assault, and the National Association of Psychiatric Survivors. By claiming to speak for all "psychiatric consumers," they have discredited the others, especially regarding the issue of involuntary treatment, which is an essential treatment strategy needed for a small number of mentally ill individuals. By claiming that mental illness does not exist or is merely an "alternate reality," this group has also discredited the recovery movement. I will return to the effect of the "survivor movement" on possible solutions to the mental illness problem in the final chapter.[3]

* * *

The good news, therefore, is that one group of individuals with serious mental illnesses is doing reasonably well. Most of them are living on their own in the community and remain stable on their medication. Some are raising families and working. This group, however, is a minority. The majority of individuals with serious mental illnesses in the United States are experiencing the effects of the misguided federal decisions made half a century ago, and the situation grows worse with each passing year.

## JAILS AND PRISONS AS THE NEW
## PSYCHIATRIC INPATIENT SYSTEM

In 1955 there were 340 public (state and county) psychiatric beds in the United States per 100,000 population. In 2010 there were 14 beds per 100,000 population, and states are continuing to close additional beds. One study estimated that the minimum number of public psychiatric beds needed in the United States is 50 per 100,000 population, almost four times the number that currently exist.[4]

The relationship between the decrease in public psychiatric beds and the subsequent increase of mentally ill persons in jails and prisons is very clear. In Atlanta following the closure of the Georgia Mental Health Institute, "the number of inmates [in the county jail] being treated for mental illness...increased 73.4 percent." After the Northwest Georgia Regional Hospital closed, the administrator of the local county jail estimated that "prisoners with mental problems...increased by 60 percent." Nationally, a 2010 survey reported that "there are now more than three times more seriously mentally ill persons in jails and prisons than in hospitals." In states like Arizona and Nevada, the difference was more than ninefold. The three largest *de facto* psychiatric inpatient facilities in the country are the county jails in Los Angeles, Chicago, and New York. In fact, there is not a single county in the United States in which the public psychiatric inpatient unit holds as many mentally ill persons as the county jail holds.[5]

How bad is the situation now? Recall that in the 1970s estimates of the number of seriously mentally ill persons in jails and prisons were around 5%. In the 1980s this had increased to around 10%, and in the 1990s, to around 15%. Estimates for 2007 to 2012 vary between 20% and 40%. Thus, 20% of Alabama prison inmates "were thought to be mentally ill"; 20% of prisoners in Michigan "had severe mental disabilities—and far more were mentally ill"; and 20% of jail inmates in the Denver metro area have "a serious mental illness."[6]

In Florida's Broward County, "23 percent of the jail system's population [are] on psychotropic drugs." In Virginia the Roanoke County sheriff claimed that "between 25 percent and 30 percent of his inmates suffer from mental illness." In the Corrections Center of Northeast Ohio, 25% of the inmates "were on psychotropic medications," which cost "nearly half of the medical budget." In Texas's Harris County Jail, 25% of inmates take psychotropic medications. In Massachusetts, 26% of all inmates in county jails have a "major mental illness." And in Illinois 28% of the inmates in the Cook County Jail "are taking serious psychotropic medications." Such estimates are consistent with a 2006 national survey by the Department of Justice that reported 24% of inmates in county jails had psychoses.[7]

Other reports have been higher. In Boone County, Missouri, "at least 30 percent of the jail population" was said to be mentally ill. Similarly, in Stark County, Ohio, "roughly 30 percent of the jail population suffers from a mental illness." At New York's Riker's Island Jail, "one in three prisoners...[is] mentally ill, and the number is climbing." And in the Tennessee prison system, "nearly one of every three inmates is mentally ill."[8]

Alarmingly, there are even higher estimates. In Texas's El Paso County Jail, 40% of the inmates are taking psychotropic medications. In Alabama's Tuscaloosa County Jail, 40% of the inmates "receive some form of psychiatric care." In Pennsylvania's Erie County Jail, 44% of inmates "have a serious mental illness." In Iowa's Black Hawk County Jail, "more than 60 percent of the inmates...are mentally ill." And in Mississippi's Hinds County Jail, "about two-thirds of the 594 inmates...take anti-psychotic medication."[9]

\* \* \*

The problems caused by the increasing number of mentally ill inmates in jails and prisons are legion. In Florida's Orange County Jail, the average stay for all inmates is 26 days; for mentally ill inmates, it is 51 days. In New York's Riker's Island Jail, the average stay for all inmates is 42 days; for mentally ill inmates, it is 215 days. The main reason mentally ill inmates stay longer is that many find it difficult to understand and follow jail and prison rules. In one study, mentally ill jail inmates were twice as likely (19% vs. 9%) to be charged with facility rule violations. In another study in the Washington State prisons, mentally ill inmates accounted for 41% of infractions although they constituted only 19% of the prison population. In a county jail in Virginia, 90% of assaults on deputies were committed by mentally ill inmates.[10]

Mentally ill inmates are also major management problems because of their impaired thought processes.

- In an Oklahoma prison, "screams, moans and chanting are normal. The noise level rises as the sun goes down....One inmate believes he is in a prisoner of war camp in Vietnam while another screams that communists are taking over the facility."
- A deputy at Mississippi's Hinds County Detention Center said: "They howl all night long. If you're not used to it, you end up crazy yourself." One inmate in this jail was described as having "tore up a damn padded cell that's indestructible, and he ate

the cover of the damn padded cell. We took his clothes and gave him a paper suit to wear, and he ate that. When they fed him food in a Styrofoam container, he ate that. We had his stomach pumped six times, and he's been operated on twice."

- Many other mentally ill inmates are quiet. In an Oklahoma prison, "one resident of the acute-care unit sculpted figurines out of his feces." In California an inmate in San Mateo County Jail's maximum security wing "lies curled up naked in a pool of urine."

- Mentally ill prisoners are also victimized much more frequently than nonmentally ill prisoners. According to a 2007 prison survey, "approximately one in 12 inmates with a mental disorder reported at least one incident of sexual victimization by another inmate over a six-month period, compared with one in 33 male inmates without a mental disorder." Among female mentally ill inmates, this difference was three times higher than among male mentally ill inmates.[11]

Not surprisingly, mentally ill inmates cost significantly more than nonmentally ill inmates. In Florida's Broward County Jail in 2007, the difference was $130 versus $80 per day. In Texas prisons in 2003, mentally ill prisoners cost $30,000 to $50,000 per year, compared to $22,000 for other prisoners. In Washington State prisons in 2009, the most seriously mentally ill prisoners cost $101,653 each, compared to approximately $30,000 per year for other prisoners. And these costs do not include the costs of lawsuits being increasingly brought against county jails, such as the suit brought in New Jersey in 2006 by the family of a "65-year-old mentally ill stockbroker [who was] stomped to death in the Camden County Jail."[12]

Sheriffs, however, originally applied for their jobs as law enforcement officials, not as custodial mental health workers, and in many counties they have begun to fight back. In Chicago, Cook County sheriff Tom Dart announced in 2011 that he was considering filing a lawsuit against the county for "allowing the jail to essentially become a dumping ground for people with serious mental health problems." In Summit County, Ohio, Sheriff Drew Alexander took it one step further in 2012 when he announced that "the county jail no longer will accept violent mentally ill and mentally disabled people arrested by area police." "We're not going to be a dumping ground anymore for these people," he said.[13]

The degree to which jails and prisons have become the nation's new psychiatric inpatient units can also be measured by bricks and mortar. It is now common—almost routine—for jails and prisons to have special sections set aside for mentally ill inmates. These units are readily identifiable by their nicknames, such as "Fantasy Island" in an Oklahoma prison. Like psychiatric hospitals, some jails and prisons have their own pharmacies; in Cleveland, the Cuyahoga County Sheriff's Department expected "to save more than $100,000" a year by opening its own pharmacy.[14]

In Maine in 2007, the governor proposed that some county jails be transformed into "specialty facilities for people with mental illnesses." That same year saw proposals in Florida's Dade and Broward Counties to provide funding for "the first county jails ever to be built specifically for inmates with chronic and severe mental illness." Also in 2007, the warden of Montana State Prison proposed "opening a special prison for the mentally ill who are now housed in the regular prison." In Raleigh, North Carolina, they are already doing this; a new, five-story hospital for 216 mentally ill prison inmates was built as part of Central Prison and opened in 2012. It sits directly across the street from Dorothea Dix State Hospital, which was simultaneously closed.[15]

But perhaps the most revealing development that illustrates how jails and prisons have become the new psychiatric inpatient system is proposals to take over closed state psychiatric hospitals and then turn them over to the Department of Corrections to become psychiatric hospitals for prisoners. In Pennsylvania the state legislature in 2010 was said to be "looking into the possibility of moving prisoners with mental illnesses into state hospitals" that were being closed. In New York State, Marcy State Psychiatric Hospital was closed many years ago and turned over to the State Department of Corrections to become the Marcy Correctional Facility. Then, in December 2009, it was announced that the Marcy Correctional Facility would open a 100-bed Residential Mental Health Unit for inmates with serious mental illness. Thus, seriously mentally ill individuals who were once treated in the psychiatric hospital may end up being treated in exactly the same building, except now it is called a prison. Office of Mental Health Commissioner Michael Hogan lauded the special unit as "a collaborative and innovative approach that to our knowledge is the first of its kind anywhere." Governor David Paterson characterized the new unit as "government at its best." Such thinking would have given Jonathan Swift much material for his satires.[16]

## SHERIFFS, POLICE, AND COURTS AS THE NEW PSYCHIATRIC OUTPATIENT SYSTEM

Just as jails and prisons have become America's new psychiatric inpatient system, the sheriffs, police, and courts have become the new psychiatric outpatient system. As a consequence of having discharged hundreds of thousands of seriously mentally ill individuals from hospitals to live in the community without adequate medications or support, psychiatric crises occur frequently. The people who respond to these crises are mostly law enforcement officials, and for many officials such calls have become a significant part of their jobs. In California's San Diego County, for example, sheriff's calls related to mentally ill individuals approximately doubled between 2009 and 2011. In 2011 police in Medford, Oregon, were dealing with "an alarming spike in the number of mentally ill people coming in contact with the police on an almost daily basis," the number of contacts having doubled since 2010. Many of the police calls were repeats, such as the 88 calls made between 2000 and 2006 by the West Des Moines, Iowa, police to the home of Joe Martens. Martens, who periodically stops taking medication for bipolar disorder, becomes violent and threatening to his neighbors. When police respond to a Martens call, "they bring two units; a third helps if things are slow."[17]

Many calls to law enforcement are to transport mentally ill people to hospitals. In Corvallis, Oregon, for example, the police handled 30 "police officer custody" cases in 2001, 58 in 2002, 113 in 2003, 140 in 2004, and 162 in 2005. In North Carolina, where state law makes county sheriffs responsible for such transport, the shortage of beds caused by the closing of state psychiatric hospitals has put an intolerable burden on the sheriffs. In 2010, 100 sheriff's departments "reported more than 32,000 trips last year to transport psychiatric patients for involuntary commitments....Fourteen sheriff's offices reported having a deputy wait with a patient for five days or more until a bed in a psychiatric unit came open." On March 25, 2010, Burke County sheriff's deputies had been with a patient in a hospital emergency room for 9 days "waiting for a bed at a mental health facility to open up." The total time spent on such tasks in North Carolina in 2009 was estimated to be 228,000 hours—time, of course, that is lost for more traditional law enforcement duties.[18]

Given the psychotic thinking and behavior of many recipients of law enforcement calls, and given the lack of mental health training of many law enforcement officers, it is inevitable that some of these encounters will turn out badly. In 2007 California's Ventura County sheriff's deputies used Taser guns to subdue people 107 times; "the majority of those shot by deputies were mentally ill." In 2008 in West Warwick, Rhode Island, a city of 29,000 people, 5 persons "described as having mental health issues" died in "police-related" incidents in a 6-month period. In California's Santa Clara County, "of the 22 officer-related shootings from 2004 to 2009 in the county, 10 involved people who were mentally ill....Many of them had numerous contacts with police before the crisis that ended in their death." In 2011 in Syracuse, three of five officer-related shootings involved "emotionally disturbed people," and in New Hampshire four of six officer-related shootings involved "mental health issues." In Albuquerque between 2010 and 2012, 11 of 24 officer-related shootings were of people with "a history of either mental illness, substance abuse or both." Although there are no national figures on such incidents, it would appear that at least one-third, and perhaps as many as one-half, of all officer-related shootings result from the failed mental illness treatment system.[19]

In 2010, in response to the numerous officer-related shootings of mentally ill people, Santa Clara County created a special task force to find ways to decrease such incidents. One member of the task force, an officer who had had 26 years' experience on the Palo Alto police force, noted that police were being repeatedly "called to the same home or situation" and said: "We want law enforcement to start looking for remedies." Significantly, the officer did not call for the local mental health center to start looking for remedies but rather the police department, which has become *de facto* the new mental health center. This reality was reflected by a conference of county sheriffs in Colorado who agreed that individuals with mental illness were "the top problem facing sheriff's departments statewide." As the Pueblo County sheriff summarized it: "By default, we've become the mental health agencies for the individual counties."[20]

There are other indicators of this ongoing shift in responsibility for seriously mentally ill individuals from traditional mental health agencies to law enforcement agencies. An increasing number of police and sheriff's departments offer specialized mental health training, usually as part of a 40-hour training course originally developed by the Memphis Police Department in 1988. The training creates Crisis Intervention Teams (CIT) of law enforcement officers who are trained to respond to crises associated with mentally ill individuals. CIT teams have spread widely; in 2011 a bill was even introduced in the New Mexico state legislature to make CIT training mandatory "for every certified police officer in New Mexico."[21]

Another indicator of the increasing responsibility for psychiatric services being assumed by law enforcement agencies is the hiring of mental health professionals by police departments. For example, in 2010 the Seattle Police Department created a new position for a mental health professional. According to the acting police chief, "the professional can conduct 'street-level assessments' and may be able to defuse threatening situations. He or she can also direct people in distress to appropriate social services." In 2012 the Burbank, California, police department hired a psychiatric social worker because their mental illness–related calls had doubled since 2009.[22]

Several law enforcement agencies are already providing social services to mentally ill individuals. In 2010 California's Ventura County Sheriff's Department began a program in which "some mentally ill inmates will be given medicine and immediate rides to their first appointments at treatment facilities upon their release from jail." A similar program in Hillsborough County, Florida, led to "a dramatic drop in recidivism." A police officer who is also a psychologist set up a program in San Rafael, California, in which the police department works jointly with the local mental health center to provide social services to mentally ill persons. Such services include having a police officer drive mentally ill persons to doctor's appointments. According to the initial evaluation of the program, "in three years, San Rafael police have closed 39 of 61 cases [and] almost a third have been moved into permanent housing." Such activities led the president of the Los Angeles County Police Chief's Association to observe: "Our local police forces have become armed social workers."[23]

Perhaps the ultimate measure of law enforcement's progressive assumption of responsibility for outpatient mental health services was the May 2011 offer by Sheriff

Ken Stolle of Virginia Beach, Virginia. City officials had voted to cut $121,596 in mental health funds from the Department of Human Services, so Stolle offered to transfer that amount of money from his jail reserve fund to cover the mental health program. He said that "the money being cut would dramatically impact the people coming into my jail with mental illness.... This is money well-spent, and it will decrease the money I'd spend housing them." By spending Department of Corrections funds on outpatient mental health services, Sheriff Stolle expects to save money in the long term. Similarly, in Tuscaloosa, Alabama, in 2012, Sheriff Ted Sexton contributed $28,000 of his department's money to help fund a mental health court.[24]

* * *

The other component of the emerging corrections-dominated psychiatric outpatient system is the courts. Traditionally, courts have adjudicated civil and criminal cases, determining guilt and meting out punishments as necessary. In 1997, in response to the increasing number of mentally ill individuals who were repeatedly charged with offenses, Florida's Broward County created the first of what are now known as mental health courts. In such courts, mentally ill defendants are given the choice of either participating in a treatment program for their mental illness or going to jail. Legally, this is done by having the prosecutor hold the charges in abeyance, requiring a guilty plea, or obtaining a conviction but then suspending the sentence, all contingent on the person's participation in the treatment program. The court then monitors the person's compliance with the program by requiring regular court visits.[25]

Mental health courts have spread quickly because they have proven to be highly successful in decreasing arrests and incarcerations of mentally ill persons. There are now at least 300 such courts throughout the United States. Initially, they were just used for mentally ill individuals charged with misdemeanors but more recently have been used for individuals charged with nonviolent felonies and even violent felonies. The courts provide primary oversight for the treatment of a significant and rapidly increasing number of seriously mentally ill individuals and are thus a vital component of the new psychiatric outpatient system controlled by the criminal justice, rather than the traditional mental health, system.[26]

## HOMELESS SHELTERS, NURSING HOMES, AND BOARD-AND-CARE HOMES

One of the salient characteristics of seriously mentally ill people in the United States is their peripatetic lives. Chris Falzone, a 28-year-old Californian with bipolar disorder, is not unusual in having "been in more than 60 facilities in 15 years.... He bounces from board-and-care homes to hospitals, from jail cells to the streets." In 2000 in

San Francisco, 30% of mentally ill jail inmates had been homeless, and 88% had been psychiatrically hospitalized. This constant changing of venues is one factor that makes the psychiatric treatment system so ineffective and expensive. For example, a 2007 Los Angeles study of mentally ill people who regularly migrate between homeless shelters, jails, emergency rooms, and psychiatric hospitals estimated the annual cost per person to be between $35,000 and $150,000.[27]

Since the early 1980s, studies have consistently reported that at least one-third of homeless individuals are seriously mentally ill. A 2010 study estimated that there are approximately 650,000 homeless persons in the United States; thus, approximately 216,000 homeless individuals have serious mental illnesses. Los Angeles and San Francisco have vied for the dubious distinction of being the "homeless capital of America." Los Angeles, with an estimated 48,000 homeless, appeared to win the award in 2005 when Mayor Antonio Villaraigosa visited Skid Row and commented: "I mean that almost looked like Bombay or something, except for more violence.... You see a complete breakdown of society." Not to be outdone, San Francisco in 2008 claimed to have "the highest per capita number of homeless in the nation.... These days, the streets of San Francisco resemble the streets of Calcutta." San Francisco had distinguished itself in 2003 when a prominent member of the American Psychiatric Association, attending the organization's annual meeting, was knocked unconscious on the street by a homeless mentally ill man, an unintended but ironic comment on the failure of psychiatrists to provide treatment for such people.[28]

Homeless mentally ill people are prominent not only in large cities. In 2007 in Roanoke, Virginia, the homeless population was estimated to be 566, of which "70 percent were receiving mental health treatment or had in the past." The number of mentally ill people being turned away from hospitals and ending up homeless had increased so markedly in Virginia by 2011 that a report by the state office of Inspector General coined a new term for it: "streeting." In 2009 in Colorado Springs, "as many as two-thirds of the 400 chronically homeless people...are said to suffer severe mental illnesses." State laws in most states also make it difficult to treat such people. For example, in Kennebec, Maine, a severely mentally ill homeless man dug a cave-like home for himself in a hillside beneath a downtown parking lot. He rejected all offers of help by police and mental health workers, and Maine law did not allow for involuntary treatment except under extreme circumstances. Finally, the overlying city parking lot began to sag because of his digging, and it was decided to arrest him because he was a threat to the parking lot, not because he was a threat to himself.[29]

Homeless mentally ill individuals are indeed threats to themselves, frequently being assaulted and otherwise victimized. In 2009 it was reported that 43 homeless people had been killed, "the highest level in a decade." Such deaths now occur almost weekly, the vast majority of victims being mentally ill.

- April 25, 2011: Stephen McGuire, 61 years old, a Marine Corps veteran, homeless and diagnosed with bipolar disorder, was beaten to death in Indianapolis by four boys and one girl.
- May 1, 2011: Chantell Christopher, 36 years old, the mother of two, homeless and "suffering from profound mental illness," was beaten to death in New Orleans. Her body was found in a crawlspace beneath the Pontchartrain Expressway, where she routinely slept.
- July 5, 2011: Kelly Thomas, 36 years old, homeless, and diagnosed with schizophrenia, was beaten to death by two policemen during a confrontation on the streets of Fullerton, California.

Our failure to protect such mentally ill people by ensuring that they receive treatment is a major miscarriage of our medical care system and a blot on our claims to be civilized.[30]

* * *

Nursing homes have continued to be heavily used for mentally ill individuals, allowing states to shift the cost of care from the state to federal Medicare and Medicaid. This is especially true in Illinois, California, Missouri, Louisiana, Ohio, and Vermont, which in 2005 had the highest percentage of nursing home admissions diagnosed with serious mental illnesses. In 2002, for the first time, the number of new nursing home admissions with mental illness as a primary diagnosis exceeded those with dementia as a primary diagnosis; by 2005 admissions with mental illness were 50% higher than those with dementia. The total number of mentally ill nursing home residents was estimated to be 560,000.[31]

Of special concern has been the rapid increase in young and middle-aged mentally ill individuals being admitted to nursing homes, thus mixing with elderly residents who have dementia. Nationally, there was a 41% increase in such admissions between 2002 and 2008, with predictable results. In one Illinois nursing home, a 21-year-old man with bipolar disorder and a history of violence raped a 69-year-old woman. In another Illinois nursing home, a 50-year-old man with a severe mental illness and a history of aggression beat to death his 77-year-old roommate, who had Alzheimer's disease.[32]

Both Illinois nursing homes were for-profit homes, as are two-thirds of all nursing homes in the United States. According to a 2007 report, for-profit homes average 33% more deficiencies than nonprofit homes during state and federal inspections. From the states' point of view, such deficiencies are of minor concern, as nursing homes allow states to save state money. For example, in 2002 in New York the annual state cost for a mentally ill patient in a state hospital was $120,000, but the state's share of the cost for the same patient in a nursing home was only $20,000; the federal government picked up the rest of the cost, and the for-profit nursing home made a handsome profit. This helps explain the cozy relationship between governors and the for-profit nursing home industry in several states, including Illinois and New York, as mentioned previously. In the latter, for example, after George Pataki had been elected governor in 1995, a "debt-retirement dinner" at an upscale New York restaurant raised an estimated $200,000 for the governor, "most of it from the nursing home industry." Subsequently, Benjamin Landa, a prominent for-profit nursing home owner and major contributor to Pataki, was appointed to the state council that regulates nursing homes.[33]

* * *

The situation of mentally ill persons in board-and-care homes is at least as bad and may well be worse than nursing homes. Nobody knows for certain, because a large and unknown number of these homes are unlicensed and thus unregulated. Like nursing homes, some operators are caring and try to provide decent services for their mentally ill residents, but many others are not. The total number of mentally ill residents in these homes is variously estimated to be several hundred thousand but is really unknown.[34]

The disgraceful depths to which board-and-care homes can descend was illustrated in 2002 by a Pulitzer Prize-winning *New York Times* series by Clifford Levy. He described for-profit homes in New York in which the owners had misappropriated thousands of dollars from residents, homes with "squalid conditions," and homes in which some residents had been raped and killed. At one home, 24 seriously mentally ill residents had been subjected to unnecessary prostate surgery, and others had been given unnecessary cataract and laser eye surgery, generating "tens of thousands of dollars in Medicaid and Medicare fees" for the physicians and the home owners. The ophthalmologist involved subsequently pleaded guilty to billings "for more than 10,000 services that were either improper, unnecessary or never conducted, ranging from cataract surgery to routine eye examinations.... He had billed for more than 400 procedures when he was actually out of the country."[35]

The fact that abuses of this magnitude could occur for many years in board-and-care homes suggests that there is virtually no state oversight of these homes. And that is indeed the case. The Empire State Association of Adult Homes, the trade group for owners of for-profit board-and-care homes in New York City, was one of the earliest and most generous donors to Pataki's campaign funds. After taking office, Pataki reduced the number of board-and-care home state inspectors in New York City from 25 to 5, reduced the staff of the Commission on Quality of Care for the Mentally Disabled in New York City from 15 to 3, and decided to not enforce a new law that would have required a report for every death occurring in a group home. As the chairman of the Commission on Quality of Care for the Mentally Disabled politely phrased it, Governor Pataki "didn't believe in government interference with the private sector."[36]

Sadly, the situation of largely unregulated board-and-care homes in New York State is far from unique. During the past decade, horrendous living conditions and abuses of the mentally ill resident have been described in many states. Most such exposés have been documented by the media rather than by state inspectors. For example, in 2004 in Kansas, an unlicensed board-and-care home was closed by federal prosecutors who accused the owners of forcing the mentally ill residents "to work on their farm and deciding who could wear clothes." The owners had been billing Medicare for nude therapy, claiming that it was beneficial for schizophrenia. In Virginia, an exposé of the state's board-and-care homes reported that "thousands of documents kept by state and local agencies reveal repeated sexual abuse, beatings, and other assaults." In 2006 in Milwaukee, the *Journal Sentinel* published a series on the city's board-and-care homes, many unlicensed, calling them "stealth mental hospitals." It described "infestations by cockroaches, mice, and rats, backed-up toilets, insufficient heat, broken smoke detectors, dangling electrical wires, filthy carpeting, a lack of proper exits, [and] a host of structural defects." In one home, a resident had been dead for 3 days before being found. In others, "building inspectors have found people begging on the streets for food because they don't get enough from landlords who take their disability checks, leaving them with next to nothing."[37]

A special problem in board-and-care homes, as in nursing homes, occurs when young individuals with serious psychiatric disorders are placed in homes with elderly residents. For example, in 2005 at a small board-and-care home in North Carolina, Tony Zichi, 25 years old, stabbed to death Ruth Terrell, age 84 years. Zichi, diagnosed with schizophrenia, had previously been evicted from seven other homes because of very violent behavior, yet he was placed in the home with four elderly women. Over a 10-month period in 2008 and 2009, four other mentally ill residents were beaten to death in North Carolina board-and-care homes, so the U. S. Department of Justice expanded its ongoing investigation into the state's mental health programs. Similar problems have been prominent in Florida. In 2007, for example, 33-year-old Darryl McGee, diagnosed with schizophrenia and with 11 previous arrests, was admitted to a board-and-care home's "locked Alzheimer's ward with people twice his age." For 4 months, "McGee terrorized the home's elderly residents during drunken rages, beating elderly men and women...before he brutally raped a 71-year-old woman in her bedroom." In an exposé of such incidents in the *Miami Herald*, it was noted that "Florida's requirements to run a home for people with mental illnesses are among the lowest in the nation: a high school diploma and 26 hours of training—less than the state requirements for barbers, cosmetologists, and auctioneers."[38]

* * *

Whether homeless, living in nursing homes, or living in board-and-care homes, individuals with serious mental illnesses who are living in the community have one thing in common—they are likely to be victimized. A 2008 review of 10 studies suggested that such victimization appears to be becoming more common. For example, among 308 patients living in community residences, 26% percent had experienced a "rape, robbery or mugging" within the previous 6 months. And among 936 seriously mentally ill outpatients, 25% had experienced a "physical assault, rape or sexual assault, [or] robbery" within the previous year. It is doubtful that any group in our society is as vulnerable as seriously mentally ill individuals living in the community. They are, in the words of one reporter, "rabbits forced to live in company with dogs."[39]

## EFFECTS ON COMMUNITY RESIDENTS

Individuals with severe mental illnesses are not the only victims of the breakdown of the mental illness treatment system. Many community residents are victims as well insofar as they no longer feel comfortable going downtown to shop or using community parks and playgrounds. Homeless individuals, especially those who are mentally ill, have expropriated public spaces in many American communities.

San Francisco provides an especially sad example. As described in 2008 by one resident:

> One is hard pressed to walk around just about any neighborhood without having to run a gantlet of panhandlers, step over passed-out drunks or drug addicts, maneuver around the mentally ill or try to avoid the stench of urine and the human feces littering the sidewalk. . . . I often feel sorry for the confused tourists who take a wrong turn off Union Square only to find themselves in the sudden squalor of the Tenderloin or the Hell-on-earth intersection of Sixth and Market streets. . . . In 2007, a homeless man snatched a woman's baby away from her and attempted to throw it over the railing above the Powell Street MUNI/ BART station, but was stopped by several onlookers.

San Francisco has no monopoly on such frightening behavior. In Los Angeles in 2011, a mother pushing her infant son down the street watched in horror as another woman grabbed the child by his leg and swung "the child over her head . . . slamming him into a metal rail." The severely mentally ill woman told police that "she tried to break off the baby's arm so she could eat it."[40]

Less dramatic variations of such scenes are being played out in every American city. Among those being victimized are shopkeepers and store owners, whose businesses suffer because customers find shopping downtown too unpleasant. For example, in Fort Lauderdale in 2008, downtown business owners complained about homeless individuals on the streets "leaving the rancid smell of urine, stealing food off plates at outdoor cafes, chasing away business and offending tourists." Such problems are completely predictable. As two observers wrote as early as 1973: "To discharge helpless, sick people into the streets is inhumane and contributes to the decline of the quality of life in the urban environment."[41]

The situation with public parks and playgrounds is even worse. Nobody has yet made a count of the number of such places that have been effectively lost to public use because they have been taken over by mentally ill homeless individuals. Walking your dog or teaching your child to ride a bike amidst men and women who are merely drunk or drugged is unpleasant, but doing so amidst psychotic men and women who are angrily shouting at unseen voices is frightening. In addition, many city parks are now devoid of benches or other places to sit because they were removed to discourage people from sleeping there. Cities such as Santa Monica, Las Vegas, Orlando, and Fort Myers have tried to restrict the use of city parks by homeless persons, arguing that such people should use the existing soup kitchens and public shelters. Such ordinances have been challenged by civil liberties advocates. In Las Vegas, for example, it was claimed that city parks are especially important for mentally ill people because "the chronically mentally ill who make up a sizeable part of the homeless population typically resist treatment and services" and often will not use public shelters.[42]

* * *

Another community facility that has been profoundly affected by the deinstitutional-ization of mentally ill individuals and our failure to provide treatment for them are the public libraries. Many libraries have become day centers for mentally ill people who are homeless or living in board-and-care homes. A 2009 survey of 124 public libraries, randomly selected from all parts of the United States, asked about "patrons who appear to have serious psychiatric disorders." The librarians reported that such individuals had "disturbed or otherwise affected the use of the library" in 92% of the libraries and "assaulted library staff members" in 28%. Eighty-five percent of the libraries had had to call the police because of the behavior of such patrons. This included benign activities such as a "patron rearranging reference books by size and refuses to stop" to less benign activities such as a man running "through the circulation area, near the children's department, repeatedly without clothing."[43]

Libraries have attempted to cope with these problems in a variety of ways. Some, such as Maryland's Hagerstown public library, have hired "security per-sonnel [who] now blend in with patrons as they keep an eye on things." A San Francisco public library, in which the majority of patrons were said to be home-less people, hired a full-time social worker. Other libraries are training staff how to respond to disturbed mentally ill individuals using a 12-hour course, "Mental Health First Aid." Despite such efforts, many people are now reluctant to use public libraries. As noted by librarians, "many, many library customers don't come downtown to our Central Library because they're afraid of these customers"; "a number of patrons have told us they will not be back because of unpleasant encounters they feel are unsafe"; "patrons are often frightened by strange behavior.... [They] hold onto their children more tightly and leave more quickly than they might have planned." Although public libraries have been an important part of American culture for two centuries, they are becoming yet another victim of the failed mental illness treatment system. As one librarian summarized it, "This problem [mentally ill persons in libraries], *not the invention of the Internet*, could prove to be the final demise of the public library as we know it."[44]

* * *

Another public space that has been markedly affected by the increasing numbers of untreated mentally ill individuals in the community are hospital emergency rooms. This problem surfaced on public radar in 2008 when Esmin Green sought psychiatric help in the emergency room of New York's Kings County Hospital Center. After having waited for 24 hours, a physician wrote an order on her chart to get blood tests and an X-ray and to use "sedation/restraints if needed." They weren't needed, because by the time the order was written, Ms. Green had been dead for more than an hour on the floor of the waiting room. Videotapes, which were widely played on television news shows, showed her lying there as two security guards and a hospital psychiatrist observed her but did nothing. In fact, in the period after she had died, notes written on her emergency room chart claimed that she was "sitting quietly," was "up and about," and "went to the bathroom." An autopsy showed that Ms. Green had died from blood clots caused by sitting too long.[45]

Perhaps the most shocking part of this episode is the fact that Ms. Green, if she had lived, would have had to wait *only* 24 hours to be seen. A national survey reported that almost 10% of all emergency room visits are now for psychiatric problems, not including substance abuse. Because there are very few remaining public psychiatric beds in the United States, emergency rooms become backed up with psychiatric patients waiting for beds.

2007: "Patients with acute mental illnesses are increasingly forced to wait up to three days in Georgia hospital emergency rooms before being admitted to state-run mental hospitals.... ERs in Georgia are already overwhelmed with the rising number of uninsured.... 'The mental health problem only exacerbates this [crowding] problem,'" said a hospital association official.

2008: A Washington State task force reported that many severely mentally ill people, including those with histories of violent behavior, "are being detained in hospital emergency rooms that aren't staffed to care for them."

2009: In Texas it was reported that nine individuals, seven of whom had "mental health issues," accounted for 2,678 visits to Austin emergency rooms between 2003 and 2008. The average cost of each visit was $1,000 and was paid by Medicaid or Medicare.

2010: In North Carolina it was reported that "on average, people in the midst of a mental health crisis can expect to languish in a medical hospital's emergency department for 2.8 days before gaining admission to a state psychiatric hospital." In the western third of the state, the average wait was 4 days. In a three-month period, Wake County had "13 people waiting a week or more."

2011: In Massachusetts "so many people seeking psychiatric help flooded Quincy Medical Center's emergency room…[that] 20 beds had to be set up in a nearby conference room to handle the surge." The chief of emergency medicine at the medical center said "he had seen the situation deteriorate dramatically" since 2002.

2011: In South Carolina "mentally ill patients are flooding into emergency departments as a direct result of deep cuts for treating these troubled individuals." One woman had been in an emergency room for 8 days awaiting a psychiatric bed, another woman 12 days. According to a Hospital Association report: "South Carolina's hospital emergency rooms have become the safety net for the mentally ill." The director of the emergency room in Pickens said: "They say it is going to get worse but I don't know how. It is really horrendous."

2012: In California, Fresno County officials were forced to reopen the county's psychiatric crisis center. Since it closed in 2009, "as many as 600 psychiatric patients visit the hospital's emergency room each month, more than double the number that went there before the crisis center closed."[46]

## VIOLENT BEHAVIORS AND HOMICIDES

The most publicly visible consequences of the failed mental illness treatment system are violent behaviors, including homicides. As previously noted, such acts became prominent in the early 1970s in California as deinstitutionalization accelerated, and they appear to have continued to increase over the subsequent 40 years.

It important to note that most acts of violence are not committed by mentally ill individuals and that most mentally ill individuals are not violent. Being a young male or a substance abuser is a much higher risk factor for predicting violent behavior than is being mentally ill. It is also true that individuals with serious mental illnesses are more likely to themselves be victimized than they are to victimize others. All this is true, but it is *also* true that a small number of individuals with serious mental illnesses, especially those who are not being treated, are responsible for a disproportionate amount of community violence, including homicides.

Between 2007 and 2009, four review studies were published on the relationship between untreated serious mental illness and violence.

- A review of 22 studies published between 1990 and 2004 "concluded that major mental disorders, per se, especially schizophrenia, even without alcohol or drug abuse, are indeed associated with higher risks for interpersonal violence." Major mental disorders were said to account for between 5% and 15% of community violence.
- After reviewing the psychiatric literature from 1970 to 2007, the author of another study concluded that "sound epidemiologic research has left no doubt about a significant relation between psychosis and violence, although one accounting for little of society's violence."
- An analysis of 204 studies of psychosis as a risk factor for violence reported that "compared with individuals with no mental disorders, people with psychosis seem to be at a substantially elevated risk for violence." Psychosis "was significantly associated with a 49%–68% increase in the odds of violence."
- A review of studies from 11 countries involving more than 18,000 patients concluded that, compared to the general population, men with schizophrenia had a two to five times greater risk for committing violent acts, and women with schizophrenia had a four times greater risk.

It should be emphasized that almost all the increased risk of violent behavior by individuals with serious mental illnesses applies only to those who are not being adequately treated with medications. For those who are being treated and take their medications, there is no evidence for any increased risk.[47]

Although most public attention regarding serious mental illness and violent behavior is focused on homicides, there are other examples of this problem. During late 2011 and early 2012, for example, Ali Shahsavari, with untreated schizophrenia, caused an emergency landing of a Southwest Airlines flight in Texas when "he intimidated crew members by screaming profanity" during the flight; Oscar Ortega, with untreated schizophrenia and a belief that he was Jesus Christ, shot at the White House in Washington; and Gregory Seifert, with a severe mental illness, used a chainsaw to cut down utility poles near Buffalo, causing a loss of power to more than 6,000 homes.[48]

But it is mental illness-related homicides that receive the most media attention. As noted in Chapter 6, there are two small, older studies in New York and California that

suggest that people with untreated serious mental illnesses are responsible for approximately 10% of homicides in the United States. A more recent study from Indiana supports this. Researchers examined the records of 518 individuals in prison who had been convicted of homicides between 1990 and 2002. Among the 518, 53 (or 10.2%) had been diagnosed with schizophrenia, bipolar disorder, or other psychotic disorders not associated with drug abuse. An additional 42 individuals had been diagnosed with mania or major depressive disorder. It should be emphasized that the study included only those individuals who had been sentenced to prison and did not include those who had committed homicides but were subsequently found to be incompetent to stand trial or not guilty by reason of insanity and therefore sent to a psychiatric facility rather than prison; thus, the 10.2% is an undercount. The authors themselves did not conclude that individuals with serious mental illnesses were responsible for at least 10% of the homicides, but given the data that seems an obvious conclusion. Studies from several other countries, including Sweden, Finland, Germany, and Singapore, have also reported that individuals with serious mental illnesses are responsible for approximately 10% of homicides.[49]

The homicides that receive the most attention are those in which there are multiple victims. As noted in the previous chapter, there are suggestions that these "rampage killings," as they are sometimes called, are becoming more common. On January 8, 2011, Jared Loughner, suffering from untreated schizophrenia, killed 6 and wounded 13 in Tucson, Arizona. Because Congresswoman Gabrielle Giffords was among the wounded, this tragedy received wide publicity. What was not publicized was the fact that in the preceding 5 years, there had been at least 11 other "rampage killings" committed by seriously mentally ill people who were not being treated. They included Matthew Colletta in New York, who killed 1 and injured 5; Lawrence Woods in Pismo Beach, California, who killed 2; Omeed Popal in San Francisco, who killed 1 and injured 14; Jennifer San Marco in Goleta, California, who killed 8; Wesley Higdon in Henderson, Kentucky, who killed 5 and injured 1; Christian Nielsen in Newry, Maine, who killed 4; Naveed Haq in Seattle, who killed 1 and injured 5; Matthew Murray in Colorado Springs, who killed 4 and injured 5; Seung-Hui Cho at Virginia Tech, who killed 32 and injured 24; Isaac Zamora in Seattle, who killed 6 and injured 4; and Jiverly Wong in Binghamton, New York, who killed 13 and injured 4. Jared Loughner became a household name because he killed six and injured Congresswoman Giffords, whereas Isaac Zamora, who also killed six in Seattle in 2008, was quickly forgotten.

This phenomenon was also illustrated in July 2012, when James Holmes, with an untreated severe mental illness and dressed as the Joker, killed 12 and injured 59 at a Batman movie in Aurora, Colorado. Because of its bizarre nature, the killings received widespread publicity. By contrast, when Jiverly Wong, with untreated paranoid schizophrenia, killed 12 and injured 4 at an immigration center in Binghamton, New York, in April 2009, the killings were reported mostly as a local story. Within 1 month of the

Aurora tragedy, Laura Sorensen shot three shoppers near Seattle, and Thomas Caffall killed two and wounded four in College Station, Texas; both Sorensen and Caffall had an untreated severe mental illness, but these stories were not widely reported. It thus appears that homicides associated with untreated severe mental illness are more common than is generally realized. Unfortunately, the FBI does not keep separate statistics differentiating such cases from other homicides, so the true magnitude of the problem is not known.[50]

Public interest in the relationship between untreated mental illness and homicides reached a new high in December 2012, following a massacre of schoolchildren in Newtown, Connecticut. Adam Lanza, a mentally ill young man whose precise diagnosis has not yet been disclosed, killed 20 elementary school children, 6 school employees, his mother, and himself. The site of the massacre was ironic, as Newtown had been the site of one of Connecticut's three state psychiatric hospitals, but the hospital there had been closed in 1996. It was in such hospitals that mentally ill individuals such as Lanza had been evaluated and treated in the past. Thus the Newtown tragedy was a symbolic coda to deinstitutionalization.

The mass killings in Connecticut were followed closely by several other homicides committed by individuals with untreated severe mental illnesses. These included a man pushed to his death beneath a subway in New York by a mentally ill woman with at least 10 past psychiatric admissions, a history of violence, and a history of failing to take medication. Coming so soon after the massacre of theatergoers in Colorado, the Newtown tragedy, and subsequent homicides elicited an unprecedented volume of calls, from President Obama down, for gun control and improved mental illness treatment laws. Whether this public outcry will results in any meaningful change remains to be determined.

Yet another indication that mental illness-related violence is increasing is the apparent increasing incidence of repeat acts of violence committed by the same person. Such acts are often eerily similar in character, suggesting that little learning is taking place among mental health officials:

- In Detroit, Paul Harrington, diagnosed with depression with psychotic features, stopped taking his medication and killed his wife and 3-year-old son. Twenty-four years earlier he had killed his wife and two daughters, ages 4 and 9 years.
- In Everett, Washington, Steven Well, diagnosed with paranoid schizophrenia, stabbed to death his landlady, who he thought was sending electrical signals into his brain. Thirty years earlier he had attacked another landlady with a knife, but she had survived. In the intervening years he had attacked a man with a hammer.
- In suburban Washington, D.C., Antoinette Starks, diagnosed with paranoid schizophrenia, stabbed a woman shopper outside a department store. Six years earlier she had stabbed another woman shopper outside a different department store.[51]

Such repeat acts of violence by mentally ill individuals were occasionally reported in past years, but they now appear to have become common. The following, for example, all took place during a 12-month period in 2007 and 2008:

- In Virginia, Johnny Hughes, diagnosed with schizophrenia, stabbed to death an elderly woman as she walked her dog. In the mid-1990s, Hughes had been found not guilty by reason of insanity of attempted murder.
- In Washington State, Daniel Tavares, diagnosed with schizophrenia, murdered a young couple. In 1991 Tavares had killed his mother.
- In Texas, Darrell Billingslea, diagnosed with schizophrenia, killed a woman he had met through the Internet. In 1989 and 1990, he had killed two men.
- In Washington State, James Williams, diagnosed with schizophrenia, killed a young woman on the street. In 1995 he had shot a stranger at a bus stop.
- In Colorado, Audrey Cahous, diagnosed with bipolar disorder, stabbed a man to death. In 1987 she had stabbed her third husband.
- In Iowa, Richard Mutchler, diagnosed with bipolar disorder, stabbed to death a man and woman. In 1991 he had killed a man.
- In California, Ofiu Foto, diagnosed with schizophrenia, beat to death an elderly woman who worked in his group home. In 2005 he had severely beaten another elderly woman and had additional charges of assault.

Such incidents, in which seriously mentally ill individuals who have proven dangerousness are not followed up and properly monitored, suggest a widespread failure of the mental illness treatment system.[52]

If, as studies suggest, seriously mentally ill individuals who are not being adequately treated are responsible for 10% percent of the nation's homicides, then how many homicides is that? In 2009, there were 13,636 total homicides in the United States, so approximately 1,300 of these might have been prevented if the mentally ill perpetrators had been adequately treated for their illness. Since 1970, there have been a total of 765,270 homicides in the United States, so approximately 76,000 of these might have been prevented. These 76,000 individuals, their families and friends, and the perpetrators of these tragedies are all victims of our failed mental illness treatment system.[53]

In summary, homicides and other violent acts committed by individuals with serious mental illnesses who are not being treated have emerged as the most visible symptom of the failed mental illness treatment system. The situation was summarized by Keith Ablow, a psychiatrist who has written a book about such cases:

We are not facing an epidemic of gun violence. We are not facing an epidemic of first-degree murder. We are facing an epidemic of mental illness, improperly triaged and treated, leading to killings with no apparent motive. They will stop when we decide to stop them—by providing robust mental health care services, targeted to those individuals whose mental illnesses include a component of violent or psychotic thinking.[54]

## WHAT ARE THE FINANCIAL COSTS?

There are many disturbing aspects to the breakdown of public psychiatric services in the United States. Not the least of these is the fact that the chaotic, unplanned system that has emerged is not only very dysfunctional—it is also very expensive. It is doubtful if there are many other areas of public services in which so much money is being spent with so little effect.

Begin, for example, with the Supplemental Security Income (SSI) and Social Security Disability Insurance (SSDI) payments. These are federal entitlement programs intended to provide living support for the aged, blind, and disabled. As noted previously, SSI is the product of President Nixon's decision in 1972 to standardize and federalize welfare and disability payments that previously had been the responsibility of the states. Nixon had no intention of making SSI into a major mental health program, but over the years it has become so. In 2009, 41% of all SSI and 28% of all SSDI recipients qualified for benefits because of their mental illness, not including mental retardation. Their total number was 4,741,970 individuals; by comparison, in 1977 the total number of mentally ill individuals receiving SSI and SSDI was estimated to be between 225,000 and 425,000. In 2009 the annual SSI and SSDI payments to mentally ill individuals was *$45.7 billion.*[55]

As a federal entitlement, the SSI and SSDI money is given to qualified individuals with no requirements. Thus, although some recipients might be able to work if they were to receive and adhere to treatment for their mental illness, there has never been any requirement for SSI or SSDI recipients to participate in a treatment program. The SSI and SSDI programs also operate independently from all other government programs for mentally ill individuals. It was the SSI and SSDI programs that spawned the board-and-care home industry, with mentally ill individuals trading their monthly stipends for "three hots and a cot" in largely unregulated facilities.

The government programs that finance mental health services are Medicare and Medicaid. These were products of President Johnson's 1965 Great Society initiatives and were originally intended to provide medical care for elderly and poor people, respectively. Medicare is funded exclusively by federal funds and pays hospital and other medical costs for people ages 65 years and older. Medicaid is funded jointly by federal and state funds and covers hospitalization in general hospitals (but in most cases not in psychiatric hospitals), outpatient services, nursing homes, medications, and a variable list of other services, such as case management, depending on the coverage offered by that particular state.

As noted previously, the architects of Medicare and Medicaid had no intention of creating mental health programs, and in fact Medicaid specifically excluded coverage for psychiatric hospitals under a provision called the institutions for mental diseases exclusion. Nevertheless, Medicaid has become "the largest payer of mental health treatment services" in the United States, with mental health costs now constituting more than 10% of the entire Medicaid program. By covering hospitalization in the psychiatric units of general hospitals but not in psychiatric hospitals, Medicaid has encouraged states to empty state hospitals, thus effectively shifting the costs of psychiatric hospitalization from exclusively state funds to a mix of federal and state funds. An analysis of deinstitutionalization in the early 1970s reported Medicaid funds to be "very strongly associated with the amount of deinstitutionalization." By covering nursing home care for mentally ill individuals, Medicaid and Medicare together acted as an additional impetus to deinstitutionalization and spawned the for-profit nursing home industry. Indeed, as economist Richard Frank and colleagues noted, "the creation of the Medicaid program in 1965 began a process that fundamentally changed the rules governing a US public mental health care system."[56]

In the almost 50 years since Medicaid was instituted, states have become increasingly sophisticated in finding ways to shift mental health costs from state funds to federal Medicaid. Widely known as "Medicaid maximization," it has been characterized by the phrase: "If it moves, Medicaid it." Medicaid now covers 55% of all state-controlled mental health costs, and for some states, such as Arizona, Alaska, Vermont, Rhode Island, and Maine, the percentage of Medicaid funds is 80% or higher. In total, based on 2005 data, Medicaid and Medicare contribute approximately *$60 billion* a year to mental health costs in the United States.[57]

The $45.7 billion in annual SSI and SSDI costs and the $60 billion in Medicare and Medicaid costs are the major contributors to public mental health costs. In addition, the federal government contributes *$5.7 billion* to mental health programs under the Department of Defense, the Veterans Administration, and a $386 million federal mental health block grant to the states. The costs of mentally ill individuals in jails and prisons must also be included. There are approximately 2 million individuals in jails and prisons; if an average of 20% of them are seriously mentally ill, then that would be 400,000 individuals. A conservative estimate of the cost of inmates in jails and prisons is $25,000 per year, although costs are higher for mentally ill inmates. Nevertheless, even at this cost, 400,000 inmates would add *$10 billion* a year to the nation's mental health costs.[58]

In addition, the costs of law enforcement, courts, and public shelters used by mentally ill persons must be included. A 2002 estimate for persons with schizophrenia cited law enforcement costs as *$2.6 billion* and public shelter costs as *$6.4 billion*. That survey also estimated the cost of family caregivers for individuals with schizophrenia at *$7.9 billion*.[59]

In total, it would appear that the direct costs of supporting and treating individuals with serious mental illnesses in the United States are presently at least *$140 billion* per year. This figure does not include indirect costs such as income lost by the mentally ill persons; in 2002 this was estimated to be $193 billion. Nor does it include the social costs of violent crimes committed by mentally ill persons, which have been estimated to be $925,000 per crime.[60]

One hundred and forty billion dollars per year is a lot of money. For purposes of comparison, it is three times the 2012 budgets of the National Institutes of Health, the National Science Foundation, and the Centers for Disease Control and Prevention *combined*. To obtain $140 billion dollars, each adult in the United States has to contribute approximately $650.

The fact that the $140 billion being spent on public mental health services in the United States is merely buying the grossly inadequate and disjointed services described in this book is mind-boggling. It suggests that something is profoundly wrong. One hundred and forty billion dollars should be more than sufficient to support excellent mental health services if the money was being used wisely. How this might be done will be the subject of the final chapter.

# 8

## SOLUTIONS: WHAT HAVE WE LEARNED
## AND WHAT SHOULD WE DO?

For more than a century, the care of individuals with serious mental illnesses had been the responsibility of state governments. The transfer of this responsibility from states to the federal government began during 1962, with the deliberations of President Kennedy's Interagency Task Force on Mental Health; this group planned the new, federally funded community mental health centers. Half a century has now passed since those meetings took place—what would members of the task force think of their plans in retrospect?

Boisfeuillet Jones, the lawyer who was the task force chairman, and Robert Manley, the Veterans Administration representative, both died without apparently publicly expressing an opinion regarding the task force's work. Daniel Moynihan is now also deceased but in 1994 expressed clear reservations about what they had done. As chairman of the Senate Committee on Finance, Moynihan convened hearings on "Deinstitutionalization, Mental Illness and Medication." In his opening statement, he criticized the failure to follow up patients after discharge from the state hospitals: "It was soon clear enough that in order for this [deinstitutionalization] to work you could not just discharge persons, they had to be looked after." The result, he said, had been a sharp increase in the number of homeless people. "To make great changes casually and not pay rigorous attention to what follows," he added, "is to invite large disturbances."[1]

Both economist members of the Interagency Task Force—Robert Atwell and Rashi Fein—are alive. Atwell later served as president of Pitzer College and president of the American Council on Education. During the 1962 discussions, he was one of the strongest voices on the task force urging the closing of state hospitals and the federalization of mental health programs. Thinking back on the program during a 2011 interview, Atwell recalled: "I really wanted this thing to work....I was a believer." When asked why the program failed, he said: "Funding was always going to be a problem and was never forthcoming." Rashi Fein has had an equally distinguished academic career and in a 2010 interview clearly recalled that members of the task force "were all troubled about the funding." In retrospect, he added, "we should have more carefully examined and discussed what it would take in dollars and commitment at the local and state levels to make the model work."[2]

The other official member of the task force, Robert Felix, was the director of the National Institute of Mental Health (NIMH) and architect of the proposed plan. Even as he was retiring from NIMH in 1964, however, he expressed some doubts about the plan, calling "essential" the "follow-up and rehabilitative services for persons returned from inpatient psychiatric care, or under foster home or similar care." Previously he had ignored such services and had not included them in the essential services for mental health centers. In 1984 Felix publicly acknowledged that "many of those patients who left the state hospitals never should have done so....The result is not what we intended, and perhaps we didn't ask the questions that should have been asked when developing a new concept but...we tried our damnedest." Until his death in 1990, Felix continued to express serious doubts about the value of his legacy.[3]

Stanley Yolles and Bertram Brown were the NIMH psychiatrists working closely with Felix at the time of the Interagency Task Force meetings. Yolles, who died in 2001, also expressed doubts about what they had created. He decried "the 'dumping' of mental hospital patients in inadequate community settings" and claimed that "the current situation results, in part, from an assumption made in 1963 that has not proved to be correct. At the time, many community psychiatrists believed that almost all mental patients could be treated in the community. This optimism was too euphoric. It now seems probable that there will always be some chronic patients—say, 15% of the total—who will require long-term, residential care." Yolles added that "it is now obvious that...aftercare and rehabilitative services *must* be available within communities."[4]

Brown, the youngest of the psychiatric triumvirate that led NIMH down the community mental health path, is alive and was willing to recount these events during extensive discussions. He said that he and his colleagues "were carrying out a public mandate to abolish the abominable conditions of insane asylums," but in doing so "the doctors were overpromising for the politicians. The doctors did not believe that community care would cure schizophrenia, and we did allow ourselves to be somewhat misrepresented." He acknowledged a "failure of appreciation of the care needed by seriously mentally ill patients." "For Yolles and me, individuals with serious mental illnesses were not a primary concern....We should have done something to cover them, but it was not a priority....We wanted to do something to help people using public health." Asked what he should have done differently, Brown said he should have hired "five good mental health superintendents as consultants." Looking back on it all, Brown characterized it as "a grand experiment" but added: "I just feel saddened by it."[5]

Fifty years after the initiation of this grand experiment, we also look with sadness upon the detritus of mental health dreams and lees of lost lives. As sociologist Andrew Scull observed, too often "the new programs remained castles in the air, figments of their planners' imaginations....The term 'community care'...merely an inflated catch phrase which concealed morbidity in the patients and distress in the relatives."[6]

As noted previously, these failed mental health programs were not conceived with malevolent intent. Their architects truly believed that closing state mental hospitals and moving patients into the community would improve everyone's lives. In a 1972 interview, Felix said that his primary motivation was to make psychiatric services available to more people, and this wish was also expressed by Yolles and Brown. As noted by columnist and psychiatrist Charles Krauthammer, the "disaster" of deinstitutionalization was not "the result of society's mean-spiritedness...[or] of mysterious determining forces, but of a failed though well-intentioned social policy. And social policy can be changed."[7]

## IMPEDIMENTS TO CHANGE

Social policy *can* indeed be changed, but change does not come easily. Psychologist Franklyn Arnhoff, writing about mental health policy in 1975, observed that "it is extremely difficult to change its course even if there is mounting evidence that its costs or its harmful effects far exceed its benefits." If we hope to change mental health policies, we must first understand the forces that impede change. These include the following[8]:

1. *Lack of understanding of serious mental illnesses.* There is a lack of public understanding, including among public officials, of the nature of serious mental illnesses. In recent decades, it has become clear that schizophrenia, bipolar disorder, and severe depression are brain diseases, just as multiple sclerosis and Alzheimer's disease are brain diseases. However, public understanding lags behind the scientific understanding. Because of the inordinate influence of Sigmund Freud's ideas on American thought in the last century, many Americans still believe that serious mental illnesses are psychological, not biological, in origin. This lack of understanding is especially acute regarding mentally ill individuals whose brain dysfunction involves the parts of the brain we use to think about ourselves—what we call anosognosia. Despite being overtly mentally ill, such individuals have no awareness of their own illness or need for medication; most such individuals will thus refuse to take medication because they honestly believe that nothing is wrong with them. It is very difficult for most people to understand this.

2. *Lack of understanding of the magnitude of the mental illness problem.* There is a lack of public understanding, including among public officials, of the magnitude of the mental illness problem as described in the preceding chapters. The deterioration of public mental illness services has been a gradually evolving disaster, like slowly rising water without any major flood to call attention to itself. The mental illness

disaster also has many manifestations, which at initial glance do not appear to be related. For example, an average American family may be aware that their county taxes are being raised to pay for the new addition to the overcrowded county jail; that they no longer allow their children to go to the public library alone because of all the strange men there talking to themselves; that people are reported by the news as sometimes doing bizarre things, like the man in Buffalo who cut down utility poles with a chainsaw; and that rampage killings, such as those carried out by Jared Loughner and James Holmes, seem to be happening more frequently. All these are consequences of a single problem—the failure to appropriately treat individuals with severe psychiatric disorders—but almost nobody makes the connection.

3. *Lack of understanding of the civil rights of people with severe mental illnesses.* Americans highly value our civil rights to live as we please and not have the government tell us what to do. Many people thus defend the rights of homeless mentally ill persons to be "free" to live on the sidewalk, under a bridge, or in jail. What they don't realize is that most such people are not "free"; rather, their actions are dictated by their delusions and auditory hallucinations, however irrational those may be. The freedom to live in the community while psychotic may also interfere with the rights of other members of the community. As psychiatrist Gary Maier phrased it, "When the personal freedom of the mentally ill is given priority over all other considerations, the tyranny of some will jeopardize the autonomy of all."[9]

4. *Public mistrust of psychiatry.* The history of psychiatry includes multiple examples of gross abuse, including the killing of mental patients in Nazi Germany, the forced psychiatric hospitalization of political dissidents in the Soviet Union, and the unconsented sterilization of patients in psychiatric hospitals under the eugenics movement in the United States. Groups opposed to psychiatry, such as the Scientologists and the "psychiatric survivors" described in the last chapter, exploit this public mistrust to block any legislation associated with involuntary treatment.

5. *Economic interests to maintain the status quo.* The nursing home industry and the board-and-care home industry have greatly profited from the discharge of hundreds of thousands of psychiatric patients, whose community care is then paid for with federal funds. Two-thirds of nursing homes and almost all board-and-care homes are for-profit operations. As the owner of seven nursing homes in Illinois inelegantly phrased it: "It's almost impossible not to make money—unless you're a total and complete idiot." In many states, the nursing home and board-and-care home industries have close financial ties to state legislators and governors, making change problematic. For-profit managed care companies have also benefited significantly by managing the care of the deinstitutionalized patients.[10]

6. *Political interests to maintain the status quo.* Politically conservative state legislators and officials have gladly ceded fiscal responsibility for seriously mentally ill persons

to the federal government, thereby reducing costs to the states. Politically liberal legislators and officials, at both the federal and state levels, assume that the federal government should take responsibility for solving most social problems, including the care of persons with serious mental illness. This combination of politically conservative and liberal bedfellows is a major impediment to change.

7. *The federal government.* Given the fact that the present mental illness disaster is a direct product of federal programs implemented half a century ago, one might think that federal officials would attempt to take corrective actions. Such an assumption would be wrong. The federal government's programs related to individuals with serious mental illnesses have continued to be a potpourri of completely uncoordinated programs, some of which counteract each other and many of which have made the problem worse. For example, in the late 1980s at the NIMH, research programs were attempting to find the causes of, and better treatments for, serious mental illnesses. Another NIMH program, the Protection and Advocacy program, was supporting public conferences at which invited speakers denied that mental illnesses exist and claimed that psychiatric medications destroy the brain.

NIMH subsequently righted itself with good leadership in the last decade, but the Protection and Advocacy program became part of another government agency, the Substance Abuse and Mental Health Services Administration (SAMHSA). In the *National Review*, I noted regarding this agency that "the health of its clients would improve if it went out of business." Although the official mission of SAMHSA is to reduce "the impact of substance abuse and mental illness in America's communities," many of SAMHSA's programs exacerbate the problem. For example, SAMHSA gives hundreds of thousands of dollars to groups in states such as California and Pennsylvania that attempt to block the implementation of laws that would make it easier to treat people with serious mental illnesses. SAMHSA also gives $330,000 a year to the National Empowerment Center in Massachusetts, whose director believes that "the covert mission of the mental health system…is social control." Such federal programs are thus impediments to change, because once started, federal programs are extremely difficult to abolish. Thus, the federal government is a major impediment to improving the mental illness treatment system.[11]

8. *Lack of leadership.* Of all the impediments to change, this may be the most significant, as change will not occur without leadership. Disorders such as cancer and heart disease have large, effective organizations that lobby for research and improved services. Serious mental illnesses have nothing comparable. Mental Health America, formerly the Mental Health Association, advocates weakly for "mental health" but says virtually nothing about mental illness. NAMI, formerly the National Alliance

for the Mentally Ill, does a creditable job of providing education and support for mentally ill persons and their families at the local level but has had virtually no effect in most states or at the federal level. The Treatment Advocacy Center, which I helped organize in 1998, focuses exclusively on the problems described in this book but is a small organization with an annual budget of just $1 million.

Other possible sources for leadership are unpromising. Three decades ago, leadership still existed among state mental health directors, but now such positions are filled by administrators whose only task is to empty the hospitals and shift state costs to the federal government. The American Psychiatric Association, which was originally organized to focus attention on the care and treatment of individuals with serious mental illnesses, has long since abandoned that population and now functions mostly as a lobby to protect the economic interests of psychiatrists. Except for Dr. Thomas Insel, director of NIMH, Washington is devoid of leadership for the problems of individuals with serious mental illnesses. Congress at one time had leaders such as Senators Pete Domenici and Paul Wellstone who provided strong support, but since Domenici's retirement and Wellstone's death, nobody has stepped forward to take their place. In summary, it is not clear where the leadership for change will come from, but until it emerges, change is unlikely.

## WHAT SHOULD WE DO?

The many impediments to change are the bad news. However, the fact that we know what to do to correct the existing mental illness disaster is the good news. There is a surprisingly broad consensus on what good services should look like, although there is less agreement on how they should be organized and funded. To illustrate the solutions, I will review the fundamental errors of deinstitutionalization—closing the hospitals, misunderstanding community treatment, and federal financing of mental health care. In doing so, I will highlight 10 lessons to be learned, lessons that should be incorporated into any future mental illness treatment system if it is to be successful.

• *Closing the Hospitals*

With the introduction of effective antipsychotic medication in the 1950s, it became possible, for the first time, to control the symptoms of many individuals hospitalized with severe mental illnesses—specifically schizophrenia, bipolar disorder, and major depression with psychotic features. These individuals constituted the majority of the patients who needed to be in state and county mental hospitals in 1955. By controlling the person's delusions, hallucinations, and other psychotic symptoms, it was possible to get many patients well enough to be moved to the community to live with their families, in nursing homes or board-and-care homes, or by themselves.

Given the fact that state mental hospitals had been the mainstay of public psychiatric care in the United States for more than a century, reversing this longstanding policy should have engendered careful planning. Many of the patients being moved to community settings had been hospitalized for 20 years or longer, so problems were predictable. Remarkably, almost no such planning took place. Rather, as noted by psychologist Franklyn Arnhoff, the emptying of the hospitals became an end in itself, "based upon the logical fallacy that since bad hospitals are bad for patients, any hospitalization is bad for patients and should be avoided entirely or made as short as possible." The radical nature of this new policy appealed to many of the psychiatric leaders and their associates, such as Mike Gorman, who played a major role in the closing of state psychiatric hospitals. Gorman described "the truly revolutionary nature of what we have wrought in altering radically the profile of American psychiatry," a change that appealed to Gorman's politically radical interests. Such thinking was also reflected in President Kennedy's historic 1963 speech to Congress, in which he said that the aim of the program "was to revolutionize the centuries-old mental health system." At ground level, such thinking motivated the NIMH troops; psychiatrist Frank Ochberg, who was a director of the community mental health centers program in the 1970s, recalled: "What a privilege to participate in breaking the back of the asylums."[12]

The emptying of state psychiatric hospitals as an end in itself became strongly reinforced by the availability of federal funds under Medicare, Medicaid, SSI, and SSDI for the patients once they had been discharged. States realized that they could save state funds by discharging patients, thereby closing state-funded hospital beds. The subsequent reduction in public psychiatric beds nationwide was indeed radical, from 340 beds to 14 beds per 100,000 population, as noted in Chapter 7. These psychiatric hospital bed closures are continuing, with many states having as a goal the closing of all public psychiatric hospitals and even the closing of the state department of mental health, which California achieved in 2012.

The closing of so many beds was a major mistake. It has become clear during the years of deinstitutionalization that a minimum number of public psychiatric beds continue to be needed. One reason they are needed is to treat patients with serious mental illnesses who are acutely ill and need to be stabilized on medication. Many such patients, if manic or otherwise acutely psychotic, must be hospitalized involuntarily and cannot be adequately treated in the psychiatric units of most general hospitals. Public psychiatric beds are also needed for a small group of seriously mentally ill patients who do not respond well to existing medications or do not take their medications. Some are repeatedly victimized in community settings and are thus a danger to themselves, whereas others are a danger to themselves because of repeated self-injury or suicide attempts.

Others are repeatedly violent and thus a danger to others. Both types of patients often shuttle between jail and the streets, because beds are not available. A 2011 study, in fact, reported that states that have fewer public psychiatric beds have higher homicide rates. As early as 1974, Aaron Rosenblatt, a psychiatric social worker, recognized the need for long-term psychiatric beds for the small number of treatment failures, calling such individuals "weary sojourner[s] in a hostile world." More recently, psychiatrist Dinesh Bhugra suggested that we revive the concept of the asylum as a place of refuge and safety: "The move of services to the community was the right thing," said Bhugra, "but we must not forget that there are always people who will need asylum."[13]

How many such psychiatric beds are needed? There has been remarkably little research on this question. In 2008, 15 psychiatric experts answered the question with a surprising consensus that about 50 (range 40–60) public psychiatric beds per 100,000 population was the minimum number needed, assuming at least adequate outpatient psychiatric services. This is approximately four times more beds than presently exist. The number will vary, of course, depending on the quality of outpatient services. What is clear, however, is that all public psychiatric hospitals cannot be completely abolished; a minimum number of beds, perhaps 40–60 per 100,000 population, are needed.[14]

---

1. Public psychiatric hospitals cannot be completely abolished. A minimum number of beds, perhaps 40 to 60 per 100,000 population, will be needed. This is approximately four times more beds than we have available today.

---

As seriously mentally ill patients were being discharged from public mental hospitals to live in communities, another major mistake was made. For most patients, antipsychotic medication had improved their symptoms. Thus, at the time these patients left the hospital, most were clinically much improved. However, antipsychotic medications help to control psychotic symptoms but do not cure the disease. Such medications are therefore similar to insulin, which controls the symptoms of diabetes but does not cure it. When the antipsychotic medications are stopped, the symptoms usually recur, and this is what happened to many discharged patients.

Why did patients stop taking their medications? Side effects of the medication are one reason. Lack of insurance coverage, lack of funds, cognitive confusion, and uncoordinated treatment are additional reasons. The most important reason, however, is that illnesses such as schizophrenia, bipolar disorder, and severe depression with psychotic features often affect the parts of the brain we use to think about ourselves, as previously discussed. Individuals with damage to these parts of the brain lose their awareness of illness and insight into their own needs. This is not a form of denial, which we all use, but rather the result of disease-related anatomical damage to specific brain areas. It is also seen in neurological patients who have strokes involving these particular brain areas and is prominent in patients with moderate or severe Alzheimer's disease, who usually have no awareness that anything is wrong. In neurology, this condition is referred to as anosognosia.[15]

As patients were being discharged from public mental hospitals, no allowance was made for the possibility that some of them would stop their medication. It was simply assumed that most patients would continue taking the medications that had improved their symptoms if they needed to do so. While in the hospital, the patients had no choice—medications were administered to them whether they wished to take them or not. Once out of the hospitals, however, the patients had a choice, and many chose not to take their medications. Why should they take them, they asked, as nothing was wrong with them? The mental health professionals who were the architects of deinstitutionalization made no allowance for this possibility.

The results have been completely predictable. At any given time, approximately half of all seriously mentally ill individuals in the United States are receiving no treatment. These are the individuals who end up living on the streets or in jails and prisons, being victimized, or perpetrating acts of violence related to their delusions, hallucinations, mania, and other untreated symptoms. Therefore, lack of awareness of illness (anosognosia) must be considered when planning any mental illness treatment system and provision made for some form of involuntary treatment, such as assisted outpatient treatment (AOT) or conditional release, for selected patients.

Studies of AOT and conditional release have reported that these approaches are very effective in maintaining seriously mentally ill individuals on medication. AOT does so by a court order that says the person must take medication as a condition for living outside the hospital. Conditional release is similar with the exception that the judicial authority is vested in the director of the psychiatric hospital. Multiple studies of AOT show that patients on AOT have a dramatic decrease in rehospitalization, victimization, and incarceration in jails and prisons. For example, one study of individuals before and after being placed on AOT reported that "the risk of any arrest was 2.66 times greater...and the risk of an arrest for a violent offense was 8.61 times greater...before AOT than it was while receiving AOT." A study in a small county in California reported that AOT reduced hospitalizations by 61% and incarcerations by 97% for those individuals on AOT; the savings to the county were $1.81 for every $1.00 spent on the program. Other studies have reported that AOT reduced homelessness from 19% to 5% and victimization from 42% to 24%.[16]

Especially impressive are studies showing the effectiveness of AOT and conditional release in reducing violent behavior among individuals with serious mental illnesses. A study in North Carolina reported that for mentally ill individuals with a history of violence, AOT reduced violent episodes from 42% to 27% when the AOT was continued for at least 6 months. In a study in New York, AOT reduced the proportion of mentally ill individuals who "physically harmed others" from 15% to 8%. In a study in New Hampshire, conditional release of mentally ill individuals reduced violent episodes by half.[17]

This raises the question of how many mentally ill individuals should be on some form of assisted treatment at any given time. Little research has been done on this questions other than estimates that approximately 10% of seriously mentally ill individuals are the most problematic (e.g., have repeated incarcerations, homelessness, repeated hospitalizations, etc.) and that 10% of those who are problematic, or 1%of the total, are a definite danger to themselves or to others. The National Institute of Mental Health estimates the total number of adults (ages 18 years and older) with severe mental illnesses (schizophrenia, severe bipolar disorder, and severe depression) in a year is 5.3% of the adult population, or about 12.3 million people. Multiplying that number by 1% gives us a total of approximately 123,000 seriously mentally ill adults who should be on some form of assisted treatment at any given time. Table 8.1 provides a breakdown of this number by state. These numbers include those who are receiving treatment in hospitals or other institutions (e.g., jails, prisons, nursing homes) at any given time. The numbers will also vary, of course, depending on the definition used for severe mental illness.[18]

Despite clear evidence of its effectiveness, AOT and conditional release are vastly underutilized. Six states—Massachusetts, Connecticut, Maryland, Tennessee, New Mexico, and Nevada—do not even have state laws permitting AOT, and most other states use it sparingly. Resistance to using any kind of involuntary treatment comes primarily from civil libertarians who appear oblivious to the fact that we routinely involuntarily confine and treat individuals with Alzheimer's disease who also suffer from anosognosia. Logical thinking, however, is not the guiding principle of America's mental health system, so we allow mentally ill individuals who are unaware of their illness to live on the streets or in jails rather than treating them, all in the name of protecting their civil rights. As our treatment system has developed over the last half-century, callousness apparently became confused with civil rights. The freedom to be insane is a cruel hoax, perpetrated on those who cannot think clearly by those who will not think clearly.

---

2. Lack of awareness of illness (anosognosia) must be considered when planning any mental illness treatment system and provision made for the implementation of some form of involuntary treatment, such as assisted outpatient treatment (AOT) or conditional release for approximately 1% of all individuals with severe mental illnesses who are living in our communities.

**Table 8.1** Number of Adults With Severe Mental Illness Who Should be on Assisted Treatment at any Given Time*

| State | Adult population (age 18 years and older) | Adults with severe mental illness who should be on assisted treatment |
|---|---|---|
| Alabama | 3,579,844 | 1,897 |
| Alaska | 514,927 | 273 |
| Arizona | 4,863,759 | 2,578 |
| Arkansas | 2,179,482 | 1,155 |
| California | 27,525,982 | 14,589 |
| Colorado | 3,796,985 | 2,012 |
| Connecticut | 2,710,303 | 1,436 |
| Delaware | 678,129 | 359 |
| District of Columbia | 485,621 | 257 |
| Florida | 14,480,196 | 7,675 |
| Georgia | 7,245,419 | 3,840 |
| Hawaii | 1,004,817 | 533 |
| Idaho | 1,126,611 | 597 |
| Illinois | 9,733,032 | 5,159 |
| Indiana | 4,833,748 | 2,562 |
| Iowa | 2,294,701 | 1,216 |
| Kansas | 2,113,796 | 1,120 |
| Kentucky | 3,299,790 | 1,749 |
| Louisiana | 3,368,690 | 1,785 |
| Maine | 1,047,125 | 555 |
| Maryland | 4,347,543 | 2,304 |
| Massachusetts | 5,160,585 | 2,735 |
| Michigan | 7,619,835 | 4,039 |
| Minnesota | 4,005,417 | 2,123 |
| Mississippi | 2,184,254 | 1,158 |
| Missouri | 4,556,242 | 2,415 |
| Montana | 755,161 | 400 |
| Nebraska | 1,344,978 | 713 |
| Nevada | 1,962,052 | 1,040 |
| New Hampshire | 1,035,504 | 549 |
| New Jersey | 6,661,891 | 3,531 |
| New Mexico | 1,499,433 | 795 |
| New York | 15,117,370 | 8,012 |
| North Carolina | 7,102,917 | 3,765 |

**Table 8.1** (*Continued*)

| State | Adult population (age 18 years and older) | Adults with severe mental illness who should be on assisted treatment |
|---|---|---|
| North Dakota | 502,873 | 267 |
| Ohio | 8,828,304 | 4,679 |
| Oklahoma | 2,768,201 | 1,467 |
| Oregon | 2,952,846 | 1,565 |
| Pennsylvania | 9,829,635 | 5,210 |
| Rhode Island | 826,384 | 438 |
| South Carolina | 3,480,510 | 1,845 |
| South Dakota | 612,767 | 325 |
| Tennessee | 4,803,002 | 2,546 |
| Texas | 17,886,333 | 9,480 |
| Utah | 1,915,748 | 1,015 |
| Vermont | 495,485 | 263 |
| Virginia | 6,035,408 | 3,199 |
| Washington | 5,094,603 | 2,700 |
| West Virginia | 1,433,328 | 760 |
| Wisconsin | 4,344,524 | 2,303 |
| Wyoming | 412,245 | 218 |
| TOTALS | 232,458,335 | 123,203 |

*According to the National Institute of Mental Health (NIMH), the number of adults with severe mental illness is 5.3% of the total adult population (age 18 years and older), or about 12.3 million individuals; this includes adults with schizophrenia, severe bipolar disorder, and severe depression. The number of adults who should be on assisted treatment is assumed to be 1% of the total number of adults with severe mental illness.

• *Misunderstanding Community Treatment*

A second fundamental error of deinstitutionalization was a misunderstanding of what is meant by "community treatment." As a universally used phrase, it is a tractable term and has been appropriated to cover a multitude of agendas. In its most elementary form, community treatment simply means having patients live anywhere but in the mental hospitals. It has been used this way by advocates who believe that mental hospitals are the ultimate iniquity. As one anti-hospital crusader phrased it, "When you have Buchenwald, you do not worry first about alternatives to Buchenwald." Many civil rights lawyers have adopted this belief; as one noted in 1974: "They [the patients] are better off outside the hospital with no care than they are inside with no care. The hospitals are what really do damage to people." Gorman also reflected this belief; when I asked him in the

1970s how he viewed the rapidly increasing numbers of mentally ill homeless persons, he replied: "No matter how bad it is for those people on the streets, it's better than it was in the hospital." Gorman even wrote a letter to the *New York Times* in 1984 suggesting that he "should be honored" for his role in emptying the state mental hospitals. Such thinking has been said to exhibit "a curious lack of regard for the fate of the individual."[19]

"Community treatment" has also been used by well-meaning social activists who viewed the community mental health center movement as a vehicle for treating social ills, as described in Chapter 4. Matthew Dumont, one of the NIMH psychiatrists who led this movement, looked back on it in a 1992 retrospective:

> The community mental health movement, which once stirred imagination and idealism like the civil rights movement, the War on Poverty, and eventually the peace and ecology movements, has become a dead leaf blown into a blind alley, its occasional rustle causing the merest sidelong glance from passersby busy with other things.

Dumont claimed that the movement failed not because of any conceptual flaw but merely because "the money ran out."[20]

Many observers have claimed that it was precisely this kind of thinking that led to the failure of deinstitutionalization in general and community treatment in particular. Community treatment became a catchword, a seductive call-to-arms for all true believers of the new program. And the emphasis was on *new*—shifting the treatment of literally hundreds of thousands of people from mental hospitals to the community had never been done before. The appeal of this newness was evident in Robert Felix's reflections on the community mental health centers when he was interviewed in 1972; he said the program had great "sex appeal" and repeatedly characterized it as "creative," "daring," "innovative," and "exciting." Frank Ochberg, an NIMH psychiatrist, similarly recalled the new program as "dazzling." Anthony Panzetta, one of the earliest and most thoughtful enthusiasts for community treatment, also noted this appeal:

> One of the sacred words in the new psychiatry is innovation. It is a cleansing word because it suggests an out with the old and in with the new mentality. It is fresh, creative, experimental, free and good....It is optimistic, egalitarian, and benevolent. In a word, it is sacred.

By 1975, however, some mental health professionals were beginning to question whether community treatment was more than a current fashion. In an article titled "Community Mental Health: A Noble Failure?" the authors observed: "The mental health profession, like American society in general, has little immunity to infatuation with fad."[21]

The misunderstanding of community treatment actually goes back to the origins of the National Institute of Mental Health. The original name of the institute was to have been the National Neuropsychiatric Institute, but early in 1946, when passage of its founding legislation was assured, Felix and his colleagues had the name changed to the National Institute of Mental Health. The change altered its essential function, from focusing on mental illnesses—diseases of the brain—to focusing on social problems thought to be relevant for mental health. Focusing on social problems inevitably led NIMH and its community mental health centers into political issues. Claudewell Thomas, an NIMH psychiatrist who directed the community mental health centers program in the 1970s, said in an interview that the sociopolitical focus of NIMH and the centers ultimately led to the demise of the centers program: "The political issue became manifest...and Republicans killed the program." In retrospect, it is clear that the change in emphasis in community treatment from mental illness to mental health was a fatal flaw.[22]

3. Community treatment of mentally ill individuals will only be successful if carried out by community mental *illness* centers, not in community mental *health* centers. The change of one word is crucial to the success of any such program. Mental illness centers may be freestanding or integrated as part of medical centers.

Another important lesson that has been learned about community treatment during the past half-century of deinstitutionalization is that continuity of care, especially the continuity of caregivers, is very important. People with normally functioning brains find it difficult to get good medical and psychiatric care when that care is provided in constantly shifting venues with constantly shifting caregivers. For people whose brains are not functioning normally, such changes are extremely difficult and usually lead to treatment failure.

The importance of continuity of care and caregivers for individuals with serious mental illnesses has long been recognized. As early as 1964 Jack Ewalt, the director of the Joint Commission on Mental Illness and Health, noted:

At the Massachusetts Mental Health Center we have found that we can greatly reduce the relapse rate by providing continuity of care.... We do not allow patients to be transferred among wards or services—the only way he can lose his doctor is if the doctor dies or goes elsewhere.

This principle was operationalized in the early 1970s by Leonard Stein and Mary Ann Test in Madison, Wisconsin, when they established the first Assertive Community Treatment

(ACT) team for patients being discharged from the state hospital. ACT teams consist of 100 to 120 patients assigned to a team of approximately 10 mental health workers, usually including a psychiatrist, psychologist, psychiatric nurses, social workers, and others. The team takes total responsibility for the patients, visiting them in their board-and-care homes or wherever they are living, making sure they continue taking their medications, and responding to crises before they lead to rehospitalizations. If patients have to be hospitalized, then team members visit the hospital. If the patients end up in jail, then team members visit the jail. Team members have a regular night and weekend call schedule, so someone is always available 24 hours a day, 365 days a year, for the patients assigned to that team. The patients thus get to know their ACT team members just as the ACT team gets to know the patients and their families. The clinical, housing, vocational, and social needs of the patients are all coordinated by the ACT team. As Mary Ann Test described it:

> The team members do not necessarily meet all the client's needs themselves (they may involve other persons or agencies). However they never transfer this obligation to someone else. The buck stops with the team.... The team remains responsible for the client no matter what his or her behavior is.[23]

ACT teams have been extensively studied over the years and have been reported to dramatically reduce rehospitalizations and the amount of time ACT patients spend in jail. They also increase the vocational success of the patients, and both patients and families have expressed great satisfaction with the ACT model. Much of the success of ACT teams comes from maintaining patients on their medication, and they do this, according to one summary, by using "access to resources such as housing and money as leverage to promote patients' adherence to treatment recommendations."[24]

Because they have been proven to be highly effective, ACT teams have been adopted in 38 states as the best model for treating people with serious mental illnesses. One study estimated that 50% of individuals with serious mental illnesses would be helped by ACT teams, as such teams are useful for individuals who do not take their medications regularly or have trouble accessing the available treatment and rehabilitation services. Because NIMH estimates that approximately 12.3 million adults have schizophrenia, severe bipolar disorder, or severe depression in a given year, that means that 6.1 million of them would benefit by ACT teams. According to a 2011 estimate, "about 60,000 persons nationwide...were being served by ACT" teams; this is about 1% of those who need it. The reason ACT teams are not used more widely 40 years after being introduced is the system of funding mental health services, as described in the next section. ACT teams do not fit well with the traditional categories of funding created for Medicare reimbursement, and because they produce less federal Medicaid revenue for the states, they are markedly underutilized.[25]

Most patients, therefore, continue to receive uncoordinated and disjointed mental illness services. They are randomly rehospitalized in whatever hospital happens to have a bed available despite the fact that the staff of that hospital may have little or no information regarding that patient's extensive and complicated medical and psychiatric history. The patients experience a high turnover of underpaid workers in their psychiatric clinics, board-and-care homes, and nursing homes. The annual staff turnover in some nursing homes, for example, is 75%. Five different psychiatrists may oversee a patient's medication on successive visits to an outpatient clinic. In 1982 Susan Sheehan created a stir when she published a book about a woman with schizophrenia who, over an 18-year period, experienced 27 separate admissions to 8 different hospitals and a total of 45 different treatment settings. Such discontinuous treatment, regarded as aberrant in 1982, is now regarded as the norm.[26]

---

4. Continuity of care, especially continuity of caregivers, is essential for good psychiatric care of individuals with serious mental illnesses.

---

Just as we have learned that continuity of care and caregivers is important, so too we have learned that medication alone is a necessary, but not sufficient, treatment for most individuals with serious mental illnesses. They also need access to decent housing, vocational opportunities, and opportunities for socialization. The best model that combines all three is the clubhouse model, based on Fountain House in New York City, which was started by six patients being discharged from a state hospital in 1948.

Clubhouses are just what they sound like—houses where mentally ill people come to hang out. A true clubhouse is open 7 days a week from morning until late evening. People do not sleep there, but most clubhouses have an associated housing program where many of the members do live. Clubhouses also have vocational programs with job training and job placement opportunities. Within the clubhouse, the members share the tasks of cooking lunch, answering phones, and keeping the clubhouse running.

Clubhouses have been widely praised for more than half a century. Studies have shown that they markedly decrease hospitalizations and incarcerations and lead to employment for many members. They are also cost-effective. Despite this apparent success, clubhouses have spread slowly across the United States. Sixty years after they began, there are still only about 200 of them, and only some of these incorporate the full clubhouse model. A few are outstanding, such as Fountain House in New York, Genesis Club in Worcester, Thresholds in Chicago, Grand Avenue Club in Milwaukee, Independence House in St. Louis, Alliance House in Salt Lake City, and Gateway House in Greenville, South Carolina. However, clubhouses provide services for, at most, 1% of those seriously mentally ill individuals who could potentially benefit from them.[27]

The major reason clubhouses have not spread more widely is the same reason ACT teams have not proliferated—the disjointed funding system. Medicaid and other federal and state funding sources are rigidly set up to support specific activities such as housing or case management, not to cover a clubhouse that is doing many useful activities simultaneously. It is thus very difficult to fund clubhouses, and as Medicaid regulations become tighter it is becoming more difficult. This became clear in 2010 when the Green Door, an excellent clubhouse that had served mentally ill individuals in the nation's capital for 30 years, was forced to close because of funding cuts. Sixty years after clubhouses began, there should be 2,000 of them, not 200, and states should be opening additional ones, not closing them down.[28]

---

5. In addition to medication, individuals with serious mental illnesses need access to decent housing, vocational opportunities, and opportunities for socialization. The clubhouse is the best model for meeting those needs.

---

The majority of seriously mentally ill individuals live in nursing homes and board-and-care homes. Some of these homes are managed by owners who provide residents with decent and humane living conditions. Many others, however, are managed by owners whose primary interest is in increasing profits, with consequent abysmal living conditions and victimization of residents, as described in previous chapters. This occurs because in most states there is little oversight of these homes; the state departments of mental health do not want to know about problems, because they would then have to close substandard facilities and find alternative living arrangements for the residents. The first rule of government is to not ask questions to which you do not want to know the answers.

Leaving nursing homes and board-and-care homes without adequate oversight has been a tragic mistake. These homes fall into the category of what are known as total institutions, which also include jails, prisons, mental hospitals, institutions for individuals with mental retardation, and orphanages. In such facilities, the staff has virtually complete power and authority over a captive and often vulnerable population. What usually happens in such total institutions was described by Philip Zimbardo in his well-known 1971 experiment with Stanford University students in which he had some students pretend to be prisoners and other students pretend to be prison guards. To the surprise of everyone, including Zimbardo, the pretend prison guards immediately began to devalue, depersonalize, dehumanize, and mistreat the pretend prisoners. Zimbardo summarized what is known about the phenomenon of total institutions in his book *The Lucifer*

*Effect: Understanding How Good People Turn Evil.* "Dehumanization," he noted, "is one of the central processes in the transformation of ordinary, normal people into indifferent or even wanton perpetrators of evil. Dehumanization is like a cortical cataract that clouds one's thinking and fosters the perception that other people are less than human."[29]

The most effective way to counteract the natural tendency for staff to dehumanize mentally ill residents in total institutions such as nursing homes and board-and-care homes is through aggressive oversight and inspections. Such inspections are only effective if they are random and unannounced. Staff should be aware that inspectors may enter their facility at any time, day or night, and hold the staff accountable for conditions there. The original model for such oversight was the Lunacy Commission that operated in England from 1845 to 1890. Commissioners, including physicians, lawyers, and lay persons, carried out unannounced inspections of all public and private mental hospitals and had the authority to order the immediate closure of a facility.[30]

In the United States, almost no unannounced inspections of nursing homes or board-and-care homes take place. The few inspections that do occur are announced well before the event, giving owners of the facility time to clean up everything. One of the few systems of unannounced inspections was implemented in 1977 in New York State as the Commission on Quality of Care for the Mentally Disabled. For two decades, members of this commission carried out unannounced inspections, publicly releasing reports resulting in headlines such as "Adult Home Abuse Found," "Report Says Home Operators Misused Funds Meant to Feed Mentally Ill," and "For Adult Homes This One Ranks among the Worst." The commission reported directly to the governor, not to the state Office of Mental Health, thus shielding it in part from the agency that was not interested in finding anything wrong.[31]

New York's brief experiment with effective oversight and unannounced inspections was terminated by Governor George Pataki when he took office in 1995. Not coincidentally, nursing home and board-and-care home operators had been major contributors to the Pataki campaign. New York thus became like most states in preferring to hear no evil and see no evil in its nursing homes and board-and-care homes. Probably more typical than New York State is Pennsylvania, which, according to Andrew Scull, "repealed its provisions for inspecting boarding homes the same year (1967) it began 'a massive deinstitutionalization program aimed at moving patients out of mental hospitals into community programs.'" The absence of such oversight virtually guaranteed that residents of those homes would be abused and victimized, and this is what has happened. [32]

---

6. To protect vulnerable mentally ill individuals living in nursing homes and board-and-care homes, there must be periodic, unannounced inspections by an independent state agency. Evaluations and corrective actions must be made public.

• *Federal Financing of Mental Health Care*

The third fundamental error of deinstitutionalization was in many ways the most egregious. For more than a century, mental health services had been the fiscal responsibility of state governments except in a few states, such as Iowa and Wisconsin, where some of the responsibility was assigned to the counties. The state department of mental health, the governor, and the legislature were ultimately responsible, and when things went wrong, as they sometimes did, they could be held accountable.

In 1963, with the passage of the community mental health centers legislation, the federal government assumed a significant role in funding mental health services for the first time in American history. With the subsequent passage of Medicare, Medicaid, SSI, and amendments to SSDI, the federal government effectively assumed responsibility for the majority of mental health funding, even if this development was mostly unplanned and unintended. In fact, the most striking aspect of the history of this massive shift in fiscal responsibility from the states to the federal government is the lack of any planning.

What has emerged is a chaotic system for funding mental health services, a system that is more thought-disordered than most of the seriously mentally ill persons it is intended to serve. As early as 1978, it was observed that "eleven major Federal departments and agencies share the task of administering 135 programs for the mentally disabled," and it has grown even worse over the years. The bewildering complexity of the system defies logical thought processes. Directors of mental health services for cities, counties, and states must be equal parts accountant, corporate executive, and mental health professional to understand what services to charge to which funding source. Providing clinical services is the easy part of such jobs compared to figuring out how to pay for the services. [33]

Out of a half-century of chaotic funding, several lessons have emerged that should be incorporated into any system of future funding. One such lesson is that turning mental illness services over to for-profit providers does not work. Some fiscal conservatives have argued that the profit motive makes human services more efficient and have thus recommended the privatization of mental health services to for-profit companies. What such people fail to note is that this has largely already been tried and failed. Some of the original community mental health center grants were given to private, for-profit entities. As psychiatrist Alan Stone observed, this development produced "a series of self-interested grabs by our colleagues to build fancy offices to pursue private patients [and] to avoid the seriously mentally ill and to exploit the federal monies." Then, in the 1970s and 1980s, for-profit corporations opened nursing homes and board-and-care homes to provide accommodations—and usually not much else—for seriously mentally ill individuals being discharged from state hospitals. [34]

The results, as detailed in preceding chapters, have been scandalous. Rather than being the wave of the future, the for-profit privatization of mental illness services has been a present-day tsunami. Anyone who doubts this need only visit North Carolina. In 2003 the state decided to privatize their entire state mental health system, which a decade earlier had been comparatively highly regarded. The results have included the closure of almost all public psychiatric beds; jails and prisons filled with mentally ill prisoners; an increase in mentally ill homeless persons; emergency rooms overflowing with mentally ill individuals waiting for nonexistent beds; board-and-care homes with thousands of largely untreated patients; and a predictable series of homicides and other tragedies attributed to individuals with untreated severe mental illnesses. Since 2003, no state has more aggressively privatized its mental health services than North Carolina, and no state has had its services deteriorate more dramatically.[35]

A more recent example is Pierce County, Washington, which in 2009 contracted for public mental health services with a for-profit company, OptumHealth. The outcome has been a massive overcrowding of the county jail with seriously mentally ill individuals, a 30% increase in mental illness-related calls to the county Fire and Rescue, and an increase in violent episodes, such as the shooting of three shoppers in August 2012 by Laura Sorensen, who was suffering from inadequately treated paranoid schizophrenia. One should never underestimate the ability of the for-profit sector to take responsibility for easy-to-treat patients and discard those who are difficult to treat, and thus more expensive, to the streets, jails, and prisons.

Scull has astutely pointed out that the for-profit privatization of mental health services currently underway in the United States is a repeat of what happened in England and, to a lesser extent in this country, during the early nineteenth century. At that time, local towns and counties turned mentally ill persons over to the highest bidders, usually private madhouses, for safe-keeping:

> In an age that saw the triumph of laissez-faire capitalism, the insane enjoyed the dubious privilege of being among the first souls (other than slaves) to have their fate heavily determined by the marketplace. The experiment was not, on the whole, adjudged a success—save perhaps by the madhouse keepers themselves, whose business was often lucrative. Indeed, it was precisely the abuses to which a profit-oriented system was prone that led to a campaign for "reform" and to the establishment of those very state asylums against which the decarceration movement is now directed.

We have thus come full circle, having emptied the asylums, which were built to reform the abuses of the for-profit system, and are again turning mentally ill persons over to the highest bidders. As Aldous Huxley noted, "That men do not learn very much from the lessons of history is the most important of all the lessons that history has to teach."[36]

> 7. For-profit funding of public mental illness services has been tried and does not work.

Another lesson that has emerged from a half-century of disjointed funding of mental health services is that it is essential to prioritize the patients for such services. As previously noted, studies have consistently shown that a relatively small subset of seriously mentally ill individuals are the ones who are repeatedly rehospitalized, become homeless, are regularly victimized, and end up in jails and prisons. One estimate of this subset is that approximately 10% of all seriously mentally ill individuals account for most of these problems. If services were to be prioritized for the 10% subset of individuals who are problematic, then most of the tragic consequences resulting from non-treatment would be avoided.[37]

Recent studies support the necessity for such prioritization. In Philadelphia 2,703 individuals were identified who were chronically homeless. Researchers calculated the cost of their medical, psychiatric, social services, public shelter, and jail costs for a year and reported that 20% of them accounted for 60% of the total group costs. Among the 20% of high users, almost all (81%) had schizophrenia or a major affective disorder. This finding is consistent with anecdotal reports from many parts of the country. The most highly publicized such report was about Murray Barr, a "chronically homeless mentally ill man" in Reno, Nevada, who in the 10 years before he died in 2005 "cost the county at least $1 million," including "at least $100,000 in emergency room fees in 6 months in one Reno hospital." Murray Barr became well known because he was portrayed in a profile, "Million-Dollar Murray," in the *New Yorker*, but in fact every urban area in the United States has several untreated, severely mentally ill, and very expensive Murray Barrs. Providing adequate psychiatric treatment to just this small group of individuals would produce enormous savings.[38]

Medicare and Medicaid data also suggest that a small number of seriously mentally ill individuals account for a strongly disproportionate share of the total costs. A study of Medicare patients who were rehospitalized within 30 days following hospital discharge reported that patients with psychoses (schizophrenia and bipolar disorder) had the second-highest rate of rehospitalization costs, behind only individuals with cardiac problems. Similarly, a study of Medicaid costs reported that "nearly 60 percent of Medicaid spending is incurred by just 5 percent of the program's beneficiaries" and that "mental illness is nearly universal among the highest-cost, most frequently hospitalized beneficiaries." Another study of Medicaid costs for individuals with one of nine different chronic diseases reported that individuals with psychoses were the most expensive, more than three times more expensive than those with diabetes or hypertension. In still another study of individuals with schizophrenia covered by Medicaid, it was estimated that the failure of these individuals to take antipsychotic medication cost Medicaid $1.5 billion in one year.[39]

It is clear, therefore, that prioritizing services for a small subset of seriously mentally ill individuals is not only humane and in the best interests of the individual but also economical and in the best interests of society. Indeed, even the 1961 report of the Joint Commission on Mental Illness and Health recommended that individuals with "major mental illnesses...should have first call" on available psychiatric services. Despite what would seem to be common sense, the prioritization of the sickest and most problematic psychiatric patients has been tried only occasionally in the United States and never with much conviction. The most ambitious attempt was in Oregon in the 1990s, when a panel of experts, appointed by the governor, prioritized by diagnoses the psychiatric services to be covered by Medicaid. When the plan reached the state legislature, however, it was promptly disemboweled by "local political wrangling" and by advocacy groups that complained, for example, that post-traumatic stress disorder was just as important as schizophrenia. Despite the support of the governor, who was a physician, political will in the state legislature was lacking.[40]

> 8. Services for mentally ill persons must be prioritized to ensure that those who are sickest, pose the greatest risk to themselves and others, and incur the greatest cost receive services as the first priority.

Another problem associated with the prioritization of patients is access to information. Very commonly, police and sheriffs, who are now the frontline mental health workers, are asked to assess mentally ill people but have no access to the person's history. As early as 1990, in an article titled "What Do Police Officers Really Want from the Mental Health System?," police officers "indicated that they most needed access to information about an individual's past history of violence or suicide attempts." Many of the sickest and most dangerous mentally ill persons travel from state to state, but critical clinical and legal information usually does not cross state lines. For example, Henry Lee Brown, with untreated schizophrenia, drifted between Mississippi, Georgia, South Carolina, Ohio, Texas, and California, "living in homeless shelters and serving jail time in mental hospitals for bizarre crimes that were increasingly violent" for 20 years before he was killed by police.[41]

The problem, of course, is confidentiality laws that prohibit the disclosure of psychiatric information. Such laws have become increasingly stringent during the same years in which untreated mentally ill individuals have increasingly flooded the community. The privacy laws have been used by mental health agencies to protect themselves when things go wrong, as they increasingly do. As one observer noted: "One of the problems in this entire realm is that of state/private agencies constantly taking the Fifth Amendment against self-incrimination by hauling out 'patient confidentiality' to say nothing at all." It is not the patient who is usually being protected but, rather, the agency.[42]

There are indications that our obsession with psychiatric privacy and confidentiality may be ameliorating somewhat, as we weigh the needs of individuals against those of society at large. In May 2011, the governor of Kansas signed a bill "that allows police to get more information on a suspect's mental health.... The new law is intended to give police the information they need to take mentally ill offenders someplace where they can be treated rather than to jail." That same month in Albuquerque, the chief of police announced that "the department is working towards building a database to catalogue where mentally ill people live ... based on information voluntarily provided by family members." This announcement followed yet another fatal encounter between a mentally ill man and a policeman. States have supported sex offender registries, available to the public, for many years and are now in the process of introducing public registries for first-degree murderers and drunken drivers. Given this trend toward making more information about potentially dangerous individuals more publicly available, the Kansas law is likely to be replicated in other states.[43]

---

9. In selected cases, psychiatric information on mentally ill individuals who have a history of dangerousness should be made available to law enforcement personnel, because they are now the frontline mental health workers.

---

The final lesson that has been learned from the past half-century of amorphous and anarchic public psychiatric services is the most important—somebody must be held ultimately accountable. Until the passage of the 1963 legislation creating the federally funded community mental health centers, states had for over a century been ultimately responsible for mental health services. Responsibility was clearly assigned, and if things went wrong, people knew in which direction to point.

All that changed after 1963, when federal officials began funding local mental health agencies directly, without going through the states. The clear message was that states were no longer responsible, which was fine with them. The states proceeded to empty their state hospitals and shift the fiscal burden to the new Medicaid and other federal programs. The states thus rapidly proved the veracity of John Talbott's warning in his 1978 book *The Death of the Asylum*: "Society will shuck off responsibility both for the state hospital system and the chronically mentally ill if given half a chance."[44]

The withdrawal of state responsibility for mental health services created a vacuum in accountability that continues to exist today. NIMH officials were happy to give away federal funds but had little ability and even less interest in monitoring how the funds were spent. Realistically, there was little capacity at the federal level to oversee the expenditure of federal funds in centers that were geographically spread from southern Florida to northern Alaska, which is why so many of the funds were so poorly spent. For human services in general, the federal government is too distant to oversee a country of 308 million people.

At the local level, city and county governments had no interest in assuming responsibility for mental health services that had traditionally been a state responsibility. The only exception to this was the few states, such as Iowa and Wisconsin, in which some responsibility for mental health services had traditionally been assigned to the counties. Thus, throughout the United States, beginning in 1963, mental health financing and services developed in a totally unplanned, random way because nobody was in charge and nobody was responsible. Money for the services arrived—and still arrives—under various federal programs such as Medicare, Medicaid, SSI, and SSDI but with neither coordination nor accountability. The tragic consequences are everywhere visible.

It is apparent, then, that the first—and most important—thing that must be done before mental illness services can be improved is to fix responsibility for the services at a specific level of government. The optimum level of government for such responsibility is to be determined. Clearly, such responsibility should not be lodged at the federal level, given the federal failure of the past half-century. Assigning the responsibility to states would seem logical, given that they had such responsibility for over a century. For small and medium-sized states, this may be the optimal level. Large states such as California, Texas, New York, Florida, and Pennsylvania may be too large and populous to administer at the state level, and such states may wish to devolve responsibility to counties or blocks of counties. Even some counties may be too large, however. For example, Los Angeles County has 9.8 million people, more than the population of the 10 smallest states combined, with a million people left over. Administering human services for 9.8 million people in such a county has nothing in common with, for example, Garfield County in Montana, which has 1,184 people in an area approximately the same size as Los Angeles County. Thus, there should be great flexibility among regions in how such programs are administered and how responsibility is assigned. The one absolute given is that responsibility *must* be assigned.

---

10. The single biggest problem with the present anarchic system of mental illness services is that nobody is accountable. It will be necessary to assign responsibility to a single level of government, and to then hold such individuals accountable, before any improvement can occur.

# HOW SHOULD MENTAL ILLNESS SERVICES
# BE ORGANIZED AND FUNDED?

How should mental illness services be organized and funded? The short answer to this question is that we do not know. The history of the last half-century has illuminated many organizational and funding mechanisms that do *not* work. For example, such services should not be organized as mental *health* services and should not be delivered by for-profit organizations. But beyond such lessons, we have learned very little regarding the best way to organize and fund such services. To find out, we should allow states and counties to experiment with different systems and then carefully assess the outcomes.

Those who are knowledgeable about the organization and funding of mental illness services in European countries often invoke them as models. To be sure, almost every European country does a better job of providing care for mentally ill individuals than does the United States. Services in countries such as Sweden and the Netherlands are significantly superior to anything that can be found in this country, but they cannot be easily imported. The organization and funding of mental illness services in countries such as Sweden and the Netherlands are intimately tied to their broader organization and funding of medical services, and this is fundamentally different from the American system. It should also be remembered that countries like Sweden and the Netherlands are much smaller and more homogeneous than the large and diverse United States. Sweden has approximately the same population as the state of Georgia, and the Netherlands has a population less than that of Florida. We can learn from the successes of these countries, but we cannot simply import their models. We have to start with what we have and ask how it can be made into a functioning mental illness services system.

Although it was never planned as such, Medicaid is the fiscal giant that dominates the funding of mental health and mental illness services. As a federal program with state-matching funds, it mandates core services that must be provided by the states and allows states to use Medicaid funds to provide additional services if they choose to do so. The share of total mental health and mental illness spending covered by Medicaid has increased from 17% in 1986 to 28% in 2005 to more than 30% today. This includes inpatient care in general hospitals, nursing homes, outpatient psychiatric and medical care, and prescription drug costs. For individuals with a diagnosis of schizophrenia, Medicaid and Medicare paid for the care of 19% of these individuals in 1977, 63% in 1996, and perhaps 90% today. The state-matching costs for Medicaid are the second largest item in most states' budgets, behind only education.[45]

The Medicaid program as currently constructed is the single largest fiscal impediment to improving services for mentally ill persons in the United States. Services at the state and local level are organized exclusively to maximize Medicaid reimbursement by the federal government, with little regard for organizational efficiency or what patients actually need. Medicaid officials in Washington have tried various strategies to control federal costs, but in every instance states have found ways to defeat these efforts. A classic example is the institution for mental disease (IMD) exclusion, by which Medicaid refuses to pay for inpatient costs in state mental hospitals. The states responded by simply emptying the state hospitals and shifting inpatient admissions to the psychiatric units of general hospitals, which are covered by Medicaid. The fact that the state hospitals already had the patients' records and were much better set up to provide care for seriously mentally ill individuals was not considered. Medicaid reimbursement, not patient needs, has been the driving force behind the organization of public psychiatric services for four decades.

States have also utilized various organizational schemes in attempts to control state Medicaid costs. At least 34 states deliver "some or all mental health services through managed care arrangements, including both carve outs and comprehensive MCOs [managed care organizations]." States such as California, Utah, Colorado, Pennsylvania, New York, and Massachusetts have used capitation funding, under which providers are paid a fixed amount to deliver all necessary services.[46]

Such funding programs have three things in common. First, the bottom line for these programs is cost savings, not patient care. Almost none of these programs make any attempt to assess quality of care or patient outcomes. Second, the sickest mentally ill patients are the ones who suffer most under such funding programs. The reason is that individuals with mental illnesses constitute only 11% of all Medicaid beneficiaries, but this 11% accounts for one-third of all high-cost beneficiaries. As described in previous chapters, seriously mentally ill individuals incur high expenses as they migrate from program to program in the present disjointed care system. When funding programs want to save Medicaid money, therefore, denying services to seriously mentally ill individuals is the easiest way to do so. Such individuals are unlikely to complain, they do not have an effective lobby of family members to advocate on their behalf, and they often end up in public shelters or jails, where they are out of sight.[47]

The third thing these funding organizations for Medicaid patients have in common is that they are very profitable. Most managed care companies are part of the highly profitable health insurance industry. For example, United Behavioral Health, part of the United Health Group company, had revenues of approximately $92 billion in 2010. United Behavioral Health claims to "oversee behavioral health services for more than 23 million beneficiaries," including Medicaid patients in California and other states. Its CEO for 17 years was Saul Feldman, a psychologist who began his career working in the NIMH Community Mental Health Centers program. In 2001 the *San Francisco Chronicle* described Feldman as being among the "super-rich" and "ultra-wealthy…living in luxury above it all" in a penthouse atop the Four Season Hotel; such penthouses rent for approximately $8,000 per day and sell for up to $14.5 million. Many other managed care executives have done equally well from the profits accrued from administering programs for mentally ill individuals. The people who have not done well, as described in this book, are the mentally ill themselves, and there is a direct cause-and-effect relationship between these two disparate outcomes.[48]

The Patient Protection and Affordable Care Act (ACA), widely referred to as Obamacare, is scheduled to take effect in 2014 but is unlikely to improve care for most mentally ill individuals. Although it expands Medicaid eligibility by an estimated 16 million people and increases Medicaid benefits, it will put more pressure on states to control costs by denying services. Thus, it is likely to lead to managed care companies finding new and creative ways to not provide services to the mentally ill individuals who need the services most. The most promising parts of the ACA are the demonstration projects being set up in some states to, for example, abolish the Institutions for Mental Disease (IMD) Medicaid exclusion on an experimental basis and to make more coherent the funding for individuals who are eligible for both Medicaid and Medicare. If these demonstration projects are carefully monitored and assessed, then they could provide very useful data.

## ALTERNATIVE FUNDING STRATEGIES

Fifty years have passed since President Kennedy planted the seeds of the community mental health centers movement, a massive federal experiment in the organization and delivery of services for mentally ill persons. The experiment destroyed the existing state system and failed tragically, as has been detailed in the preceding chapters. At this time, we appear to be stuck with the resulting dysfunctional system, making modifications to Medicaid reimbursement that improve the fiscal bottom line for managed care organizations but do not improve services for mentally ill individuals. All attempts to improve services over the past three decades have essentially been tinkerings with the status quo.

If we have any hope of improving such services, then we need to think much more broadly and creatively. We know that our present system is failing, but we do not know what system would work better. Therefore, we should be willing to take risks and think outside the traditional Medicaid box. In doing so, it is essential to measure the results of our trials and objectively assess the results. A research component must therefore be included in each mental illness services experiment, a component that has been largely missing from past attempts to change the system.

What should be measured? Many methods for assessing treatment outcomes for mentally ill persons have been proposed but infrequently used. They include subjective and objective measures of the effect of the services on patients, such as quality-of-life scales and severity of symptoms. They also include measures of the effects on the community, such as the rehospitalization, homelessness, and incarceration rates. A substantial literature describing such measures and rating systems exists but is rarely used. Such measures should be included in all experiments in mental illness services, with data collected before the experiment begins and again after it is underway.[49]

What kind of trials might take place? One such experiment would involve block granting all federal Medicaid funds to two or three small states or large counties without any federal strings attached. Baseline measures would be collected before the program began, then periodically for perhaps 5 years. By the end of that time, it should become clear whether states and counties can deliver more effective and economic mental illness services without federal guidelines.

Another experiment might involve completely abolishing the state or county department of mental health and giving all Medicaid and other mental illness-related funds to the state or county department of corrections. Because the police and sheriffs have de facto become the frontline mental health workers and the jails have become the primary psychiatric inpatient units, why not let corrections take complete responsibility, along with the funds, and measure the outcome? What would most likely happen is that corrections personnel would focus resources on the most severely mentally ill patients, which would almost certainly be an improvement over the present system.

Still another experiment might involve altering the rules on the use of SSI and SSDI payments. Currently, these payments are given to disabled mentally ill individuals automatically, regardless of whether these individuals are participating in treatment programs. For selected mentally ill individuals who are aware of their illness and need for treatment, it would be a useful experiment to tie such payments, or part of such payments, to the patients' active participation in treatment programs. This would guarantee that more patients would continue to take the medication needed to keep them well, thereby decreasing rehospitalization, homelessness, incarceration, victimization, and violence. Such outcomes would be comparatively easy to measure. Making selected mentally ill individuals more personally responsible for the outcome of their illness is similar to proposals put forth in some states to make nonmentally ill individuals more personally responsible for the outcome of their illness, such as charging higher copayments to people who smoke or are grossly overweight.

These are merely examples of many possible experiments that could be carried out with careful outcome measures. Innovation would be encouraged. All such experiments would be done on relatively small populations—small states or large counties—on a time-limited basis, so that outcomes could be accurately assessed. Such experiments should never be instituted on a national basis, as the community mental health centers program was. It may well be that, in the long run, some states may opt for one kind of mental illness program whereas other states opt for another kind, which would be consistent with the diversity of our country and population.

What would be the role of the federal government in such experiments? The overall organization of experiments could be assigned to the NIMH or to the Institute of Medicine, with assessments contracted to universities or private groups such as the RAND Corporation. Beyond such tasks, the federal government should probably play little role.

* * *

So here we are, 50 years after the dream of Robert Felix crossed paths with the needs of the Kennedys to assuage their family guilt. In retrospect, it was a fateful encounter. At that time, the total funds being spent on mental health services in the United States was approximately $1.0 billion, which would be $7.6 billion today. As noted in Chapter 7, we are now spending approximately $140 billion on mental health services. Even allowing for the increase in population in the intervening years, we are now spending approximately 12 times more on mental health services than we were at that time. What we are purchasing with those funds is a disgrace.[50]

For the majority of people with serious mental illnesses, the situation is little better today than it was in 1947, when Frank Wright, in *Out of Sight, Out of Mind*, noted:

Throughout history the problem of the mentally ill has been dodged. We have continually avoided mental patients—we have segregated them, ostracized them, turned our backs on them, tried to forget them. We have allowed intolerable conditions to exist for the mentally ill through our ignorance and indifference. We can no longer afford to disregard their needs, to turn a deaf ear to their call for help. We must come face to face with the facts.

Isn't it time to finally do so?[51]

# NOTES

## Preface

1. T. Vargas, "Disabled Man Found in Filth, Jury in Neglect Case Is Told," *Washington Post*, March 13, 2007.
2. President Kennedy's message on Mental Illness and Mental Retardation, February 5, 1963, in Henry A. Foley and Steven S. Sharfstein, *Madness and Government: Who Cares for the Mentally Ill?* (Washington, DC: American Psychiatric Press, 1983), 165.

## Chapter 1

1. Michael R. Beschloss, *Kennedy and Roosevelt: An Uneasy Alliance* (New York: W. W. Norton, 1980), 190.
2. Ibid., 164, 189.
3. Doris Kearns Goodwin, *The Fitzgeralds and the Kennedys: An American Saga* (New York: St. Martin's Press, 1987), 688–689; Peter Collier and David Horowitz, *The Kennedys: An American Drama* (New York: Warner Books, 1984), 117.
4. Goodwin, *The Fitzgeralds and the Kennedys*, 689.
5. Alfred W. Crosby, *America's Forgotten Pandemic: The Influenza of 1918* (Cambridge: Cambridge University Press, 1989), 39–40; K. A. Menninger, "Psychoses Associated with Influenza, I: General Data: Statistical Analysis," *Journal of the American Medical Association 72*, no. 4 (1919): 235–241; K. A. Menninger, "Psychoses Associated with Influenza, II. Specific Data, An Expository Analysis," *Archives of Neurology and Psychiatry 2*, no. 3 (1919): 291–337; K. A. Menninger, "Melancholy and Melancholia," *Journal of the Kansas Medical Society 21* (1921): 44–50; K. A. Menninger, "Reversible Schizophrenia: A Study of the Implications of Delirium Schizophrenoides and Other Post-influenzal Syndromes," *American Journal of Psychiatry 78*, no. 4 (1922): 573–588; K. A. Menninger, "Influenza and Schizophrenia: An Analysis of Post-influenzal 'Dementia Praecox,' as of 1918, and Five Years Later: Further Studies of the Psychiatric Aspects of Influenza," *American Journal of Psychiatry 5*, no. 4 (1926): 469–529.
6. Crosby, *America's Forgotten Pandemic*, 20; N. Takei et al., "Prenatal Exposure to Influenza Epidemics and Risk of Mental Retardation," *European Archives of Psychiatry and Clinical Neuroscience 245*, no. 4–5 (1995): 255–259; W. Erikson, J. M. Sundet, and K. Tambs, "Register Data Suggest Lower Intelligence in Men Born the Year after Flu Pandemic," *Annals of Neurology 66*, no. 3 (2009): 284–289; S. A. Mednick et al., "Adult Schizophrenia following Prenatal Exposure to an Influenza Epidemic," *Archives of General Psychiatry 45*, no. 2 (1988): 189–192. In addition to her exposure to the influenza virus, Rosemary was said to have had a hard delivery, with her "head trapped in the birth canal." This may have contributed to her subsequent mild mental retardation but is unlikely to have been a cause of her later psychosis, based on what is now known; see Edward Shorter, *The Kennedy*

*Family and the Story of Mental Retardation* (Philadelphia: Temple University Press, 2000), 30–31.

7. Laurence Leamer, *The Kennedy Women: The Saga of an American Family* (New York: Ballantine Books, 1994), 143; Goodwin, *The Fitzgeralds and the Kennedys*, 414–415; Collier and Horowitz, *The Kennedys*, 68.

8. Leamer, *The Kennedy Women*, 170; Goodwin, *The Fitzgeralds and the Kennedys*, 415.

9. Leamer, *The Kennedy Women*, 173, 212–213; Goodwin, *The Fitzgeralds and the Kennedys*, 576–577.

10. Leamer, *The Kennedy Women*, 237–238; Goodwin, *The Fitzgeralds and the Kennedys*, 422; V. Dawson, "Eunice Shriver and the Power of the Possible," *Washington Post*, August 3, 1987; Shorter, *The Kennedy Family*, 32.

11. Leamer, *The Kennedy Women*, 239; Goodwin, *The Fitzgeralds and the Kennedys*, 420, 577; Robert Dallek, *An Unfinished Life: John F. Kennedy, 1917–1963* (Boston: Little, Brown, and Company, 2003), 72.

12. Leamer, *The Kennedy Women*, 267–271, 284–285; Will Swift, *The Kennedys amidst the Gathering Storm* (New York: HarperCollins, 2008), 82; Goodwin, *The Fitzgeralds and the Kennedys*, 630.

13. Goodwin, *The Fitzgeralds and the Kennedys*, 415, 704; Beschloss, *Kennedy and Roosevelt*, 197; Leamer, *The Kennedy Women*, 312–313.

14. Ronald Kessler, *The Sins of the Father: Joseph P. Kennedy and the Dynasty He Founded* (New York: Warner Books, 1996), 217; Leamer, *The Kennedy Women*, 316.

15. Beschloss, *Kennedy and Roosevelt*, 221, 209; Seymour M. Hersh, *The Dark Side of Camelot* (Boston: Little, Brown, and Company, 1997), 39; Alonzo L. Hamby, *Liberalism and Its Challenges: FDR to Reagan* (New York: Oxford University Press, 1985), 184.

16. Collier and Horowitz, *The Kennedys*, 132; Leamer, *The Kennedy Women*, 319.

17. Goodwin, *The Fitzgeralds and the Kennedys*, 741; Leamer, *The Kennedy Women*, 240; Collier and Horowitz, *The Kennedys*, 133.

18. Goodwin, *The Fitzgeralds and the Kennedys*, 741–742; Leamer, *The Kennedy Women*, 335–336; Shorter, *The Kennedy Family*, 32. Shorter cites as his reference for this fact Leamer, *The Kennedy Women*, 318–319, but I do not find that information there; it thus may have come from the private records to which he had access.

19. Doris Drummond, John F. Kennedy Library Foundation, letter to the author, October 18, 2010; Kessler, *The Sins of the Father*, 250; Rose F. Kennedy, *Times to Remember* (New York: Doubleday, 1974), 286; Bertram S. Brown, interview by John F. Stewart for the John F. Kennedy Library, August 6, 1968, 11; V. A. Morgan et al., "Intellectual Disability Co-occurring with Schizophrenia and Other Psychiatric Illness: Population-Based Study," *British Journal of Psychiatry 193*, no. 5 (2008): 364–372; P. Nettelbladt et al., "Risk of Mental Disorders in Subjects with Intellectual Disability in the Lundby Cohort 1947–97," *Nordic Journal of Psychiatry 63*, no. 4 (2009): 316–321.

20. Beschloss, *Kennedy and Roosevelt*, 42; Collier and Horowitz, *The Kennedys*, 38, 7.

21. Aaron J. Rosanoff, *Manual of Psychiatry and Mental Hygiene* (New York: John Wiley and Sons, 1938), 526; E. Fuller Torrey and Judy Miller, *The Invisible Plague: The Rise of Mental Illness from 1750 to the Present* (New Brunswick, NJ: Rutgers University Press, 2001), 239. Some of the excess psychiatric hospitalization of Irish immigrants was later found to be due to demographic differences, such as more young people among the immigrants.

22. Walter Freeman, "Psychosurgery," in *American Handbook of Psychiatry*, vol. II, ed. Silvano Arieti (New York: Basic Books, 1959), 1528; Jack El-Hai, *The Lobotomist: A Maverick*

*Medical Genius and His Tragic Quest to Rid the World of Mental Illness* (New York: John Wiley and Sons, 2005), 168.

23. Goodwin, *The Fitzgeralds and the Kennedys*, 742. John White is quoted in Collier and Horowitz, *The Kennedys*, 133–134.

24. Kessler, *The Sins of the Father*, 75.

25. El-Hai, *The Lobotomist*, 151–154.

26. Ibid., 106, 227, 163–164.

27. In *The Patriarch: The Remarkable Life and Turbulent Times of Joseph P. Kennedy* (New York: Penguin Press, 2012), 535, author David Nasaw claimed that the lobotomy was done between November 12 and 28, based on the Kennedy correspondence to which he had access. Kessler, *The Sins of the Father*, 242–246.

28. Collier and Horowitz, *The Kennedys*, 134 (the quotation is from Timothy Shriver, Eunice Kennedy Shriver's son); Kessler, *The Sins of the Father*, 255; Collier and Horowitz, *The Kennedys*, 69; Leamer, *The Kennedy Women*, 338.

29. Kessler, *The Sins of the Father*, 255; Swift, *The Kennedys*, 514; Leamer, *The Kennedy Women*, 342, 390.

30. Amanda Smith, ed., *Hostage to Fortune: The Letters of Joseph P. Kennedy* (New York: Viking, 2001), 515–516; Goodwin, *The Fitzgeralds and the Kennedys*, 745.

31. Leamer, *The Kennedy Women*, 433, 712, 795; G. Zielinski, "A Life Outside the Spotlight: Rosemary Kennedy Lived Quietly for Decades as Her Family Made History," *Milwaukee Journal Sentinel OnLine*, January 9, 2005, http://nl.newsbank.com/sites/mwsb/; Nasaw, *The Patriarch*, 628.

32. Edgar Allan Poe, *The Raven* (New York: J. K. Wellman, 1845); Kessler, *The Sins of the Father*, 247; Nasaw, *The Patriarch*, 536, 629–631; El-Hai, *The Lobotomist*, 174.

33. Laurence Leamer, *The Kennedy Men* (New York: William Morrow, 2001), 170.

## Chapter 2

1. R. H. Felix, "Psychiatry in Prospect," *American Journal of Psychiatry 103*, no. 5 (1947): 600–606. Felix's original 1942 master's thesis on the organization of a national mental health program is no longer available, according to officials at the Johns Hopkins School of Public Health. Felix's many published papers on this subject from 1945 to 1949 presumably reflect his earlier ideas.

2. F. J. Braceland, "Robert Hanna Felix, Eighty-Ninth President, 1960–61: A Biographical Sketch," *American Journal of Psychiatry 118*, no. 1 (1961): 9–14.

3. Henry A. Foley and Steven S. Sharfstein, *Madness and Government: Who Cares for the Mentally Ill?* (Washington, DC: American Psychiatric Publishing, 1983), 18; G. N. Grob, "Creation of the National Institute of Mental Health," *Public Health Reports 111*, no. 4 (1996): 378–381; G. N. Grob, "Government and Mental Health Policy: A Structural Analysis," *Milbank Quarterly 72*, no. 3 (1994): 471–500; A. D. Miller, "Hindsight in Retrospect: Learning the Lessons of History," *Psychiatric Quarterly 62*, no. 3 (1991): 213–231; Bertram S. Brown, interview by author, October 15, 2010; *Mental Illness and Retardation, Hearings on S. 755 and 756, Before the Subcomm. on Health, Comm. on Labor and Public Welfare*, 88th Cong. 193 (1963).

4. Grob, "Government and Mental Health Policy."

5. Murray Levine, *The Theory and Politics of Community Mental Health* (New York: Oxford University Press, 1981), 16; John A. Talbott, *The Death of the Asylum* (New York: Grune and Stratton, 1978), 17; Grob, "Government and Mental Health Policy"; E. M. Gruenberg

and J. Archer, "Abandonment of Responsibility for the Seriously Mentally Ill," *Milbank Memorial Fund Quarterly/Health and Society 57*, no. 4 (1979): 485–506.

6. Foley and Sharfstein, *Madness and Government*, 2; Grob, "Government and Mental Health Policy."

7. R. H. Felix, "Psychiatric Plans of the United States Public Health Service," *Mental Hygiene 30* (1946): 381–389; R. H. Felix, "The Relation of the National Mental Health Act to State Health Authorities," *Public Health Reports 62*, no. 2 (1947): 41–49.

8. R. H. Felix, "Mental Hygiene as Public Health Practice," *American Journal of Orthopsychiatry 21*, no. 4 (1951): 707–716; *Mental Health Study Act of 1955, Hearings on H.J. Res. 230, Before the Subcomm. on Health and Science, Comm. on Interstate and Foreign Commerce*, 84th Cong. 10 (1955).

9. R. H. Felix and R. V. Bowers, "Mental Hygiene and Socio-environmental Factors," *Milbank Memorial Fund Quarterly 26*, no. 2 (1948): 125–147; *ADAMHA News*, January 25, 1978; Derek Freeman, *Margaret Mead and Samoa: The Making and Unmaking of an Anthropological Myth* (Cambridge: Harvard University Press, 1983); E. Fuller Torrey, *Freudian Fraud: The Malignant Effect of Freud's Theory on American Thought and Culture* (New York: HarperCollins, 1992), 75–83.

10. R. H. Felix, "Mental Hygiene and Public Health," *American Journal of Orthopsychiatry 18*, no. 4 (1948): 679–684; Felix, "The Relation of the National Mental Health Act"; R. H. Felix, "The National Mental Health Act: How It Can Operate to Meet a National Problem," *Mental Hygiene 31*, no. 3 (1947): 363–374.

11. E. Fuller Torrey, *Nowhere to Go: The Tragic Odyssey of the Homeless Mentally Ill* (New York: Harper and Row, 1988), 58–59.

12. Torrey, *Nowhere to Go*, 55–57. See also Alex Sarayan, *The Turning Point: How Men of Conscience Brought about Major Change in the Care of America's Mentally Ill* (Washington, DC: American Psychiatric Publishing, 1994).

13. Torrey, *Nowhere to Go*, 52–53; "Proposed Institute for Research on Nervous and Mental Disease," *Science 89*, no. 2298 (1939): 7.

14. G. N. Grob, "Foreword," in *Mind, Brain, Body, and Behavior: Foundations of Neuroscience and Behavioral Research at the National Institutes of Health*, eds. Ingrid G. Farreras, Caroline Hannaway, and Victoria A. Harden (Washington, DC: IOS Press, 2004); L. D. Ozarin, "His Vision Led to NIMH's Birth," *Psychiatric News*, August 3, 1990, 21.

15. *National Neuropsychiatric Institute Act, Hearings on S. 1160, Before the Subcomm. on Health and Education, Comm. on Education and Labor*, 79th Cong. 134 (1946); Torrey, *Nowhere to Go*, 68–69.

16. Grob, "Foreword."

17. *National Neuropsychiatric Institute Act, Hearings on H.R. 2550, Before the Subcomm. on Public Health, Comm. on Interstate and Foreign Commerce*, 79th Cong. 77–78, 84 (1945).

18. Felix, "Mental Hygiene and Public Health"; R. H. Felix, "Evolution of Community Mental Health Concepts," *American Journal of Psychiatry 113*, no. 8 (1957): 673–679.

19. Foley and Sharfstein, *Madness and Government*, 29; Samuel H. Beer, "Foreword," in Henry A. Foley, *Community Mental Health Legislation: The Formative Process* (Lexington, MA: Lexington Books, 1975), xi.

20. Foley and Sharfstein, *Madness and Government*, 18.

21. J. R. Ewalt, "The Community Stake in the Mental Health Program," *American Journal of Psychiatry 112*, no. 4 (1955): 248–251; Foley, *Community Mental Health Legislation*, 19.

22. Robert Felix, interview by Henry Foley, February 1972; William C. Menninger, "Presidential Address," *American Journal of Psychiatry 106*, no. 1 (1949): 1–12.

23. *National Neuropsychiatric Institute Act, Hearings on H.R. 2550*, 79th Cong. 28 (1945) (statement of Francis Braceland).

24. M. Gorman, "Mental Illness: Legislative and Economic Considerations," *American Journal of Public Health 53*, no. 3 (1963): 403–408; M. Gorman, "Oklahoma Attacks Its Snake Pits," *Reader's Digest 53* (1948): 139–160.

25. Federal Bureau of Investigation records from 1952 investigation of Thomas Francis (Mike) Gorman, obtained July 29, 2011.

26. Ibid.; Mike Gorman, *Every Other Bed* (Cleveland: World Publishing, 1956), 12.

27. E. B. Drew, "The Health Syndicate: Washington's Noble Conspirators," *Atlantic Monthly*, December 1967, 75–82; Mike Gorman Papers, 1946–1989, National Library of Medicine, History of Medicine Division, call number MS C 462; Brown, interview by author, October 15, 2010.

28. Jack Ewalt, interview by Henry Foley, 1972; Daniel A. Felicetti, *Mental Health and Retardation Politics: The Mind Lobbies in Congress* (New York: Praeger, 1975), 53; M. Gorman, "Community Mental Health: The Search for Identity," *Community Mental Health Journal 6*, no. 5 (1970): 347–355; *Mental Illness and Retardation, Hearings on S. 755 and 756*, 88th Cong. 46 (1963) (statement of Mike Gorman).

29. Felix, interview; *Mental Health, Hearings on S.J. Res. 46, S. 724, S. 848, and S. 886 (title VI), Before the Subcomm. on Health, Comm. on Labor and Public Welfare*, 84th Cong. 55 (1955).

30. *Mental Health, Hearings on S.J. Res. 46, S. 724, S. 848, and S. 886 (title VI)*, 84th Cong. 111 (1955); *Mental Health Study Act of 1955, Hearings on H.J. Res. 230*, 84th Cong. 36, 124 (1955).

31. Foley and Sharfstein, *Madness and Government*, 35.

32. Ibid., 37; Felix, interview.

33. David Mechanic, *Mental Health and Social Policy*, 3rd ed. (Englewood Cliffs, NJ: Prentice Hall, 1989), 90.

34. *Action for Mental Health: Final Report of the Joint Commission on Mental Illness and Health* (New York: John Wiley and Sons, 1961), 268, 284, 286, 287.

35. Mike Gorman, "Community Absorption of the Mentally Ill: The New Challenge," *Community Mental Health Journal 12*, no. 2 (1976): 119–127; Mike Gorman Papers.

36. N. W. Winkelman, "Chlorpromazine in the Treatment of Neuropsychiatric Disorders," *Journal of the American Medical Association 155*, no. 1 (1954): 18–21.

37. *Mental Health Study Act of 1955, Hearings on H.J. Res. 230*, 84th Cong. 73 (1955); W. Gronfein, "Psychotropic Drugs and the Origins of Deinstitutionalization," *Social Problems 32*, no. 5 (1985): 437–454.

38. Shorter, *The Kennedy Family*, 35–36; Kessler, *The Sins of the Father*, 249.

39. Shorter, *The Kennedy Family*, 41–42.

40. Ibid., 36, 42.

41. Kessler, *The Sins of the Father*, 365.

42. Shorter, *The Kennedy Family*, 45, 67–73.

43. Ibid., 34; Ted Swarz, *Joseph P. Kennedy* (New York: John Wiley, 2003), 306.

## Chapter 3

1. Anthony J. Celebrezze, interview by William Geoghegan for the John F. Kennedy Library, September 27, 1968; Robert Cooke, interview by John F. Stewart for the John F. Kennedy Library, July 25, 1968, 29.

2. Leamer, *The Kennedy Women*, 519.

3. "Presidential Candidate Kennedy Opens Key Primary Drive Here," *Daily Union* (Fort Atkinson/Jefferson County, WI), February 16, 1960.

4. Ibid.; Leamer, *The Kennedy Women*, 519; Christine Spangler (editor of the *Daily Union*), interview by author, July 22, 2011.

5. Elizabeth M. Boggs, interview by John F. Stewart for the John F. Kennedy Library, February 17, 1969, 4.

6. Eunice Shriver, "Hope for Retarded Children," *Saturday Evening Post*, September 1962, 71–74; Kessler, *The Sins of the Father*, 254.

7. Foley, *Community Mental Health Legislation*, 33; Ibid., 31, quoting Stanley Yolles; Foley and Sharfstein, *Madness and Government*, 44.

8. Eunice Shriver, interview by John F. Stewart for the John F. Kennedy Library, May 7, 1968, 1; Cooke, interview, 7.

9. Shorter, *The Kennedy Family*, 87–88.

10. Ibid., 80–81.

11. Edward D. Berkowitz, *Mr. Social Security: The Life of Wilbur J. Cohen* (Lawrence: University of Kansas Press, 1995), 154; Shorter, *The Kennedy Family*, 81, 83, 84.

12. Shorter, *The Kennedy Family*, 96; Patrick Doyle, interview by John F. Stewart for the John F. Kennedy Library, March 4, 1968, 19; Cooke, interview, 44; Kessler, *The Sins of the Father*, 252.

13. Felicetti, *Mental Health and Retardation Politics*, 73; David L. Bazelon, interview by William McHugh for the John F. Kennedy Library, March 5, 1969, 14–15.

14. Bazelon, interview, 15–16; Kessler, *The Sins of the Father*, 253.

15. Foley, *Community Mental Health Legislation*, 59.

16. Ibid., 34; Felix, interview; Boisfeuillet Jones, interview by Henry Foley, April 1972.

17. Boisfeuillet Jones and Daniel Moynihan, interviews by Henry Foley, April 1972; Rashi Fein, personal communication to author, December 21, 2010.

18. Brown, interviews by author, October 15, 2010, and March 2, 2011.

19. Ibid.

20. Brown, interview by author, December 22, 2010.

21. R. Slovenko and E. D. Luby, "On the Emancipation of Mental Patients," *Journal of Psychiatry and Law 3*, no. 2 (1975): 191–213.

22. Miller, "Hindsight in retrospect"; Brown, interview by author, October 15, 2010; R. H. Felix, "Bright New Era for Mental Health Care," *Hospitals 38* (1964): 46–49; *Research Facilities, Mental Health Staffing, Continuation of Health Programs, and Group Practice, Hearings on H.R. 2984, Before the Comm. on Interstate and Foreign Commerce*, 89th Cong. 58 (1965) (statement of Stanley Yolles); Stanley Yolles, interview by Henry Foley, March 1972; Bob Smucker, *Promise, Progress, and Pain: A Case Study of America's Community Mental Health Movement from 1960 to 1980* (Washington, DC: Center for Lobbying in the Public Interest, 2007), 9; Foley, *Community Mental Health Legislation*, 37.

23. Robert Atwell, interview by Henry Foley, January 1972; Robert Atwell, interview by author, March 9, 2011; Foley and Sharfstein, *Madness and Government*, 46; Grob, "Government and Mental Health Policy."

24. Foley, *Community Mental Health Legislation*, 39; Fein, personal communication; Felix, interview; Atwell, interview by Foley.

25. Gerald Caplan, *An Approach to Community Mental Health* (New York: Grune and Stratton, 1961), 42, 232.

26. Robert Felix, "Foreword," in Gerald Caplan, *Principles of Preventive Psychiatry* (New York: Basic Books, 1964); Robert H. Felix et al., *Mental Health and Social Welfare* (New York: Columbia University Press, 1961), 10–11.

27. Felix and Bowers, "Mental Hygiene and Socio-environmental Factors"; Caplan, *An Approach*, book jacket; Felix et al., *Mental Health and Social Welfare*, 3.

28. Yolles, interview.

29. Felix, "Mental Hygiene and Public Health."

30. A. D. Miller, J. B. Margolin, and S. F. Yolles, "Epidemiology of Reading Disabilities; Some Methodologic Considerations and Early Findings," *American Journal of Public Health 47*, no. 10 (1957): 1250–1256; Notes on Mental Health Study Center, Bertram S. Brown files, MSC 493, container 11, folder 10, National Library of Medicine; Miller, "Hindsight in Retrospect."

31. J. McCord, "Crime in Moral and Social Contexts—The American Society of Criminology, 1989 Presidential Address," *Criminology 28*, no. 1 (1990): 1–26; J. McCord, "Consideration of Some Effects of a Counseling Program," in *New Directions in the Rehabilitation of Criminal Offenders*, eds. Susan E. Martin, Lee B. Sechrest, and Robin Redner (Washington, DC: National Academy Press, 1981), 394–405; J. McCord, "A Thirty-Year Follow-Up of Treatment Effects," *American Psychologist 33*, no. 3 (1978): 284–289.

32. *Research Facilities, Mental Health Staffing, Continuation of Health Programs, and Group Practice, Hearings on H.R. 2984*, 89th Cong. 97 (1965) (statement of Boisfeuillet Jones); Atwell, interview by Foley; Foley, *Community Mental Health Legislation*, 37.

33. Foley, *Community Mental Health Legislation*, 44.

34. Briefing book on proposed CMHC legislation for the Secretary of HEW, Bertram S. Brown files, MSC 493, container 11, folder 11, National Library of Medicine.

35. Foley, *Community Mental Health Legislation*, 39; Atwell, interview by author; Franklin Chu and Sharland Trotter, *The Madness Establishment* (New York: Grossman Publishers, 1974), 18.

36. Allen J. Matusow, *The Unraveling of America: A History of Liberalism in the 1960s* (New York: Harper and Row, 1984), 100–107; Hamby, *Liberalism and Its Challenges*, 205.

37. Foley and Sharfstein, *Madness and Government*, 166.

38. G. N. Grob, "Mental Health Policy in 20th-Century America," in *Mental Health, United States, 2000*, eds. Ronald W. Manderscheid and Marilyn J. Henderson (Rockville, MD: Substance Abuse and Mental Health Services Administration, 2001), 3–14.

39. A. K. Bahn and V. B. Norman, "First National Report on Patients of Mental Health Clinics," *Public Health Reports 74*, no. 11 (1959): 943–956; V. B. Norman, B. M. Rosen, and A. K. Bahn, "Psychiatric Clinic Outpatients in the United States, 1959," *Mental Hygiene 46*, no. 3 (1959): 321–343.

40. R. M. Glasscote et al., *The Community Mental Health Center: An Analysis of Existing Models* (Washington, DC: Joint Information Services of the American Psychiatric Association and National Association for Mental Health, 1964), xiv; W. T. Vaughn and M. G. Field, "New Perspectives of Mental Patient Care," *American Journal of Public Health 53*, no. 2 (1963): 237–242.

41. I. Zwerling and J. F. Wilder, "An Evaluation of the Applicability of the Day Hospital in Treatment of Acutely Disturbed Patients," *Israel Annals of Psychiatry and Related Disciplines 2* (1964): 162–185; T. T. Friedman, A. Becker, and L. Weiner, "The Psychiatric Home Treatment Service: Preliminary Report of Five Years of Clinical Experience," *American Journal of Psychiatry 120*, no. 8 (1964): 782–788; R. H. Felix, "Community Mental Health,"

*American Journal of Orthopsychiatry 33*, no. 5 (1963): 788–795; "Characteristics of Community Mental Health Services Acts," files of Bertram S. Brown, MSC 493, container 11, folder 10, National Library of Medicine; *Mental Illness and Retardation, Hearings on S. 755 and 756*, 88th Cong. 47–48 (1963) (statement of Mike Gorman).

42. Foley and Sharfstein, *Madness and Government*, 54; Brown, interview by Stewart, 20.

43. Aide-Memoire, Bertram S. Brown files, MSC 493, container 11, folder 10, National Library of Medicine; Leamer, *The Kennedy Women*, 601.

44. Foley and Sharfstein, *Madness and Government*, 163–169.

45. *Mental Illness and Retardation, Hearings on S. 755 and 756*, 88th Cong. 45, 191 (1963).

46. Felicetti, *Mental Health and Retardation Politics*, 57, 82n19.

47. Foley and Sharfstein, *Madness and Government*, 67; *Mental Health (Supplemental), Hearings on H.R. 1576, Before the Subcomm. on Public Health and Safety, Comm. on Interstate and Foreign Commerce*, 88th Cong. 72 (1963).

48. Paul Hoch, letter to Jacob Javits, May 7, 1963, Bertram S. Brown files, MSC 493, container 11, folder 15, National Library of Medicine; H. Brill and R. E. Patton, "Clinical-Statistical Analysis of Population Changes in New York State Mental Hospitals since Introduction of Psychotropic Drugs," *American Journal of Psychiatry 119*, no. 1 (1962): 20–35.

49. Hoch, letter to Javits.

50. J. K. Wing, "Pilot Experiment in the Rehabilitation of Long-Hospitalized Male Schizophrenic Patients," *British Journal of Preventive and Social Medicine 14*, no. 4 (1960): 173–180; J. K. Wing et al., "Morbidity in the Community of Schizophrenic Patients Discharged from London Mental Hospitals in 1959," *British Journal of Psychiatry 110*, no. 4 (1964): 10–21; C. M. Parkes, G. W. Brown, and E. M. Monck, "The General Practitioner and the Schizophrenic Patient," *British Medical Journal 1*, no. 5283 (1962): 972–976; J. R. Ewalt, "Needs of the Mentally Ill: Types of Effective Action between the Community and Its Hospital Facilities," *Mental Hospitals 12*, no. 2 (1961): 12–15.

51. Grob, "Government and Mental Health Policy."

52. *Mental Illness and Retardation, Hearings on S. 755 and 756*, 88th Cong. 190–91 (1963) (statement of Robert Felix); R. H. Felix, "Our Present Prospects and the Task Ahead," *Comprehensive Psychiatry 4*, no. 6 (1963): 368–374.

## Chapter 4

1. Foley and Sharfstein, *Madness and Government*, 69–70; Hamby, *Liberalism and Its Challenges*, 257.

2. Foley and Sharfstein, *Madness and Government*, 72, 79; *Research Facilities, Mental Health Staffing, Continuation of Health Programs, and Group Practice, Hearings on H.R. 2984*, 89th Cong. 52 (1965).

3. Foley, *Community Mental Health Legislation*, 89; J. F. Wilder, "Strengths of the Community Mental Health Center in Urban Areas," in *An Assessment of the Community Mental Health Movement*, eds. Walter E. Barton and Charlotte J. Sanborn (Lexington, MA: Lexington Books, 1977), 67.

4. Chu and Trotter, *The Madness Establishment*, 26; Grob, "Government and Mental Health Policy."

5. Bertram S. Brown, interview by Henry Foley, 1972; Foley and Sharfstein, *Madness and Government*, 260; Miller, "Hindsight in Retrospect."

6. S. F. Yolles, "Psychiatry, Mental Health, and Society: A View of the Future," *Biological Psychiatry 1*, no. 1 (1969): 5–12.

7. S. F. Yolles, "Intervention against Poverty: A Fielder's Choice for the Psychiatrist," *American Journal of Psychiatry 122*, no. 3 (1965): 324–325; S. F. Yolles, "Community Mental Health: Issues and Policies," *American Journal of Psychiatry 122*, no. 9 (1966): 979–985; S. F. Yolles, "Social Policy and the Mentally Ill," *Hospital and Community Psychiatry 20*, no. 2 (1969): 37–42; D. F. Musto, "Whatever Happened to 'Community Mental Health'?" *Public Interest 39* (1975): 53–79.

8. Frank Baker, Cecil D. Isaacs, and Herbert C. Schulberg, *Study of the Relationship between Community Mental Health Centers and State Mental Hospitals* (Boston: Socio-Technical Systems Associates, Inc., 1972), NIMH contract no. HSM-42-70-107.

9. Wilder, "Strengths of the Community Mental Health Center"; A. M. Vayda and F. D. Perlmutter, "Primary Prevention in Community Mental Health Centers: A Survey of Current Activity," *Community Mental Health Journal 13*, no. 4 (1977): 343–351; H. Harris, "Planning Community Mental Health Services in an Urban Ghetto," in *The Community Mental Health Center*, eds. Allan Biegel and Alan I. Levenson (New York: Basic Books, 1972), 53; Anthony Panzetta, *Community Mental Health: Myth or Reality* (Philadelphia: Lea and Febiger, 1971), 111, 146.

10. Yolles, "Social Policy and the Mentally Ill"; Wilder, "Strengths of the Community Mental Health Center"; Panzetta, *Community Mental Health*, 113, 114, 124.

11. Yolles, "Psychiatry, Mental Health, and Society."

12. L. J. Duhl, "The Shame of the Cities," *American Journal of Psychiatry 124*, no. 9 (1968): 1184–1189; L. J. Duhl, "Psychiatry and the Urban Poor," in *Distress in the City*, ed. William Ryan (Cleveland: Press of Western Reserve University, 1969), 118; Leonard J. Duhl and Robert J. Leopold, *Mental Health and Urban Social Policy* (San Francisco: Jossey-Bass, 1968), 4, 14.

13. Matthew Dumont, *The Absurd Healer: Perspectives of a Community Psychiatrist* (New York: Science House, 1968), 52, 53, 80.

14. H. P. Rome, "Psychiatry and Foreign Affairs: The Expanding Competence of Psychiatry," *American Journal of Psychiatry 125*, no. 6 (1968): 725–730; James L. Sundquist, *Politics and Policy: The Eisenhower, Kennedy, and Johnson Years* (Washington, DC: Brookings Institution, 1968), 119.

15. Foley, *Community Mental Health Legislation*, 117.

16. Yolles, "Psychiatry, Mental Health, and Society."

17. H. W. Dunham, "Community Psychiatry: The Newest Therapeutic Bandwagon," *Archives of General Psychiatry 12*, no. 3 (1965): 303–313.

18. B. Rubin, "Community Psychiatry: An Evolutionary Change in Medical Psychology in the United States," *Archives of General Psychiatry 20*, no. 5 (1969): 497–507; M. O. Wagenfeld, "The Primary Prevention of Mental Illness: A Sociological Perspective," *Journal of Health and Social Behavior 13*, no. 2 (1972): 195–203; W. G. Burrows, "Community Psychiatry—Another Bandwagon," *Canadian Psychiatric Association Journal 14*, no. 2 (1969): 105–114, quoting Davidson; D. W. DeWild, "Toward a Clarification of Primary Prevention," *Community Mental Health Journal 16*, no. 4 (1980): 306–316.

19. Seymour R. Kaplan and Melvin Roman, *The Organization and Delivery of Mental Health Services in the Ghetto* (New York: Praeger, 1973), 213–214; Duhl and Leopold, *Mental Health and Urban Social Policy*, 17.

20. "Community Takes over Control of Bronx Mental Health Services," *New York Times*, March 6, 1969. See also Kaplan and Roman, *Mental Health Services in the Ghetto*, and R. Shaw and C. J. Eagle, "Programmed Failure: The Lincoln Hospital Story," *Community Mental Health Journal 7*, no. 4 (1971): 255–263.

21. Leopold Bellak, *Community Psychiatry and Community Mental Health* (New York: Grune and Stratton, 1964), 12; L. Bellak, "Toward Control of Today's Epidemic of Mental Disease," *Medical World News*, February 6, 1970.

22. C. McCabe, "On Looney Leaders," *San Francisco Chronicle*, September 30, 1969.

23. Matusow, *The Unraveling of America*, 227; David G. Smith and Judith D. Moore, *Medicaid Politics and Policy 1965–2007* (New Brunswick, NJ: Transaction Publishers, 2008), 21, 44, 45.

24. Brown, interview by author, October 15, 2010; Comptroller General of the United States, Report to Congress, *Returning the Mentally Ill to the Community: Government Needs to Do More* (Washington, DC: Comptroller General of the US, January 7, 1977), 46.

25. Brown, interview by author, January 13, 2011.

# Chapter 5

1. D. Robinson, "Conspiracy USA: The Far Right Fights against Mental Health," *Look*, January 26, 1965, 30–32.

2. Arnold A. Rogow, *The Psychiatrists* (New York: G. P. Putnam's Sons, 1970), 126; Henry Pinsker, "'Goldwater Rule' History" (letter), *Psychiatric News*, August 3, 2007, 33.

3. Matthew Dumont, *The Absurd Healer*, 80.

4. M. Greenblat and E. Glazier, "The Phasing Out of Mental Hospitals in the United States," *American Journal of Psychiatry 132*, no. 11 (1975): 1135–1140.

5. National Institute of Mental Health, *Provisional Data on Federally Funded Community Mental Health Centers* (Rockville, MD: National Institute of Mental Health, annual reports 1968–1978); Baker et al., *Study of the Relationship*, iii; Report of the Inspector General of DHEW, *A Service Delivery Assessment on Community Mental Health Centers* (Washington, DC: Department of Health, Education and Welfare, 1979).

6. *Legislative and Administrative Changes Needed in Community Mental Health Centers Program* (Washington, DC: General Accounting Office, 1979); Chu and Trotter, *The Madness Establishment*, 38.

7. *Community Mental Health Centers: The Federal Investment*, DHEW publication no. (ADM) 78-677 (Washington, DC: Department of Health, Education and Welfare, 1978); John F. Bean Jr., Michael M. Makowiecki, and Mark R. Yessian, *A Service Delivery Assessment on Community Mental Health Centers: Executive Report* (Washington, DC: Department of Health, Education and Welfare, 1979).

8. Task Panel on Community Mental Health Centers Assessment, *The President's Commission on Mental Health* (Washington, DC: US Government Printing Office, 1978), 2:319; B. C. Holland, "An Evaluation of the Criticisms of the Community Mental Health Movement," in Barton and Sanborn, *An Assessment*, 101; Comptroller General, *Returning the Mentally Ill to the Community*; Anthony Lehman, interview by author, July 22, 2010.

9. E. F. Torrey, "Community Mental Health Policy—Tennis, Anyone?" *Wall Street Journal*, March 29, 1990; E. Fuller Torrey and Robert L. Taylor, *A Minuet of Mutual Deception: NIMH and the Community Mental Health Centers* (Bethesda, MD: National Institute of Mental Health, 1972); Chu and Trotter, *The Madness Establishment*, 116.

10. Lawrence S. Kubie, "Pitfalls of Community Psychiatry," *Archives of General Psychiatry 18*, no. 3 (1968): 257–266.

11. Torrey and Taylor, *A Minuet*; E. Fuller Torrey, Sidney M. Wolfe, and Laurie M. Flynn, *Fiscal Misappropriations in Programs for the Mentally Ill: A Report on Illegality and Failure of*

the Federal Construction Grant Program for Community Mental Health Centers, publicly released by the Public Citizen Health Research Group, Washington, DC, and the National Alliance for the Mentally Ill, Arlington, Va., March 23, 1990.

12. C. Windle and D. Scully, "Community Mental Health Centers and the Decreasing Use of State Mental Hospitals," Community Mental Health Journal 12, no. 3 (1976): 239–243; J. R. Doidge and C. W. Rodgers, "Is NIMH's Dream Coming True? Wyoming's Centers Reduce State Hospital Admissions," Community Mental Health Journal 12, no. 4 (1976): 399–404; Comptroller General, Returning the Mentally Ill to the Community.

13. Robert F. Rich, Bypassing State Government to Meet National Needs: Assessing Federal Initiatives of the 1960s through the Lens of the 1980s, report of NIMH grants MH 30792 and 37799, mimeo, 1985; B. Brown, "Ousted NIMH Chief Responds to Criticism," U.S. Medicine 14, no. 1 (1978), 14; B. Brown, "Psychiatric Practice and Public Policy," American Journal of Psychiatry 125, no. 2 (1968): 141–146; Brown, interviews by author, October 15 and December 22, 2010.

14. Foley and Sharfstein, Madness and Government, 91; Chu and Trotter, The Madness Establishment, 29.

15. Community Mental Health Centers—Oversight, Hearings Before the Subcomm. on Public Health and Environment, Comm. on Interstate and Foreign Commerce, Serial no. 93-39, 93rd Cong. 9 (1973) (statement of Bertram S. Brown); NIMH official, interview by author, reported in E. Fuller Torrey, Nowhere to Go, 188.

16. Public Health Service Act Extension, Hearings on S. 1136, Before the Subcomm. on Health, Comm. on Labor and Public Welfare, 93rd Cong. 39–41 (1973).

17. S. Feldman, "Promises, Promises or Community Mental Health Services and Training: Ships That Pass in the Night," Community Mental Health Journal 14, no. 2 (1978): 83–91; F. M. Ochberg, "Community Mental Health Center Legislation: Flight of the Phoenix," American Journal of Psychiatry 133, no. 1 (1976): 56–61.

18. Chu and Trotter, The Madness Establishment, 106–107; Comptroller General of the United States, Report to Congress, Need for More Effective Management of Community Mental Health Centers Program (Washington, DC: Comptroller General of the US, August 27, 1974), 33.

19. Torrey and Taylor, A Minuet; E. F. Torrey, "Stealing from the Mentally Ill," Public Citizen, July/August 1990, 22–23.

20. Feldman, "Promises, Promises."

21. Task Panel, The President's Commission, 2:315.

22. Ibid., 4:1855; Ibid., 2:367.

23. "'Diluted' Care Ascribed to Mental Health Clinic," U.S. Medicine 13 (1977): 1, 27; Musto, "Whatever Happened"; J. C. Turner and W. J. TenHoor, "The NIMH Community Support Program: Pilot Approach to a Needed Social Reform," Schizophrenia Bulletin 4, no. 3 (1978): 319–344.

24. Bruce J. Ennis, Prisoners of Psychiatry (New York: Harcourt, Brace, Jovanovich, 1972), 232; Wikipedia, King of Hearts (1966 film), en.wikipedia.org/wiki/King_of_Hearts_(1966_film).

25. S. M. Rose, "Deciphering Deinstitutionalization: Complexities in Policy and Program Analysis," Milbank Memorial Fund Quarterly/Health and Society 57, no. 4 (1979): 429–460.

26. Murray Levine, Theory and Politics, 199.

27. H. E. Cauvin, "President Offered in '83 to Meet with Hinckley," Washington Post, June 12, 2004; K. Horak, "In 'Perfect American Family,' Tragedy Hits Twice in 2 Years," Washington Post, March 27, 1983.

28. R. H. Felix, "Mental Hygiene and Public Health."

29. Bahn and Norman, "First National Report."

30. Smucker, *Promise, Progress, and Pain*, 27; Rich, *Bypassing State Government*.

31. Levine, *Theory and Politics*, 91; *Proceedings of the National Governors' Association Annual Meeting: Governors' Policy Position on Mental Health, Mental Retardation, and the Elderly* (Washington, DC: National Association of Mental Health, September 9, 1977).

32. R. Slovenko and E. D. Luby, "From Moral Treatment to Railroading Out of the Mental Hospital," *Bulletin of the American Academy of Psychiatry and the Law 2*, no. 4 (1974): 223–236; Comptroller General, *Returning the Mentally Ill to the Community*; Turner and TenHoor, "The NIMH Community Support Program"; Gruenberg and Archer, "Abandonment of Responsibility"; Levine, *Theory and Politics*, 92.

33. Matusow, *The Unraveling of America*, 220, 260, 263.

34. *Community Mental Health Centers Amendments of 1969, Hearings on S. 2523, Before the Subcomm. on Health, Comm. on Labor and Public Welfare*, 91st Cong. 98 (statement of Horace G. Whittington); A. F. Panzetta, "Whatever Happened to Community Mental Health: Portents for Corporate Medicine," *Hospital and Community Psychiatry 36*, no. 11 (1985): 1174–1179.

## Chapter 6

1. E. F. Torrey et al., *Care of the Seriously Mentally Ill: A Rating of State Programs* (Washington, DC: Public Citizen Health Research Group and the National Alliance for the Mentally Ill, 1990), 25.

2. H. R. Searight and P. J. Handal, "Psychiatric Deinstitutionalization: The Possibilities and the Reality," *Psychiatric Quarterly 58*, no. 3 (1986–87): 153–166; R. Reich and L. Siegel, "Psychiatry under Siege: The Chronically Mentally Ill Shuffle to Oblivion," *Psychiatric Annals 3* (1973): 35–55; Subcommittee on Long-Term Care of the Special Committee on Aging, US Senate, *Nursing Home Care in the United States: Failure in Public Policy, Supporting Paper No. 7. The Role of Nursing Homes in Caring for Discharged Mental Patients (and the Birth of a For-Profit Boarding Home Industry)* (Washington, DC: US Government Printing Office, 1976), 719.

3. G. L. Klerman, "Better But Not Well: Social and Ethical Issues in the Deinstitutionalization of the Mentally Ill," *Schizophrenia Bulletin 3*, no. 4 (1977): 617–631; E. N. Goplerud, "Unexpected Consequences of Deinstitutionalization of the Mentally Disabled Elderly," *American Journal of Community Psychiatry 7*, no. 3 (1979): 315–328.

4. H. R. Lamb and V. Goertzel, "Discharged Mental Patients—Are They Really in the Community?" *Archives of General Psychiatry 24*, no. 1 (1971): 29–34 (this report was originally presented at a meeting in 1969 and then published in 1971).

5. Greenblatt and Glazier, "The Phasing Out of Mental Hospitals"; H. R. Lamb, "The New Asylums in the Community," *Archives of General Psychiatry 36*, no. 2 (1979): 129–134; J. Chase, "Where Have All the Patients Gone?" *Human Behavior*, October 1973, 14–21.

6. E. Fuller Torrey, *The Insanity Offense: How America's Failure to Treat the Seriously Mentally Ill Endangers Its Citizens* (New York: W. W. Norton, 2008), 43–44.

7. "The Discharged Chronic Mental Patient," *Medical World News*, April 12, 1974, 47–58; Riech and Siegel, "Psychiatry under Siege"; J. A. Talbott, "Deinstitutionalization: Avoiding the Disasters of the Past," *Hospital and Community Psychiatry 30*, no. 9 (1979): 621–624.

8. M. F. Abramson, "The Criminalization of Mentally Disordered Behavior: Possible Side-Effect of a New Mental Health Law," *Hospital and Community Psychiatry 23*, no. 4 (1972): 101–105.

9. Dennis G. Amundsen et al., *A Study of the Need for and Availability of Mental Health Services for Mentally Disordered Jail Inmates and Juveniles in Detention Facilities* (Sacramento: Arthur Bolton Associates, 1976); G. Swank and D. Winer, "Occurrence of Psychiatric Disorder in a County Jail Population," *American Journal of Psychiatry 133*, no. 11 (1976): 1331–1333; W. Bromberg and C. B. Thompson, "The Relation of Psychosis, Mental Defect and Personality Types to Crime," *Journal of Criminal Law and Criminology 28* (1937): 70–88; Torrey, *The Insanity Offense*, 45.

10. L. Sosowsky, "Explaining the Increased Arrest Rate among Mental Patients: A Cautionary Note," *American Journal of Psychiatry 137*, no. 12 (1980): 1602–1605; J. C. Bonovitz and J. S. Bonovitz, "Diversion of the Mentally Ill into the Criminal Justice System: The Police Intervention Perspective," *American Journal of Psychiatry 138*, no. 7 (1981): 973–976.

11. Torrey, *The Insanity Offense*, 40–41, 48.

12. Testimony of Dr. Andrew Robertson before the Select Committee on Proposed Phaseout of State Hospital Services, May 18–October 10, 1973, California State Archives (also quoted in Chase, "Where Have All the Patients Gone?").

13. "Denying the Mentally Ill" (editorial), *New York Times*, June 5, 1981; R. D. Lyons, "How Release of Mental Patients Began," *New York Times*, October 30, 1984.

14. Rebecca Tarkington Craig and Barbara Wright, *Mental Health Financing and Programming: A Legislator's Guide* (Denver, CO: National Conference of State Legislatures, 1988), 4–5.

15. Subcommittee on Long-Term Care, *Nursing Home Care in the United States*; M. Snowden and P. Roy-Byrne, "Mental Illness and Nursing Home Reform: OBRA-87 Ten Years Later," *Psychiatric Services 49*, no. 2 (1998): 229–233.

16. "9 Ex-patients Kept in Primitive Shed in Mississippi," *New York Times*, October 21, 1982; "Fire Raises Questions about Mental Patients," *New York Times*, March 25, 1984; A. Scull, "A New Trade in Lunacy: The Recommodification of the Mental Patient," *American Behavioral Scientist 24*, no. 6 (1981): 741–754; A. F. Lehman and L. S. Linn, "Crimes against Discharged Mental Patients in Board-and-Care Homes," *American Journal of Psychiatry 141*, no. 2 (1984): 271–274.

17. E. L. Bassuk, L. Rubin, and A. Lauriat, "Is Homelessness a Mental Health Problem?" *American Journal of Psychiatry 141*, no. 12 (1984): 1546–1550.

18. R. K. Farr, *The Homeless Mentally Ill and the Los Angeles Skid Row Mental Health Project* (Los Angeles, CA: Department of Mental Health, 1985).

19. P. Gold, "Revolving Door Traps Mentally Ill," *Insight*, October 19, 1987, 22–23.

20. R. E. Drake, M. A. Wallach, and J. S. Hoffman, "Housing Instability and Homelessness among Aftercare Patients in an Urban State Hospital," *Hospital and Community Psychiatry 40*, no. 1 (1989): 46–51; J. R. Belcher, "Rights versus Needs of Homeless Mentally Ill Persons," *Social Work 33*, no. 5 (1988): 398–402; H. R. Lamb, "Deinstitutionalization at the Crossroads," *Hospital and Community Psychiatry 39*, no. 9 (1988): 941–945.

21. R. Jemelka, E. Trupin, and J. A. Chiles, "The Mentally Ill in Prisons: A Review," *Hospital and Community Psychiatry 40*, no. 5 (1989): 481–491; "Virginia Study Urges Stronger Community Supports to Keep Mentally Ill Out of Jail," *Hospital and Community Psychiatry 36* (1985): 420, 429; H. J. Steadman et al., "A Survey of Mental Disability among State Prison Inmates," *Hospital and Community Psychiatry 38*, no. 10 (1987): 1086–1090; M. Collett, "The Crime of Mental Health: Mental Patients Freed from Hospitals Are Winding Up in Jail, Where They Aren't Safe," *Valley Times* (Pleasanton, CA), December 15, 1981; H. W. Neighbors et al., *The Prevalence of Mental Disorder in Michigan Prisons* (Lansing: Report submitted to the Michigan Department of Corrections, July 2, 1987); E. Guy et al., "Mental

Health Status of Prisoners in an Urban Jail," *Criminal Justice and Behavior 12*, no. 1 (1985): 29–53; Torrey et al., *Care of the Seriously Mentally Ill.*

22. J. R. Belcher, "Are Jails Replacing the Mental Health System for the Homeless Mentally Ill?" *Community Mental Health Journal 24*, no. 3 (1988): 185–195; H. R. Lamb, "Incompetency to Stand Trial," *Archives of General Psychiatry 44*, no. 8 (1987): 754–758; L. Kilzer, "Jails as a 'Halfway House' or Long-Term Commitment?" *Denver Post*, June 3, 1984; Collett, "The Crime of Mental Health"; D. A. Treffert, "The Obviously Ill Patient in Need of Treatment," *Hospital and Community Psychiatry 36*, no. 3 (1985): 259–264.

23. R. Blumenthal, "Emotionally Ill Pose Growing Burden to Police," *New York Times*, November 16, 1989; S. Cochran, M. W. Deane, and R. Borum, "Improving Police Response to Mentally Ill People," *Psychiatric Services 51*, no. 10 (2000): 1315–1316.

24. T. L. Kuhlman, "Unavoidable Tragedies in Madison, Wisconsin: A Third View," *Hospital and Community Psychiatry 43*, no. 1 (1992): 72–73.

25. A. Karras and D. B. Otis, "A Comparison of Inpatients in an Urban State Hospital in 1975 and 1982," *Hospital and Community Psychiatry 38*, no. 9 (1987): 963–967.

26. D. E. Wilcox, "The Relationship of Mental Illness to Homicide," *American Journal of Forensic Psychiatry 6*, no. 1 (1985): 3–15; F. Grunberg, B. I. Klinger, and B. R. Grumet, "Homicide and Community-Based Psychiatry," *Journal of Nervous and Mental Disease 166*, no. 12 (1978): 868–874; F. Grunberg, B. I. Klinger, and B. Grumet, "Homicide and Deinstitutionalization of the Mentally Ill," *American Journal of Psychiatry 134*, no. 6 (1977): 685–687.

27. National Association of State Mental Health Program Directors Research Institute, "Closing and Reorganizing State Psychiatric Hospitals: 2003," *State Profile Highlights*, March 2004.

28. This and the related information on the Illinois nursing homes was taken from a series by Michael J. Berens in the *Chicago Tribune*, September 27–October 28, 1998 ("Dangerous Bedfellows"; "With State Help, Nursing Homes Open Door to Mentally Ill"; "A History of Violence"; "A Tragic Path toward Death"; "Mentally Ill 'Vanish' "; "The Bed Brokers"; "State Moves to Separate Mentally Ill, Elderly"; "Inquiry Set on Housing Mentally Ill"; "State Cashes in on Sham Diagnoses").

29. "Nursing Home Patients Were Killed, State Says," *Riverside (CA) Press-Enterprise*, August 14, 1995; M. Winerip, "For Adult Homes This One Ranks among the Worst," *New York Times*, August 17, 1990; R. Winton and P. Y. Hong, "Woman Found Locked Away Had Fallen through System," *Los Angeles Times*, April 7, 1997.

30. Torrey et al., *Care of the Seriously Mentally Ill*, 167; E. Fuller Torrey, *Out of the Shadows: Confronting America's Mental Illness Crisis* (New York: John Wiley and Sons, 1997), 62–65.

31. H. G. Cisneros, "The Lonely Death on My Doorstep," *Washington Post*, December 5, 1993; L. A. Goodman, M. A. Dutton, and M. Harris, "Episodically Homeless Women with Serious Mental Illness: Prevalence of Physical and Sexual Assault," *American Journal of Orthopsychiatry 65*, no. 4 (1995): 468–478.

32. B. Mandel, "The Homeless Are a Cancer on City's Soul," *San Francisco Examiner*, January 14, 1990; L. Ludlow, "Over the Edge and on the Streets: Mentally Ill Homeless near Crisis in S.F.," *San Francisco Chronicle*, December 27, 1987; Letter to the author, August 1992.

33. C. W. Dugger, "Threat Only When on Crack, Homeless Man Foils System," *New York Times*, September 3, 1992.

34. M. Fiegel, "The Rip Van Winkle of Psychiatry" (letter), *Wall Street Journal*, March 30, 1994; S. Sandler, "The West Side Has Lost Patience," *New York Times*, November 17, 1992;

Matthew P. Dumont, *Treating the Poor: A Personal Sojourn through the Rise and Fall of Community Mental Health* (Belmont, MA: Dymphna Press, 1992), 2; L. Holloway, "Airport Homeless: A Long Pleasant Layover," *New York Times*, February 3, 1995; G. F. Will, "A Right to Live on the Sidewalk?" *Washington Post*, November 19, 1987.

35. S. Robitaille, "Statistics Paint Picture of a System in Distress," *Mercury News* (San Jose, CA), February 16, 1992; D. Gamino, "Jail Rivals State Hospital in Mentally Ill Population," *Austin American-Statesman*, April 17, 1993; "Mentally Ill and Ignorant" (editorial), *Cleveland Plain Dealer*, September 8, 1994; M. Hornbeck, "Mentally Ill Flood Prisons," *Detroit News*, December 4, 1997; D. Romboy, "S. L. Urged to Tackle Mental-Health Issue," *Deseret News* (Salt Lake City, UT), October 19, 1999; R. L. Elliott, "Jailing Mentally Ill for Minor Offenses Helps No One," *Atlanta Journal-Constitution*, April 4, 2002; D. Schanche Jr., "Prisons: A Costly Answer to Mental Health Care," *Macon (GA) Telegraph*, January 28, 2002.

36. Y. C. Hammett, "Prisons Fail to Help Mentally Ill," *Stuart News/Port St. Lucie News* (FL), April 29, 1998; "1 in 10 inmates in Dallas Jail Is Mentally Ill," *Austin American-Statesman*, May 31, 1992; M. J. Grinfeld, "Report Focuses on Jailed Mentally Ill: L.A. Task Force Seeks Change, Tight Budgets May Delay Reform," *Psychiatric Times*, July 1993; S. Downing, "A Third of Inmates in County Jails Mentally Ill, Survey Finds," *Commercial Appeal* (Memphis, TN), March 30, 1999; Paula M. Ditton, *Mental Health and Treatment of Inmates and Probationers* (Washington, DC: Bureau of Justice Statistics Special Report, US Department of Justice, July 1999).

37. J. R. Husted, R. A. Charter, and B. Perrou, "California Law Enforcement Agencies and the Mentally Ill Offender," *Bulletin of the American Academy of Psychiatry and the Law 23*, no. 3 (1995): 315–329; E. Bumiller, "In Wake of Attack, Giuliani Cracks Down on Homeless," *New York Times*, November 20, 1999; S. Downing, "Mentally Ill Woman Sent to State Facility," *Commercial Appeal* (Memphis, TN), March 10, 1999.

38. Ventura County Grand Jury Report, *Fatal Shootings in Ventura County by Law Enforcement Officers, 1992–2001* (Ventura County, CA: Office of the Ventura County District Attorney, undated); Anthony Baez Foundation, *Stolen Lives, Killed by Law Enforcement* (New York: National Lawyers Guild, 1999); J. J. Fyfe, "Policing the Emotionally Disturbed," *Journal of the American Academy of Psychiatry and the Law 28*, no. 3 (2000): 345–347; "Mental Illness Frequently Deepens the Tragedy of Police Shootings," *Seattle Post-Intelligencer*, May 25, 2000; B. P. Kraft, "Suspect Pleads Guilty in Slaying of Police Officer," *Jackson (MS) Clarion-Ledger*, July 10, 1993; C. N. Hart, "Tragedy Raises Many Questions," *Mental Health Advocate* (Alliance for the Mentally Ill of Minnesota), September/October 1993; "Cop Killer Was Hostile Loner Who Liked to Feed Birds," *Kalispell (MT) Daily Inter Lake*, October 3, 1994; "N.M. Gunfire Kills Three," *Denver Post*, May 28, 1994; D. Holden, "Relatives Say Zmyewski Was Severely Mentally Ill," *Huntsville (AL) Times*, November 27, 1994; C. Quinn, "Officer Dies of Gunshot Wound," *Winston-Salem Journal* (NC), March 1, 1995. Russell E. Weston Jr., a man with paranoid schizophrenia, shot two Capitol police officers to death at the US Capitol building on July 24, 1998. Francis Mario Zito, a forty-two-year-old man with a long history of mental illness, was convicted of murdering a Queen Anne's County, Maryland, sheriff's deputy and a Centreville, Maryland, police officer on February 13, 2001. James Logan, a twenty-three-year-old with schizophrenia, shot and killed two Prince George's County, Maryland, sheriff's deputies in August 2001, when they came to his home and attempted to take him for an emergency psychiatric evaluation. See M. Roig-Franzia, "Suspect Battled Schizophrenia: Man Held in Officers' Slayings Has History of Violent Outbursts," *Washington Post*, February 15, 2001, and "Suspect Sought in

Deaths of Deputies," WBAL Channel News (MD), August 30, 2002, http://www.wbalchan-nel.com.

39. Donald M. Steinwachs, Judith D. Kasper, and Elizabeth A. Skinner, *Family Perspectives on Meeting the Needs for Care of Severely Mentally Ill Relatives: A National Survey* (Arlington, VA: National Alliance for the Mentally Ill, 1992); B. G. Link, H. Andrews, and F. T. Cullen, "The Violent and Illegal Behavior of Mental Patients Reconsidered," *American Sociological Review 57*, no. 3 (1992): 275–292; J. Monahan, "Mental Disorder and Violent Behavior," *American Psychologist 47*, no. 4 (1992): 511–521.

40. Keith Ablow, *The Strange Case of Dr. Kappler: The Doctor Who Became a Killer* (New York: Free Press, 1994); B. Miller, "Woman Freed on Insanity Plea Held in New Slaying," *Washington Post*, July 10, 1993, and P. Davis and B. Miller, "Police Had Warning of Violence," *Washington Post*, July 13, 1993; B. Coddington, "Attorneys: Spare Man Death Penalty; Murderer Is No Threat to Public, Other Inmates," *Spokesman-Review* (Spokane, WA), September 30, 1998; T. Alex, "Truck Hits Car, Killing 1," *Des Moines Register*, September 29, 1998; Associated Press, "Need Seen to Plug Holes in Care of Mentally Ill," February 21, 1999.

41. F. Fessenden, "Rampage Killers: They Threaten, Seethe and Unhinge, Then Kill in Quantity," *New York Times,* April 9, 2000.

42. In 1900, there were 150,000 hospitalized patients and a population of 76 million. In 1955, there were 559,000 patients and a population of 165 million. In 2000, there were 55,000 patients and a population of 281 million; Scull, "A New Trade in Lunacy"; J. A. Talbott, "Deinstitutionalization: Avoiding the Disasters of the Past," *Hospital and Community Psychiatry 30*, no. 9 (1979): 621–624.

## Chapter 7

1. L. Davidson et al., "Peer Support among Adults with Serious Mental Illness: A Report from the Field," *Schizophrenia Bulletin 32*, no. 3 (2006): 443–450; A. O. Ahmed et al., "Peers and Peer-Led Interventions for People with Schizophrenia," *Psychiatric Clinics of North America 35*, no. 3 (2012): 699–715.

2. L. Davidson et al., "The Top Ten Concerns about Recovery Encountered in Mental Health System Transformation," *Psychiatric Services 57*, no. 5 (2006): 640–645. See also S. A. Peebles et al., "Recovery and Systems Transformation for Schizophrenia," *Psychiatric Clinics of North America 30*, no. 3 (2007): 567–583, and F. J. Frese, E. L. Knight, and E. Saks, "Recovery from Schizophrenia: With Views of Psychiatrists, Psychologists, and Others Diagnosed with This Disorder," *Schizophrenia Bulletin 35*, no. 2 (2009): 370–380.

3. D. J. Rissmiller and J. H. Rissmiller, "Evolution of the Antipsychiatry Movement into Mental Health Consumerism," *Psychiatric Services 57*, no. 6 (2006): 863–866.

4. E. Fuller Torrey et al., *No Room at the Inn: Trends and Consequences of Closing Public Psychiatric Hospitals* (Arlington, VA: Treatment Advocacy Center, 2012); E. Fuller Torrey et al., *The Shortage of Public Hospital Beds for Mentally Ill Persons* (Arlington, VA: Treatment Advocacy Center, 2008).

5. A. Simmons, "Prisons See More Inmates Requiring Mental Health Care," *Gwinnett (GA) Daily Post*, July 30, 2006; "Jail Situation Is Insane" (editorial), *Rome (GA) News Tribune*, December 19, 2011; E. Fuller Torrey et al., *More Mentally Ill Persons Are in Jails and Prisons Than Hospitals: A Survey of the States* (Arlington, VA: Treatment Advocacy Center, 2010).

6. Associated Press, "Official Says State Prisons Like a 'Mental Health Center,'" *Athens (AL) News Courier*, December 21, 2007; "After Closing Psychiatric Hospitals, Michigan

Incarcerates Mentally Ill," *Detroit Free Press*, November 27, 2011; A. Schrader, "Better to Aid Mentally Ill Outside of Jail, Report Says," *Denver Post*, April 19, 2008.

7. J. Mozingo, "Jailing the Ill," *Miami Herald*, November 15, 2007; L. Hammack, "Jail Can Offer Temporary Refuge for Those Suffering from Mental Illness," *Roanoke (VA) Times*, October 15, 2007; N. Satija, "Toledo Area Jails Facing Growing Numbers of the Mentally Ill: Inmate Influx Is Attributed to Fewer Hospitals," *Toledo Blade* (OH), August 30, 2009; B. Grissom, "Sheriffs Worry over Proposed Mental Health Cuts," *Texas Tribune*, December 16, 2010; "Mentally Ill Need Treatment, Not Jail," *WWLP* (Boston), February 2, 2012, http://www.wwlp.com/dpp/news/politics/state_politics/Mentally-ill-need-treatment-not-jail; C. Dettro, "Mentally Ill Create 'Crisis' for Law Enforcement, Officials Say," *State Journal-Register* (IL), September 19, 2012; D. J. James and L. E. Glaze, *Mental Health Problems of Prison and Jail Inmates* (Washington, DC: Bureau of Justice Statistics, US Department of Justice, 2006).

8. A. Hermes, "Boone County Struggles to Meet Mental Health Care Needs for Inmates," *Missourian*, December 17, 2007; L. Monsewicz, "Stark County Jail Can Be a Dangerous Place," *CantonRep.com* (OH), October 19, 2011, http://www.cantonrep.com/news/x984143026/Stark-County-Jail-can-be-a-dangerous-place; C. Gross, "Rikers Island Struggles with Record Mental Illness Numbers," NY1.com, September 30, 2011, http://www.ny1.com/content/top_stories/148187/rikers-island-struggles-with-record-mental-illness-numbers; B. Hall, "Mentally Ill Fill Prisons with Sometimes Deadly Results," *NewsChannel 5* (TN), May 9, 2011, http://www.newschannel5.com/story/14602818/mentally-ill-fill-prisons-with-sometimes-deadly-results?clienttype=printable.

9. Grissom, "Sheriffs Worry"; L. S. Avant, "Mentally Ill Crowding in Jails, Officials Say," *TuscaloosaNews.com* (AL), April 19, 2012, http://www.tuscaloosanews.com/article/20120419/NEWS/120419722; J. Last, "Shocking Stats from Erie County Prison," *ErieTVNews.com* (PA), July 11, 2012, http://www.erietvnews.com/story/19003869/shocking-stats-from-erie-county-prison; M. Geary, "Mentally Ill Inmates Fill Black Hawk County Jail," *KCRG* (IA), April 3, 2011, http://www.kcrg.com/news/local/Mentally-Ill-Inmates-Fill-Black-Hawk-County-Jail-119160659.html; J. Mitchell, "Jail No Place for Mentally Ill, Advocates Say," *Clarion Ledger* (Jackson, MS), January 31, 2011.

10. Criminal Justice/Mental Health Consensus Project, Fact Sheet: "Mental Illness and Jails," http://consensusproject.org/downloads/fact_jails.pdf; C. Turner, "Ethical Issues in Criminal Justice Administration," *American Jails* 20, no. 6 (2007): 49–53; F. Butterfield, "Study Finds Hundreds of Thousands of Inmates Mentally Ill," *New York Times*, October 22, 2003; K. Connolly, "Mentally Ill Increasing Strain on US Prison System," *BBC News*, February 22, 2011, http://www.bbc.co.uk/news/world-us-canada-12532538.

11. G. Fields, "No Way Out: Trapped by Rules, the Mentally Ill Languish in Prison," *Wall Street Journal*, May 3, 2006; M. Parker, "Mentally Ill Jailed, Awaiting Therapy," *Clarion Ledger* (Jackson, MS), August 16, 2010; J. Dearen, "Mental Patients Languish in Jail," *Oakland Tribune* (CA), September 22, 2005; N. Wolff, C. L. Blitz, and J. Shi, "Rates of Sexual Victimization in Prison for Inmates with and without Mental Disorders," *Psychiatric Services* 58, no. 8 (2007): 1087–1094.

12. C. M. Miller and A. Fantz, "Special 'Psych' Jails Planned," *Miami Herald*, November 15, 2007; E. Bender, "Community Treatment More Humane, Reduces Criminal Justice Costs," *Psychiatric News*, October 3, 2003, 28; A. Rathbun, "Inmates with Mental Illness Bring Extra Costs to Monroe Prison," *Everett (WA) Herald*, November 23, 2009; A. J. Gottschlich and G. Cetnar, "Drug Bills at Jail Top Food Costs," *Springfield (OH) News Sun*, August 20, 2002.

13. B. Bradley, "Sheriff Dart Considers Suing the State over Health Issue," *ABC7News.com*, May 20, 2011, http://abclocal.go.com/wls/story?section=news/local&id=8143042; R. Armon, "Sheriff Closes Jail to Violent Mentally Ill," *Akron (OH) Beacon Journal*, February 13, 2012.

14. Fields, "No Way Out"; R. Exner, "Sheriff Runs Own Pharmacy Unit in Jail," *Cleveland Plain Dealer*, November 5, 2011.

15. " 'Edge of Crisis' for Jails," *Sun Journal* (Lewiston, ME), August 31, 2007; Miller and Fantz, "Special 'Psych' Jails Planned"; J. McKee, "Lack of Mental-Health Treatment Options Clogs Criminal Justice System," *Helena (MT) Independent Record*, October 2, 2007; N. Barnett, "At Central Prison in Raleigh, a New Mental Hospital Reflects Rise in Mentally Ill Inmates," *Independent News* (NC), February 3, 2011.

16. M. Scott, "State Hospitals as Alternative to Prison?" *WHYY* (Philadelphia), January 27, 2010, http://whyy.org/cms/news/health-science/2010/01/27/state-hospitals-as-alternative-to-prison/29099; New York State Office of Mental Health press release, DOCS, "OMH Open Residential Mental Health Unit at Marcy Correctional Facility," December 15, 2009, http://www.omh.state.ny.us/omhweb/News/2009/pr_rmhu.html.

17. D. Ramsey, "Sheriff's Dept Sees Rise in Calls Relating to the Mentally Ill," *Village News* (CA), August 18, 2011; C. Conrad, "Incidents Involving Mentally Ill Increase," *Mail Tribune* (Medford, OR), May 2, 2011; J. Strong, "Battling Their Demons: A Man with Mental Illness and His West Des Moines Neighbors Live in Fear of Each Other," *Des Moines Register*, September 14, 2006.

18. M. Booth, "Police Get Training on Dealing with Mentally Ill," *Corvallis (OR) Gazette-Times*, May 1, 2008; R. Sheehan, "Shuttling Patients Burdens Deputies," *News and Observer* (Raleigh, NC), January 15, 2010; J. N. Chang, "Deputies on Day 9 with Commitment Patient," *News Herald* (Morgantown, NC), March 26, 2010.

19. J. Scheibe, "Injuries Drop for Officers with Tasers, Officials Say," *Ventura County (CA) Star*, March 27, 2008; T. Buford, "Questions Linger about Man's Death in Police Custody," *Providence (RI) Journal*, July 1, 2008; L. Goldston, "Former Cops Changing Way Santa Clara County Deals with Mentally Ill in Crisis," *Mercury News* (San Jose, CA), November 4, 2010; K. Gibas, "Syracuse Police Say Encounters with Emotionally Disturbed People Are on the Rise," *YNN* (NY), December 19, 2011, http://centralny.ynn.com/content/top_stories/567616/syracuse-police-say-encounters-with-emotionally-disturbed-people-are-on-the-rise/; "Are Some Police Shootings Linked to Lapse in Mental Health Care?," *WMUR 9* (NH), September 22, 2011, http://news.yahoo.com/video/manchesterwmur-18211745/are-some-police-shootings-linked-to-mental-health-lapses-26713713.html; J. Proctor, "Database to Warn Cops of Mental Illness Red Flags," *PoliceOne.com* (NM), May 8, 2012, http://www.policeone.com/edp/articles/5504604-Database-to-warn-cops-of-mental-illness-red-flags/.

20. Goldston, "Former cops"; P. Malone, "Mentally Ill Inmates Pose Big Problems, Sheriffs Say," *Pueblo (CO) Chieftan*, September 22, 2007.

21. M. Simonich, "Bill Would Require Police to Train for Mentally Ill," *Las Cruces (NM) Sun-News*, February 10, 2011.

22. S. Krishnan, "Mental-Health Professional Added to Seattle Police Department," *Seattle Times*, May 18, 2010; M. Hsin, "Social Worker to Help Police Department Tackle Mental Health Calls," *Burbank (CA) Leader*, May 29, 2012.

23. A. Foxman, "Jail Officials to Escort Some Inmates to Treatment," *Ventura County (CA) Star*, August 1, 2010; J. Sly, "Police Helping Mentally Ill Find Treatment," *Modesto (CA) Bee*, October 22, 2002; *NAMI E-News*, Vol. 01-20, September 22, 2000.

24. J. Jiggetts, "Va. Beach Sheriff Offers to Aid Mental Health Program," *Virginian-Pilot* (Norfolk, VA), May 5, 2011; S. Taylor, "County to Test Mental Health Court," *Tuscaloosa News* (AL), May 17, 2012.

25. P. A. Griffin, H. J. Steadman, and J. Petrila, "The Use of Criminal Charges and Sanctions in Mental Health Courts," *Psychiatric Services 53*, no. 10 (2002): 1285–1289; H. J. Steadman, S. Davison, and C. Brown, "Mental Health Courts: Their Promise and Unanswered Questions," *Psychiatric Services 52*, no. 4 (2001): 457–458.

26. V. A. Hiday and B. Ray, "Arrests Two Years after Exiting a Well-Established Mental Health Court," *Psychiatric Services 61*, no. 5 (2010): 463–468; H. J. Steadman et al., "Effect of Mental Health Courts on Arrests and Jail Days," *Archives of General Psychiatry 68*, no. 2 (2011): 167–172; H. R. Lamb and L. E. Weinberger, "Mental Health Courts as a Way to Provide Treatment to Violent Persons with Severe Mental Illness," *Journal of the American Medical Association 300*, no. 6 (2008): 722–724.

27. J. Marquis and D. Morain, "A Tortuous Path for the Mentally Ill," *Los Angeles Times*, November 21, 1999; D. E. McNiel, R. L. Binder, and J. C. Robinson, "Incarceration Associated with Homelessness, Mental Disorder, and Co-occurring Substance Abuse," *Psychiatric Services 56*, no. 7 (2005): 840–846; H. R. Lamb et al., "Treatment Prospects for Persons with Severe Mental Illness in an Urban County Jail," *Psychiatric Services 58*, no. 6 (2007): 782–786; P. F. Mangano and G. Blasi, "Stuck on Skid Row: L.A. Should Do What Other Cities Are: Move the Homeless into Permanent Housing, and Stop Just Managing the Problem," *Los Angeles Times*, October 29, 2007.

28. A. Foster, J. Gable, and J. Buckley, "Homelessness in Schizophrenia," *Psychiatric Clinics of North America 35*, no. 3 (2012): 717–734; A. Nagourney, "Los Angeles Seeking to Shed Reputation for Homelessness," *New York Times*, December 13, 2010; S. Lopez, "Now Comes the Heavy Lifting," *Los Angeles Times*, October 23, 2005; C. Stillwell, "Homeless by the Bay," *San Francisco Chronicle*, March 5, 2008; K. Seligman, "Street Attack Stuns Visiting Doctors," *San Francisco Chronicle*, May 23, 2003.

29. L. Hammack and M. Adams, "Roanoke Turns Its Focus on Homeless," *Roanoke (VA) Times*, December 16, 2007; V. Chufo, "200 High-Risk Patients Locked Out of Mental Health Treatment," *Daily Press* (VA), June 1, 2011; B. Newsome and L. Benzel, "Mental Health Troubles Dog the Chronically Homeless," *Colorado Springs Gazette*, January 6, 2009; G. Remal, "Police May Arrest Homeless Man," *Kennebec (ME) Journal*, September 28, 2005.

30. E. Lichtblau, "Killings of Homeless Rise to Highest Level in a Decade," *New York Times*, August 19, 2010; J. Tuohy, "Deadly Beating of Homeless Man Shows 'The Ultimate Form of Cowardice,'" *IndyStar* (IN), May 6, 2011; J. DeBerry, "At Memorial for New Orleans Murder Victim, a Heavenly Hope Takes on New Meaning," *Nola.com* (LA), May 1, 2011, http://www.nola.com/opinions/index.ssf/2011/05/at_memorial_for_new_orleans_mu.html; "2 Cops Charged in Beating Death of Homeless Man," *CBSNews.com*, September 21, 2011, http://www.cbsnews.com/8301-201_162-20109623.html.

31. D. C. Grabowski et al., "Mental Illness in Nursing Homes: Variations across States," *Health Affairs 28*, no. 3 (2009): 689–700; C. A. Fullerton et al., "Trends in Mental Health Admissions to Nursing Homes, 1999–2005," *Psychiatric Services 60*, no. 7 (2009): 965–971.

32. C. K. Johnson, "Nursing Homes Patients Endangered by Mentally Ill," *Pottstown (PA) Mercury*, May 4, 2009.

33. R. Pear, "Report Finds Violations at Most Nursing Homes," *New York Times*, September 30, 2008; W. Barrett, "Scandal Cash," *Village Voice* (NY), June 4, 2002; C. J. Levy, "Mentally Ill and Locked Up in New York Nursing Homes," *New York Times*, October 6, 2002.

34. M. Fleishman, "The Problem: How Many Patients Live in Residential Care Facilities?" *Psychiatric Services 55*, no. 6 (2004): 620–622.

35. C. J. Levy and S. Kershaw, "For Mentally Ill, Chaos in an Intended Refuge," *New York Times*, April 18, 2001; C. J. Levy, "Doctor Admits He Did Needless Surgery on the Mentally Ill," *New York Times*, May 20, 2003; C. J. Levy, "Home for Mentally Ill Settles Suit on Coerced Prostate Surgery for $7.4 Million," *New York Times*, August 5, 2004; L. Eisenberg, "Violence and the Mentally Ill: Victims, Not Perpetrators," *Archives of General Psychiatry 62*, no. 8 (2005): 825–826.

36. Barrett, "Scandal Cash."

37. "Group-Home Owners Charged with Resident Abuse, Fraud," *Washington Post*, November 8, 2005; D. S. Fallis, "In Va.'s Assisted Living Homes, Violent Preyed on the Vulnerable," *Washington Post*, May 24, 2004; M. Kissinger, "Mentally Ill Suffer Deadly Neglect," *Milwaukee Journal Sentinel*, March 18, 2006; M. Kissinger, "Promise of Care Made But Broken," *Milwaukee Journal Sentinel*, March 19, 2006.

38. L. Ahearn, "Mental Health Reform Flaws, Laid Bare," *Greensboro (NC) News Record*, April 13, 2008; M. Biesecker, "Feds Will Probe Mental Health," *Charlotte-Observer* (NC), November 25, 2010; C. M. Miller, R. Barry, and M. Sallah, "At Homes for the Mentally Ill, a Sweeping Breakdown in Care," *Miami Herald*, May 4, 2011.

39. J. Y. Choe, "Perpetration of Violence, Violent Victimization, and Severe Mental Illness: Balancing Public Health Concerns," *Psychiatric Services 59*, no. 2 (2008): 153–164; "A Ferocious Crime against the Helpless," *Cape Cod Times*, July 22, 1984.

40. Stillwell, "Homeless by the Bay"; R. Vaillancourt, "Woman Attacks Infant in Stroller," *Los Angeles Downtown News*, July 27, 2011.

41. B. Wallman, "Leaders Angered by Homeless in Fort Lauderdale," *Sun Sentinel* (FL), February 22, 2008; Reich and Siegel, "Psychiatry under Siege."

42. R. C. Archibold, "Please Don't Feed Homeless in Parks, Las Vegas Says in Ordinance," *New York Times*, July 28, 2006.

43. E. F. Torrey, R. Esposito, and J. Geller, "Problems Associated with Mentally Ill Individuals in Public Libraries," *Public Libraries*, March/April 2009.

44. E. Julius, "Homeless in Hagerstown," *Hagerstown (MD) Herald Mail*, September 22, 2009; Associated Press, "San Fran Library Hires Social Worker for Homeless," *New York Times*, February 20, 2010; A. Ball, "Public Workers Given Mental Health Training in Austin," *Austin American-Statesman*, September 6, 2010; Torrey et al., "Public Libraries."

45. J. Dwyer, "After a Death Seen on Tape, Change Is Promised," *New York Times*, July 12, 2008.

46. M. Moran, "Mental Illness Accounts for Large Portion of ED Resources," *Psychiatric News*, August 20, 2010; A. Judd and A. Miller, "Mental Patient Backlog Jams ER," *Atlanta Journal Constitution*, November 28, 2007; C. Smith, "Task Force Recommends Changes to State's Involuntary Commitment Laws," *Seattle Post-Intelligencer*, October 9, 2008; "9 Patients Made Nearly 2,700 ER Visits in Texas," Associated Press Archive, April 1, 2009; M. Biesecker, "Mentally Ill Wait Longer in ERs," *News and Observer* (Raleigh, NC), January 20, 2011; K. Brown, "Fewer Beds at S.C. Psychiatric Hospitals Mean More Mentally Ill Patients End Up in Emergency Rooms," *Independent Mail* (Anderson, SC), April 2, 2011; K. Alexander, "Fresno County to Reopen Mentally Ill Crisis Center," *Fresno (CA) Bee*, March 11, 2012.

47. P. J. Taylor, "Psychosis and Violence: Stories, Fears, and Reality," *Canadian Journal of Psychiatry 53*, no. 10 (2008): 647–659; C. C. Joyal et al., "Major Mental Disorders and Violence: A Critical Update," *Current Psychiatry Reviews 3*, no. 1 (2007): 33–50; K. S. Douglas, L. S. Guy, and S. D. Hart, "Psychosis as a Risk Factor for Violence to

Others: A Meta-analysis," *Psychological Bulletin 135*, no. 5 (2009): 679–706; S. Fazel et al., "Schizophrenia and Violence: Systematic Review and Meta-analysis," *PLoS Medicine 6*, no. 8 (2009): e1000120.

48. T. Ruiz, "Was Schizophrenia to Blame for Emergency Landing?," *ConnectAmarillo.com* (TX), October 20, 2011, http://www.connectamarillo.com/news/story.aspx?id=677065#. UIr9tIZ0bNg; W. Yardley, "White House Shooting Suspect's Path to Extremism," *New York Times*, November 20, 2011; J. Mobilia, "Man Suspected of Taking Chainsaw to Utility Poles in Court," *YNN.com* (NY), January 26, 2012, http://jamestown.ynn.com/content/all_news/571597/man-suspected-of-taking-chainsaw-to-utility-poles-in-court/.

49. J. C. Matejkowski, S. W. Cullen, and P. L. Solomon, "Characteristics of Persons with Severe Mental Illness Who Have Been Incarcerated for Murder," *Journal of the American Academy of Psychiatry and the Law 36*, no. 1 (2008): 74–86; S. Fazel and M. Grann, "Psychiatric Morbidity among Homicide Offenders: A Swedish Population Study," *American Journal of Psychiatry 161*, no. 11 (2004): 2129–2131; S. Fazel et al., "Homicide in Discharged Patients with Schizophrenia and Other Psychoses: A National Case-Control Study," *Schizophrenia Research 123*, no. 2–3 (2010): 263–269; M. Eronen, J. Tilhonen, and P. Hakola, "Schizophrenia and Homicidal Behavior," *Schizophrenia Bulletin 22*, no. 1 (1996): 83–89; P. Gottlieb, G. Gabrielson, and P. Kamp, "Psychotic Homicides in Copenhagen from 1959 to 1983," *Acta Psychiatrica Scandinavica 76*, no. 3 (1987): 285–292; M. Erb et al., "Homicide and Schizophrenia: Maybe Treatment Does Have a Preventive Effect," *Criminal Behavior and Mental Health 11*, no. 1 (2011): 6–26; K. G. W. W. Koh, K. P. Gwee, and Y. H. Chan, "Psychiatric Aspects of Homicide in Singapore: A Five-Year Review (1997–2001)," *Singapore Medical Journal 47*, no. 4 (2006): 297–304.

50. M. Graczyk and J. A. Lozano, "Family: Texas Shootout Gunman Had Mental Illness," Associated Press, August 14, 2012; "Family Thwarted in Getting Laura the Help She So Desperately Needs," *News Tribune* (Tacoma, WA), August 15, 2012.

51. S. James, "After '75 Murders of His Family, Detroit Man Again Accused of Killing Family," *Detroit Free Press*, January 28, 2000; "Suspect in Everett Stabbing Committed Nearly Identical Crime in 1980," *King5.com* (WA), July 20, 2010, http://www.king5.com/news/local/Suspect-in-Everett-stabbing-has-attacked-before-98833949.html; D. Morse and M. P. Flaherty, "Woman Again Accused of Stabbing Shoppers," *Washington Post*, October 13, 2011.

52. J. Walker and J. Nolan, "Slaying Suspect Was Off His Meds," *Richmond (VA) Times Dispatch*, October 29, 2007; L. Crimaldi, "A Killer's Release," *Boston Herald*, December 17, 2007; J. Emily, "Three-Time Murderer Gets 50 Years in '08 Lake Highlands Slaying," *Dallas Morning News*, July 29, 2009; J. Sullivan, J. Martin, and C. Clarridge, "DNA Links Felon to Slaying on Capitol Hill," *Seattle Times*, January 26, 2008; K. Mitchell, "Fatal Knife Attack Not a Shock," *Denver Post*, June 15, 2008; T. Alex, "Suspect in Des Moines Killings Strangled Colo. Man in '91," *Des Moines Register*, July 16, 2008; A. Furillo, "Sacramento Homicide Spotlights Gap in Mental Health Care," *Sacramento Bee*, November 23, 2008.

53. Bureau of Justice Statistics, "Homicide Trends in the United States" (Washington, DC: Federal Bureau of Investigation, Uniform Crime Reports, 1950–2005), http://bjs.ojp.usdoj.gov/content/homicide/tables/totalstab.cfm.

54. K. Ablow, "Mental Illness May Have Prompted Empire State Building Shooting," *FoxNews.com*, August 24, 2012, http://www.foxnews.com/opinion/2012/08/24/prediction-empire-state-building-shooter-will-turn-out-to-be-mentally-ill/.

55. "Table 38, Percentage Distribution of Recipients by Diagnostic Group, by State or Other Area, December 2009," *SSI Annual Statistical Report* (Washington, DC: Social Security

Administration, 2009), http://www.ssa.gov/policy/docs/statcomps/ssi_asr/2009/sect06. html#table38 (the total number of SSI recipients was multiplied by the percentage with "mental disorders, other" for each state); "Table 10, Number, by State or Other Area and Diagnostic Group, December 2009," *Annual Statistical Report on the Social Security Disability Insurance Program, 2009* (Washington, DC: Social Security Administration, 2009), http://www.ssa.gov/policy/docs/statcomps/di_asr/2009/sect01b.html#table10; H. H. Goldman, A. A. Gattozzi, and C. A. Taube, "Defining and Counting the Chronically Mentally Ill," *Hospital and Community Psychiatry 32*, no. 1 (1981): 21–27.

56. T. L. Mark et al., "Changes in US Spending on Mental Health and Substance Abuse Treatment, 1986–2005, and Implications for Policy," *Health Affairs 30*, no. 2 (2011): 284– 292; W. Gronfein, "Incentives and Intentions in Mental Health Policy: A Comparison of the Medicaid and Community Mental Health Programs," *Journal of Health and Social Behavior, 26*, no. 3 (1985): 192–206; R. G. Frank, H. H. Goldman, and M. Hogan, "Medicaid and Mental Health: Be Careful What You Ask For," *Health Affairs 22*, no. 1 (2003): 101–113.

57. D. Rowland, R. Garfield, and R. Elias, "Accomplishments and Challenges in Medicaid Mental Health," *Health Affairs 22*, no. 5 (2003): 73–83; Frank et al., "Medicaid and Mental Health"; "Table 24, SMHA-controlled Mental Health Revenues, by Revenue Source and by State, FY 2008," *NASMHPD Research Institute 2008 State Survey* (Falls Church, VA: NRI Inc., 2008), http://www.nri-inc.org/projects/profiles/RevExp2008/T24.pdf; Mark et al, "Changes in US Spending."

58. Mark et al., "Changes in US Spending"; J. J. Stephan, *State Prison Expenditures, 2001* (Washington, DC: US Department of Justice, Bureau of Justice Statistics, 2004).

59. E. Q. Wu et al., "The Economic Burden of Schizophrenia in the United States in 2002," *Journal of Clinical Psychiatry 66*, no. 9 (2005): 1122–1129.

60. T. R. Insel, "Assessing the Economic Costs of Serious Mental Illness," *American Journal of Psychiatry 165*, no. 6 (2008): 663–665; D. E. Marcotte and S. Markowitz, "A Cure for Crime? Psycho-pharmaceuticals and Crime Trends," Working Paper 15354 (Cambridge, MA: National Bureau of Economic Research, 2009), http://www.nber.org/papers/w15354.

## Chapter 8

1. *Deinstitutionalization, Mental Illness, and Medications, Senate Hearings Before the Comm. on Finance*, 103rd Cong. 1–3 (1994).

2. Atwell, interview by author; Atwell, personal communication to author, March 10, 2011; Rashi Fein, personal communication to author, December 21, 2010.

3. R. H. Felix, "A Model for Comprehensive Mental Health Centers," *American Journal of Psychiatry 54*, no. 12 (1964): 1964–1969; R. D. Lyons, "How Release of Mental Patients Began," *New York Times*, October 30, 1984; Bertram S. Brown, personal communication to author, March 11, 1988.

4. S. F. Yolles, "The Future of Community Psychiatry," in Barton and Sanborn, *An Assessment*, 169–185.

5. Lyons, "Release of Mental Patients"; Brown, interviews by author, October 15 and December 22, 2010.

6. A. Scull, "A New Trade in Lunacy"; A. T. Scull, "The Decarceration of the Mentally Ill: A Critical View," *Politics and Society 173*, no. 2 (1976): 173–212, quoting George W. Brown.

7. Felix, interview; C. Krauthammer, "For the Homeless: Asylum," *Washington Post*, January 4, 1985.

8. F. N. Arnoff, "Social Consequences of Policy toward Mental Illness," *Science 188*, no. 4195 (1975): 1277–1281.

9. G. J. Maier, "The Tyranny of Irresponsible Freedom," *Hospital and Community Psychiatry 40*, no. 5 (1989): 453.

10. M. J. Berens, "Mentally Ill 'Vanish'" (6n28).

11. E. F. Torrey, "Bureaucratic Insanity," *National Review*, July 20, 2011.

12. Arnoff, "Social Consequences"; Felicetti, *Mental Health and Retardation Politics*, 32, quoting Mike Gorman; Frank Ochberg, interview by author, March 21, 2011.

13. S. P. Segal, "Civil Commitment Law, Mental Health Services, and US Homicide Rates," *Social Psychiatry and Psychiatric Epidemiology 47*, no. 9 (2012): 1449–1458; A. Rosenblatt, "Providing Custodial Care for Mental Patients: An Affirmative View," *Psychiatric Quarterly 48*, no. 1 (1974): 14–25; "The Need for Asylum," *Lancet 378*, no. 9785 (2011): 1.

14. Torrey et al., *Shortage of Public Hospital Beds*.

15. Xavier Amador and Anthony David, eds., *Insight and Psychosis: Awareness of Illness in Schizophrenia and Related Disorders* (Oxford: Oxford University Press, 2004).

16. B. G. Link et al., "Arrest Outcomes Associated with Outpatient Commitment in New York State," *Psychiatric Services 62*, no. 5 (2011): 504–508; *Kendra's Law: Final Report on the Status of Assisted Outpatient Treatment* (Albany, NY: New York State Office of Mental Health, 2005); V. A. Hiday et al., "Impact of Outpatient Commitment on Victimization of People with Severe Mental Illness," *American Journal of Psychiatry 159*, no. 8 (2002): 1403–1411; G. Tsai, "Assisted Outpatient Treatment: Preventive, Recovery-Based Care for the Most Seriously Mentally Ill," *Resident's Journal 7*, no. 6 (2012): 16–18.

17. J. W. Swanson et al., "Involuntary Out-Patient Commitment and Reduction of Violent Behaviour in Persons with Severe Mental Illness," *British Journal of Psychiatry 176*, no. 4 (2000): 324–331; *Kendra's Law*; C. O'Keefe, D. P. Potenza, and K. T. Mueser, "Treatment Outcomes for Severely Mentally Ill Patients on Conditional Discharge to Community-Based Treatment," *Journal of Nervous and Mental Disease 185*, no. 6 (1997): 409–411.

18. Torrey, *The Insanity Offense*, 179–180; D. A. Regier et al., "The De Facto Mental and Addictive Disorders Service System. Epidemiologic Catchment Area Prospective 1-Year Prevalence Rates of Disorders and Services," *Archives of General Psychiatry 50*, no. 2 (1993): 85–94.

19. Slovenko and Luby, "On the Emancipation of Mental Patients"; "The Discharged Chronic Mental Patient," *Medical World News*, April 12, 1974; Torrey, *Nowhere to Go*, xiv, quoting an interview of Mike Gorman. The Gorman letter to the *New York Times*, dated November 5, 1984, is among the Mike Gorman papers in the National Library of Medicine; it was apparently never published.

20. Dumont, *Treating the Poor*, 16, 26.

21. Felix, interview; Ochberg, interview; Panzetta, *Community Mental Health*, 28; W. G. Smith and D. W. Hart, "Community Mental Health: A Noble Failure?," *Hospital and Community Psychiatry 26*, no. 9 (1975): 581–583.

22. Claudewell R. Thomas, interview by author, March 30, 2011.

23. J. R. Ewalt, "Services for the Mentally Ill: Rational or Irrational?," *Mental Hygiene 15*, no. 2 (1964): 63–66; M. A. Test, "Continuity of Care in Community Treatment," *New Directions for Mental Health Services*, no. 2 (1979): 15–23; E. F. Torrey, "Continuous Treatment Teams in the Care of the Chronic Mentally Ill," *Hospital and Community Psychiatry 37*, no. 12 (1986): 1243–1247.

24. B. J. Burns and A. B. Santos, "Assertive Community Treatment: An Update of Randomized Trials," *Psychiatric Services 46*, no. 7 (1995): 669–675; P. S. Appelbaum and S. Le Melle, "Techniques Used by Assertive Community Treatment (ACT) Teams to Encourage

Adherence: Patient and Staff Perceptions," *Community Mental Health Journal 44*, no. 6 (2008): 459–464; R. E. Clark et al., "Cost-Effectiveness of Assertive Community Treatment versus Standard Case Management for Persons with Co-occurring Severe Mental Illness and Substance Abuse Disorders," *Health Services Review 33*, no. 5 (1998): 1285–1308; S. M. Essock, L. K. Frisman, and J. Kontos, "Cost-Effectiveness of Assertive Community Treatment Teams," *American Journal of Orthopsychiatry 68*, no. 2 (1998): 179–190; G. S. Cuddeback, J. P. Morrissey, and P. S. Meyer, "How Many Assertive Community Treatment Teams Do We Need?," *Psychiatric Services 57*, no. 12 (2006): 1803–1806.

25. D. K. Padgett and B. F. Henwood, "Moving into the Fourth Decade of ACT," *Psychiatric Services 62*, no. 6 (2011): 605.

26. B. C. Vladeck, *Unloving Care: The Nursing Home Tragedy* (New York: Basic Books, 1980), 21; S. Sheehan, *Is There No Place on Earth for Me?* (Boston: Houghton, Mifflin, 1982).

27. G. R. Bond et al., "The Effectiveness of Psychiatric Rehabilitation: A Summary of Research at Thresholds," *Psychosocial Rehabilitation Journal 7*, no. 4 (1984): 6–22.

28. K. Sheppard, "Programs That Work," *American Prospect*, July/August 2008, A15–A17.

29. Philip Zimbardo, *The Lucifer Effect: Understanding How Good People Turn Evil* (New York: Random House, 2007), xii.

30. D. J. Mellett, "Bureaucracy and Mental Illness: The Commissioners in Lunacy, 1845–90," *Medical History 221*, no. 3 (1981): 221–250. As an aside, one of the commissioners was Robert Lutwidge, the uncle and close friend of Lewis Carroll. When Lutwidge was killed by a patient during a hospital inspection, Carroll memorialized his death in a poem, *The Hunting of the Snark*. For an account of this, see E. F. Torrey and J. Miller, "The Capture of the Snark," *Knight Letter*, *73*, no. 2 (2004), 21–25.

31. S. J. Schultz, "Adult Home Abuse Found," *Legislative Gazette* (Albany, NY), June 15, 1992; S. Raab, "Report Says Home Operators Misused Funds Meant to Feed Mentally Ill," *New York Times*, June 14, 1992; M. Winerip, "For Adult Homes This One Ranks among the Worst," *New York Times*, August 17, 1990.

32. A. Scull, "Deinstitutionalization and the Rights of the Deviant," *Journal of Social Issues 37*, no. 3 (1981): 6–20.

33. E. L. Bassuk and S. Gerson, "Deinstitutionalization and Mental Health Services," *Scientific American 238*, no. 2 (1978): 46–53.

34. Alan A. Stone, personal communication to author, June 1, 2010; W. R. Shadish Jr., "Private-Sector Care for Chronically Mentally Ill Individuals," *American Psychologist 44*, no. 8 (1989): 1142–1147.

35. J. Merchant, "The State of Mental Health Care," *Smoky Mountain News* (NC), January 16, 2008; *North Carolina's Mental Health Care Crisis and the Resulting Challenges Facing Mission Hospital* (Asheville, NC: Mission Health System, January 2011); "Family Thwarted"; C. Hill, "Where to Put Pierce County's Mentally Ill Jail Inmates?," *News Tribune* (Tacoma, WA), September 11, 2012; K. Hamilton, "OptumHealth's Mad Medicine," *Seattle Weekly*, May 23, 2012.

36. Scull, "The Rights of the Deviant"; Aldous Huxley, *Collected Essays* (New York: Harper, 1959), 308.

37. Torrey, *The Insanity Offense*, 179–180.

38. S. R. Poulin et al., "Service Use and Costs for Persons Experiencing Chronic Homelessness in Philadelphia: A Population-Based Study," *Psychiatric Services 61*, no. 11 (2010): 1093–1098; J. O'Malley, "$15 Million Tab for the Homeless," *Reno (NV) Gazette Journal*, December 12, 2007; M. Gladwell, "Million-Dollar Murray," *New Yorker*, February 3, 2006.

39. S. F. Jencks, M. V. Williams, and E. A. Coleman, "Rehospitalizations among Patients in the Medicare Fee-for-Service Program," *New England Journal of Medicine 360*, no. 14

(2009): 1418–1428; C. Boyd et al., "Faces of Medicaid: Clarifying Multimorbidity Patterns to Improve Targeting and Delivery of Clinical Services for Medicaid Populations," Center for Health Care Strategies Data Brief, December 2010, http://www.chcs.org/publications3960/publications_show.htm?doc_id=1261201; S. X. Sun et al., "Review and Analysis of Hospitalization Costs Associated with Antipsychotic Nonadherence in the Treatment of Schizophrenia in the United States," *Current Medical Research and Opinions 23*, no. 10 (2007): 2305–2312; R. I. Garis and K. C. Farmer, "Examining Costs of Chronic Conditions in a Medicaid Population," *Managed Care 11*, no. 8 (2002): 43–50.

40. *Action for Mental Health*, 262; "Oregon Plan: Future of MH Services Up in the Air," *Psychiatric News*, May 19, 1995, 1, 30; D. A. Pollack et al., "Prioritization of Mental Health Services in Oregon," *Milbank Quarterly 72*, no. 3 (1994): 515–550.

41. P. M. Gillig et al., "What Do Police Officers Really Want from the Mental Health System?" *Hospital and Community Psychiatry 41*, no. 6 (1990): 663–665; M. Tran, K. Pang, and H. G. Reza, "Shocked Family of O.C. Sniper Says He Was 'a Sweetheart,'" *Los Angeles Times*, June 16, 2004.

42. P.-R. Noth, "Care, Safety of Patients Should Trump Cost Issue," *Rome (GA) News-Tribune*, March 13, 2011.

43. J. Lambe, "New Kansas Law Lets Police Know If Offenders Are Mentally Ill," *Kansas City Star*, May 29, 2011; M. Sharpe, "APD to Train Officers to Better Deal with Mentally Ill," *KOB.com* (Albuquerque, NM), May 11, 2011; E. Goode, "States Seeking New Registries for Criminals," *New York Times*, May 21, 2011.

44. Talbott, *The Death of the Asylum*, 174.

45. T. L. Mark et al., "Changes in US Spending on Mental Health and Substance Abuse Treatment, 1986–2005, and Implications for Policy," *Health Affairs 30*, no. 2 (2011): 284–292; R. Frank et al., "Medicaid and Mental Health"; Rowland et al., "Accomplishments and Challenges."

46. C. Shirk, "Medicaid and Mental Health Services," National Health Policy Forum Background Paper No. 66 (Washington, DC: George Washington University, 2008); J. R. Bloom et al., "Capitation of Public Mental Health Services in Colorado: A Five-Year Follow-up of System-Level Effects," *Psychiatric Services 62*, no. 2 (2011): 179–185.

47. Rowland et al, "Accomplishments and Challenges."

48. "UnitedHealth Group Reports First Quarter Results" (press release) (Minneapolis: UnitedHealth Group, April 20, 2010); C. Zinko, "Ultra-wealthy Enjoy Living in Luxury Above It All in S.F.," SFGate.com, April 8, 2001, http://www.sfgate.com/realestate/article/Ultra-Wealthy-Enjoy-Living-in-Luxury-Above-It-All-2933852.php.

49. See, for example, Torrey, *Out of the Shadows*, 131–140; A. A. Miles, R. Walter-Heinrichs, and N. Ammari, "'Real World' Functioning in Schizophrenia Patients and Healthy Adults: Assessing Validity of the Multidimensional Scale of Independent Functioning," *Psychiatry Research 186*, no. 1 (2010): 123–127; R. Richieri et al., "The Schizophrenia Caregiver Quality of Life Questionnaire (S-CGQoL): Development and Validation of an Instrument to Measure Quality of Life of Caregivers of Individuals with Schizophrenia," *Schizophrenia Research 126*, no. 1–3 (2010): 192–201; and T. Lutterman et al., *Sixteen-State Study on Mental Health Performance Measures*, DHHS Publication No. (SMA) 03-3835 (Rockville, MD: Center for Mental Health Services, Substance Abuse and Mental Health Services Administration, 2003).

50. *Action for Mental Health*, 301.

51. Frank L. Wright, *Out of Sight Out of Mind* (Philadelphia: National Mental Health Foundation, 1947), 45.

# INDEX